SATURN RETURN

MARK HALPERT

Saturn Return
Copyright © 2021 by Mark Halpert

All rights reserved. This book or any portion thereof
may not be reproduced or used in any manner whatsoever
without the express written permission of the publisher
except for the use of brief quotations in a book review.

All lyrics and quotations included are for review, study, or critical purposes.

For inquiries, contact saturnreturn5762@gmail.com

Printed in the United States of America and Canada

Cover Art and Illustrations: Donna Jean Bishop
Book Design: Carla Green, Clarity Designworks

ISBN paperback: 978-1-7774404-0-4
ISBN ebook: 978-1-7774404-1-1

To Lunatic
For showing me where to look

Contents

Contents		v
Playlist		vii
Author's Note		ix
MAP	Nepal and India	x
CHAPTER 1	Going to Kathmandu	1
CHAPTER 2	Annapurna	6
CHAPTER 3	Pokhara: One	14
CHAPTER 4	Pokhara: Creep	22
CHAPTER 5	Varanasi: Divali	28
CHAPTER 6	Varanasi: Tabla	32
CHAPTER 7	Varanasi: Shiva's City	39
CHAPTER 8	Varanasi: George	44
CHAPTER 9	Palolem: Home	50
CHAPTER 10	Palolem: Choose Your Own Adventure	56
CHAPTER 11	Palolem: Free Person	63
CHAPTER 12	Om Beach: Shiva's Eye	69
CHAPTER 13	Hampi: Ravi Chandra	75
CHAPTER 14	Hampi: Treehouse	82
CHAPTER 15	Hampi: Little Wing	88
CHAPTER 16	Palolem: Suzanne	95
CHAPTER 17	Palolem: Grateful	99
CHAPTER 18	Palolem: Ashtanga	106
CHAPTER 19	Palolem: This Has All Been Wonderful	112
CHAPTER 20	Kochin: Jew Town	119
CHAPTER 21	Kochin: Attachment	125

CHAPTER 22	Kochin: Full Moon	131
CHAPTER 23	Varkala: Leaf in the Wind	137
CHAPTER 24	Neyyar Dam: Decorate Time	142
CHAPTER 25	Varkala: Paradise Waits	150
CHAPTER 26	Varkala: Sin City	157
CHAPTER 27	Mysore: Gurus	163
CHAPTER 28	Palolem: Breathe	171
CHAPTER 29	2,673 km: General Class	179
CHAPTER 30	2,673 km: Second Class	184
CHAPTER 31	Rishikesh: Light Workers	188
CHAPTER 32	Rishikesh: The Deeper You Go, The Higher You Fly	195
CHAPTER 33	Shimla Happens (Part One)	203
CHAPTER 34	Shimla Happens (Part Two)	209
CHAPTER 35	Himalayan Honeymoon	215
CHAPTER 36	Dharamsala and Delhi: Karma Yoga	222
CHAPTER 37	Dharamsala: Sivaratri	228
CHAPTER 38	Dharamsala to Delhi: Compassion	235
CHAPTER 39	Varanasi: Bhakti	243
CHAPTER 40	Varanasi: Permission to Exit	250
MAP	Thailand, Laos, and Cambodia	258
CHAPTER 41	Koh Lanta: Libro Abierto	259
CHAPTER 42	Bangkok to Chiang Mai: Baggage	264
CHAPTER 43	Around Chiang Mai: Arjuna	270
CHAPTER 44	Mae Hong Son: The Buddhist Spirit	276
CHAPTER 45	Laos: Life Happens Now	282
CHAPTER 46	Koh Chang: A Gift	289
CHAPTER 47	Chiang Mai: Solo	295
CHAPTER 48	Koh Phangan and Koh Tao: Enjoy Being	300
MAP	Western Canada and United States	308
CHAPTER 49	Canada: Man of Honor	309
CHAPTER 50	Saturn Return	315
EPILOGUE	Eighteen Years Later	323

Acknowledgements 329

Playlist

Extended Playlist on Spotify: https://sptfy.com/saturnreturn

Kathmandu – Bob Seger
One – U2
Creep – Radiohead
All Things Must Pass
 – George Harrison
Norwegian Wood – The Beatles
Love You To – The Beatles
50 Ways to Leave Your Lover
 – Paul Simon
With A Little Help From My Friends
 – The Beatles
Little Wing – Jimi Hendrix
Suzanne – Leonard Cohen
Feel like a Stranger – Grateful Dead
Foolish Heart – Grateful Dead
Castles Made of Sand
 – Jimi Hendrix
Down With Disease – Phish
Mike's Song – Phish
Fee – Phish
Help on the Way – Grateful Dead
Speak to Me – Pink Floyd
Breathe (In the Air) – Pink Floyd
Shine On You Crazy Diamond
 – Pink Floyd

Dear Prudence – The Beatles
Everybody's Got Something to Hide
 Except Me and My Monkey
 – The Beatles
Here Comes The Sun – The Beatles
Sexy Sadie – The Beatles
Get Up I Feel Like Being A Sex
 Machine – James Brown
The Rain Song – Led Zeppelin
Cowgirl in the Sand – Neil Young
Wait Until Tomorrow
 – Jimi Hendrix
Dark Star – Grateful Dead
Across the Universe – The Beatles
God – John Lennon
Beautiful Boy (Darling Boy)
 – John Lennon
Within You Without You
 – The Beatles
When I'm Sixty Four – The Beatles
Ship of Fools – Grateful Dead
Going to California – Led Zeppelin
Truckin' – Grateful Dead
Once In a Lifetime – Talking Heads
Om Namah Shivaya – Krishna Das

Author's Note

I've been writing the story of my year in Asia since I arrived in Kathmandu many years ago. I referred to my journals and emails when preparing this book. There are no composite characters and I've changed people's names. I haven't included everything that happened, but everything here did happen. At least, I think it did.

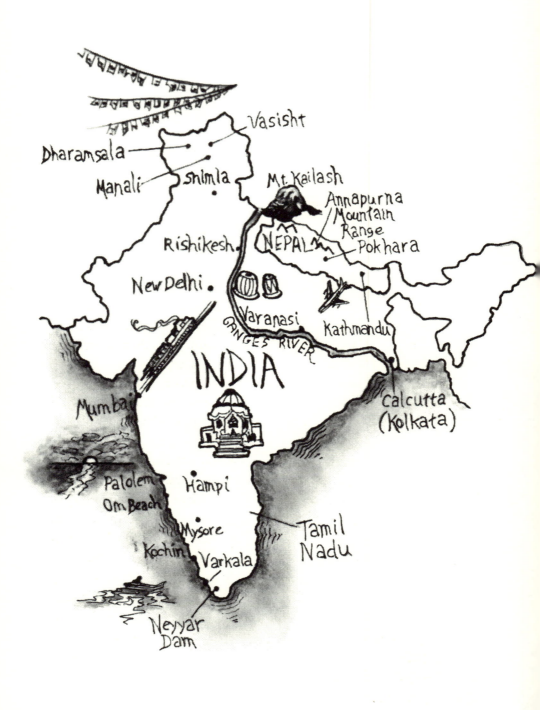

CHAPTER 1

Going to Kathmandu

The first taste of air in a new country can tell you a lot. In Kathmandu, it was heavy and damp, even inside the airport. My girlfriend and I had aimed to arrive in Nepal after the rainy season but Mother Nature had other plans: power washing the mountain kingdom.

Ronit and I had been on planes for more than a day and were relieved to finally begin a long-planned adventure. It was August 2001, and we'd left home on one-way tickets, planning to hike in the Nepali Himalayas and then explore India.

We took a taxi through a manic flow of mini-cars and motorbikes to the tourist area to find a guesthouse. On foot, we passed a kaleidoscope of crafts while vendors and pitchmen strained for our attention. Temples and shrines to Hindu gods stood out among a concentrated cluster of inconsistent architecture. Bustling businessmen bowed briefly at these holy places, praying and proceeding as if they were grabbing a morning coffee.

The locals were dedicated to their work and their gods, and they were also grieving the sudden and shocking death of their king. Two and a half months before our arrival, the crown prince of Nepal had shot and killed his family and himself in their Kathmandu palace, allegedly in a dispute over his choice of bride. The prince's father, King Birendra, had been enormously popular. He was known as a benevolent leader and was revered as a god. His photo was in every shop we entered and many still referred to him as the king, though his surviving brother was now in charge. As rain drenched the cobblestone streets, it felt as though the nation was crying.

Ronit and I were going through a difficult time as well. Though we'd been together for three years, our relationship was strained leading up to our trip.

We first met at a mutual friend's house in my hometown of Edmonton, Canada. Ronit had just returned from studying in Australia, but was already planning her next adventure. She spoke with the emphasis of a woman who knew her priorities, and I was drawn in by her spirit. Her wavy brown hair, olive-brown skin, and elegant jaw made me wonder, "Where are you from, originally?" But as she got up to leave, I focused on a more pressing question and asked for her number.

"I don't have a phone yet," she said, and then hopped on her bicycle and rode away. When she did get a phone, I obtained her number from another mutual friend. I had to talk her into going out with me, but once she agreed, we hit it off. I learned that her Mexican mom and Israeli dad separated when she was two, and that she'd grown up in nearby Calgary. She had half brothers and stepsiblings, but was clearly one of a kind.

Ronit had an exotic beauty. She wasn't tall, but had long legs. She wanted her torso to be just as long and would stop at full-length mirrors to push her hands down on her hips, encouraging the mirror to stretch out her upper body. The mirrors didn't comply, but that only mattered to Ronit. Everyone else would notice her radiant energy when she was excited about something. Traveling was often that thing.

Ronit worked at a travel shop. When people asked her for advice on an upcoming journey, her smile would brighten the store. After receiving Ronit's guidance on gear and books, the customers' anxiety would turn to anticipation.

We were both in our midtwenties, and I was studying accounting. Ronit had an arts degree, and mused about becoming a lawyer, a doctor, or an artist. She had the talent to be all of them at once.

Both of us liked music. I played hand drums and Ronit sang and played guitar. We'd go to concerts and travel together to music festivals. We made mixtapes for each other and, though we were both busy, we made sure to go out for dinner once a month in celebration of our first date.

On Friday nights, we'd often have dinner with my parents. When Ronit and I floated the idea of a yearlong trip to Asia, my parents were supportive, expecting that afterwards, we'd return home to settle down. My dad had traveled to Europe as a young man and we had his blessing to go, *after* my accounting exams were completed. The caveat was significant. I was training in his office to become a Chartered Accountant like he was. As long as I earned my certification first, he didn't care if I went to Kathmandu or Timbuktu.

Ronit's family was spread around the world, so I was grounding for her. I played hockey and rode my mountain bike, but I also spent a *lot* of time watching hockey on TV and even more time getting high. Pot was my escape from the monotony of working as an auditor. My daily grind involved penciling numbers onto long green sheets of paper and asking clients to pull files. A joint was my reward at the end of the day, but it created a distance between Ronit and me. When she wanted to be present and learning, I was often distant and buzzing.

Still, we pressed on with plans for our trip. In anticipation, Ronit printed business cards with a photo of a dragon pendant that a friend had made for her. The card included her name and email address along with the title "Nomad." I admired her worldliness, but Ronit's wanderlust was also local. She was often looking at the next table or into the next room, seeking someone more interesting, or more interested in her.

While I was still studying for my final accounting exam, Ronit accepted a humanitarian position in El Salvador and went there for six months. She was in a rural area without email or even a reliable telephone. We didn't talk often and when we did, the phone connection was lousy. I noticed that Ronit's closest friends in El Salvador were all guys and, meanwhile, I found companionship in an attractive neighbor with a penchant for massages. Though the time and distance caused our relationship to fade, we kept our plan to travel to Asia together once I passed my exam and Ronit returned home. We both believed that the adventure would strengthen our bond.

One morning in early 2001, I awoke prepared to learn my exam results. The pass rate hovered around fifty percent, and I was half-confident and half-afraid. The grades would be released in a white tile and glass office building in downtown Edmonton. In my Jewish family, a profession was a ticket for release from perpetual guilt and judgment. After studying for most of my life, the pressure to achieve could finally be off.

I bowed my head under the winter air as I approached the building. Once inside, I had no interest in talking with any of the other suitclad aspiring accountants in the hallway. Rather, I was on an extraction mission: Get the envelope and get out. I planned to open it in the privacy of my car just in case the news was bad.

The glass doors opened and I bolted to the desk. "Halpert, Mark," I said, as I'd rehearsed with eyes open in bed many nights—last name first for maximum efficiency.

"Halpert, Mark," she repeated, handing me the envelope of truth. "Good luck!"

In the hallway, I abandoned my plan to steal away to the car and jammed my finger under the envelope flap. As people began to flow out of the glass doors, I wrestled a stack of papers from the envelope. A third of the way down the page on top, I read:

PASS

I made the instinctual fist pump of a hockey player and walked back to the car, sighing breaths of relief. Despite the growing murkiness between us, Ronit and I had our ticket to ride. Within months, I would quit my job, move out of my house, and fly to the Himalayas with her. I turned up the volume on the radio and this song came on:

"K-k-k-k-k-k Kathmandu. I think that's really where I'm going to.
If I ever get out of here, I'm going to Kathmandu."
– *Kathmandu*, Bob Seger

As that first day in Kathmandu turned to night, swelling rain subdued the sounds of mopeds, bike bells, and car horns. We sought shelter in a concrete hotel room and heard a depressing weather forecast. The monsoon was expected to last for at least another couple of weeks and roads were too muddy for travel outside of Kathmandu. No one was hiking in the mountains yet.

Ronit sat on the bed's scratchy wool blanket and sought purpose in the Kathmandu chapter of our guidebook. I stood on the tiny balcony and watched sheets of grey soak the ancient city. I wondered if we could begin to rebuild our relationship in a city wet with rain and tears. I was pretty sure that I already knew the answer, but I really wanted to be wrong.

CHAPTER 2

Annapurna

The days dripped into one another. When the monsoon rains eased a bit, Ronit and I rode a bus through mudslides to Pokhara, a lakeside tourist trap with no tourists. While we waited to trek around the Annapurna Himalayan mountain range, our hiking boots served only to avoid puddles between continental breakfasts and used bookstores. Still, it was nice to be together, and away from the pressures and responsibilities of home.

About a week into our stay in Pokhara, the owner of our guesthouse looked to the clearing sky, declared that the monsoon was over, and said it was safe for Ronit and I to begin our two-hundred-kilometer trek. We bought a map and set out on our way. The trail was a dirt footpath with no motorized vehicles, promising views of the world's second-tallest mountain range, rushing rivers, and a high mountain pass. As we climbed, we'd stop in villages to rest our heads and eat *dahl baht*, the ubiquitous Nepali dish of rice and lentils with vegetable curry.

Hiking up felt like a journey into the past. We ate by candlelight and shared the trail with donkeys and human porters hauling food, beverages, and supplies. Beer and soda prices went up with the altitude.

There were a few other hikers, often with porters or guides, but Ronit and I went for hours walking in silence, absorbing the pristine mountain air. On our third day, Ronit's back started to hurt from wearing her pack, so we interviewed a porter named Karma Sherpa. He'd lived in the mountains for all of his twenty years and couldn't tell me how many treks he'd done. A quiet smile graced his broad face as he spoke of the beauty of the mountains. He said that he could carry up to thirty kilograms (sixty-six pounds) and we offered him the job.

The Sherpas are an ethnic group from the Mount Everest region and are known around the world for their mountain climbing abilities. I'd often spot Karma with a cigarette in the guesthouse kitchens and say with a smile, "Sherpas don't smoke." He'd look embarrassed and proclaim that he was quitting the next day. We played card games together in the evenings. Ronit was relieved to have Karma carrying her pack and we enjoyed the simplicity of hiking together, day after day.

One morning, we ascended a narrow canyon to a town with a row of coffee can-sized prayer wheels on waist-high white concrete structures. Karma demonstrated how to spin the wheels as he led us to a hotel lined with colored prayer flags strung across the sky. The owner showed us to a room with a view of two waterfalls. When she shook dust from the blankets, we assumed that we were the first guests of the season.

Other guests arrived a moment later: Doug from "outside of Toronto" and his soft-spoken Nepali guide, Ganesh. Both men were around my age, and Ganesh's English was excellent. He traveled with a small backpack that made it look like he was out for one day, not twenty. As we chatted over dinner at the guesthouse's outdoor tables, I asked Ganesh what the writing on the prayer wheels represented.

"*Om Mani Padme Hum* is a blessing for enlightenment. You spin the wheel and send the blessing out to the world. The prayer flags send the same blessing when they blow in the wind."

The five of us hiked together the following day and Ganesh, named for the Hindu god of travelers, identified each mountain for me. At one

point, I surprised Ganesh when I realized that I knew his last name. I remembered that my friend Josh had recommended a guide with that name, but only put it all together when I realized that Josh was from the same town as Doug. We celebrated the serendipity while walking through clouds where an opening revealed side sections of a massive mountain. The layered grey triangles looked like the underbellies of Imperial Star Destroyers from *Star Wars*. When I asked Ganesh what we were looking at, he said, "Manasulu Mountain. Eighth tallest in the world."

Four days later, the eighth of our trek, our group approached Manang, a tiny town at an elevation of 3,450 meters. The rarified air and pine needles reminded me of the Canadian Rockies. Midday sun reflected off of the snowy heads of enormous Annapurna II and III. We took our first rest day of the trip to adjust to the altitude.

Ganesh advised us to do an acclimatization hike to prepare for the upcoming high pass.

The next morning, Doug, Ronit, and I climbed to a glacier viewpoint where thick clouds painted in white and grey patterns crossed our path. As we descended, both of my knees started to hurt with each step. It was a new sensation and particularly troubling since I wasn't even wearing my pack.

On the final steps back to Manang, I was surprised to see a dreadlocked Chicagoan named Huck, whom we knew from our guesthouse in Manang, running toward us. He was shouting, "Did you hear what happened? Did you hear what happened in America?"

"We were hiking. What happened in America?" I asked.

"Pearl Harbor was nothing, man! Planes flew into the World Trade Center and the Pentagon. Maybe the White House, too…"

I shrugged because it was unbelievable. It sounded like a movie, not reality. But Huck looked stern, his dreadlocks bouncing as he nodded and said, "I'm not fucking kidding, man. Someone blew up the World Trade Center. Both buildings!"

We walked together into Manang as Huck told us that he'd located a satellite phone in the village and called his parents. His family was fine, but thousands of people had died in the attacks. Ronit and I thought for a moment of calling home as Huck had, but he was from Chicago, a big American city. Our families were in Canada, far from the devastation. They knew that we were on a three-week hike, so I didn't feel that it was necessary to hunt down the satellite phone to check in with them.

Oops.

I learned later that there is an instinctual reaction to tragic events, where families gather their own to ensure that all are safe and accounted for. Had I known it then, I would have found that phone. At the time though, I was more interested in tending to my sore knees and hearing further details of the attacks.

A hiker at the guesthouse had a battery-powered radio. We huddled on wooden benches to listen to a brief BBC report, with facts filtered through British accents and static. We knew that 9/11 would have wide-ranging effects, but what could we do about it? We were more than a week from a road in either direction. Our only option was to keep hiking. I couldn't find another porter to help with my knees at that altitude, but Karma took some weight from my pack.

Three days later, at 4,540 meters, the landscape became barren of trees. In the clouds, we saw only rocks, yaks, yak herders living in tents, and lots of yak poop. We were as high as the peaks of most North American and European mountains already, with another thousand meters to climb in order to cross the mountain pass called Thorung La. The pass connected the Manang valley to Mustang valley on the other side of the Annapurna range.

Sweat cooled on my neck as we arrived at a lodge in Thorung Phedi, perched on a mountainside among grey slabs of rock. I was relieved to rest my knees, which stung in pain with each step. I wore tensor bandages and used walking sticks from local whittlers.

Immersed in cloud, we couldn't see the restaurant next door but found our way to it, being careful not to fall off the mountain. I was nauseous from the altitude as we sat at a table with a unique heating system: thick blankets hung over our legs to retain heat from the hot coals that the lodge staff placed under the tables. I managed to force down some dahl baht.

Ronit was in good spirits and her back was feeling better. Others had altitude sickness like I did, but the room was ripe with anticipation for the next day's challenge. Crossing the pass had to be done in one day, a far longer hike than any we'd done yet. We would leave before sunrise and gain 1,000 meters of altitude on a long, continuous climb, then descend another 1,600 meters to Muktinath on the Mustang side. We planned to arrive in Muktinath by mid-afternoon.

Wind whistled through the walls of our hut all night as Ronit and I cuddled to keep warm. I slept only a little before Ganesh knocked on our door with a 4 a.m. wakeup call. In the restaurant, hikers wore serious stares and their warmest clothing. Ganesh asked if I wanted another day to acclimatize to the altitude. I looked out the window, knowing that daytime would only reveal more clouds and rocks. "No," I said, "let's move."

Ganesh knew that our group would travel at different speeds and that I was likely to be slow due to my sore knees and altitude sickness. He put a hand on my shoulder and said, "We will do this together."

I powered upward for the first hour in darkness, looking only at my feet. We arrived at a landing called High Camp, drank some water, and noticed the first cracks of sunlight. Clouds parted just long enough to

reveal glimpses of the mighty Annapurna mountains. Doug and Ganesh took items from my bag to make it lighter, and Doug asked if I wanted to borrow his Walkman. I hadn't heard any of my favorite music in almost two weeks. The percussive jams of the Talking Heads helped me to ignore the pain in my knees as I trod upward.

Hours later, I had lost sight of everyone and was staring at my shoes when Doug startled me mid-stride by tapping my arm. "Look behind you and give me your camera."

The sun had evaporated the clouds and the path was framed by a spectacular view of a jagged range of snowy incisors. Doug jogged ahead and snapped a picture of me trudging along with my trekking poles. With the music off, I listened to the crunching of icy rocks under my feet while Doug led me forward. After a few minutes, I realized that he didn't have his pack. He had been to the pass and then come back to check on me. We were close.

My stomach was grinding and my knees numb from the continuous pain. Then Ganesh appeared, also without a pack. He lifted mine off of my back, put it on his, and fell in line behind me. "Ronit?" I asked Ganesh over my shoulder.

"At the pass, with Karma."

That update and their kindness lifted me enough to appreciate the stunning setting. I took a few more pictures before ascending into clouds that obscured the Himalayan jaws.

Thorung La announces its 5,415 meters with a friendly handpainted sign next to a mini-mountain of flapping prayer flags. After Ganesh alerted Ronit of my arrival, our group took an obligatory photo. She'd been resting in a tiny hut, where one hearty fellow boiled tea over a woodstove. I ordered lemon tea. The price was double what it was in the towns below, but felt like a bargain. We huddled along the soot-covered wall, sipping from tall steel cups, watching light snow fall outside. The thermometer on the door confirmed that it was zero degrees Celsius.

My knees pulsed with the satisfaction of rest, and my stomach and mind were soothed by the warm tea. I was giddy with relief and laughed for the first time in days. I'd battled my way up and was now confident that I could make it down the other side.

Ronit was tired but smiling. Neither of us had anticipated how hard the trek would be, but we'd adapted and supported each other. We hiked together for the long descent from the pass, watching Doug and Ganesh far ahead in the distance. Ronit struggled with the downward angles and even passed out from fatigue at one point. Our twelve-day climb felt like a rite of passage for our relationship. We'd persevered through adversity and were closer for it.

After a rest day, Doug was feeling done, so we said goodbye to him and Ganesh. Ronit and I needed to let our bodies recover. My knees were improving with the lower altitude, but Ronit's back trouble had flared up again. When she felt well enough to move on toward Pokhara, we hiked with optimism for our future, talking about cities, jobs, and even marriage and kids. Though the monsoon had slowed us at first, traveling *was* bringing us together as we'd hoped. The trek around Annapurna was the manifestation of a long-held shared dream. I didn't want to let go of that connection, but eventually we came to the end of the trail and had no choice but to restore contact with the world. Neither of us had any idea how jarring that would turn out to be.

CHAPTER 3

Pokhara: One

The first honk was the worst. After twenty-three days of traveling on foot, I cringed at the noise and exhaust smoke when our hiking trail met up with a road. The shock wore off by the time we'd showered in our familiar guesthouse room in Pokhara. We delighted in eating food that wasn't dahl bhat, and when the clouds cleared occasionally, we could see the mighty mountain view that the town is famous for. But when we used the guesthouse phone to call home, my father sounded more like a field general than an accountant, saying through the scratchy telephone connection, "You need to get out of there!"

I hadn't checked email yet, so I hadn't realized how unnerved he was about not hearing from us immediately after the September 11th terrorist attacks. When I read his messages later, I could see my parents' exasperation. Cable news had stoked their fear of terrorism for weeks while we were on the mountain, away from phones and computers.

Talking to me now, my dad sounded irrational. "They're going to start bombing soon in your part of the world!"

"Who is bombing? Where?"

"The Americans! In Afghanistan."

I reminded him that India and Pakistan separated Nepal from Afghanistan. He warned that the coming war might involve Nepal, too. I countered with a lie packaged between two convenient truths: "Nepalis are mostly Buddhist and Hindu. There aren't any Muslims here. The Nepali government supports the Americans."

As he paused to write down that information, I considered how strange the conversation felt. My dad had always given me strong guidance about school, work, and life in general, but this time seemed different. It was as though *Breaking News* had washed the logic from his brain. I looked out at the road as locals and tourists strolled, seemingly unconcerned with impending war or terrorist attacks. My dad then handed the phone to my mom who said, "Can you two just hurry up, find yourselves, and come home?"

I didn't like defying my dad, but with my mom, it was more of a plea than a power struggle. I didn't want to cause her pain, but I couldn't fathom giving up on a journey that had only just begun. Besides, I had no idea what I'd do at home if I returned; there was no way that I would go right back to work. Ronit and I wanted to go to India next, explore for up to a year, and perhaps even find jobs abroad. I didn't have to be home until my sister's wedding the following June and, besides, the whole point of this trip was to pivot toward something new. Returning home so soon would eliminate that possibility.

I agreed to contact the Canadian consulate and ask what they were advising Canadians in Nepal to do. When I called later that day, the diplomat advised me to tell my parents not to worry—Nepal was still considered safe for traveling. Ronit's mom wasn't panicking, so we decided to stay. I felt bad for going against my parents' wishes, but it was also liberating. Working in my dad's office was great for my career, but it had delayed my independence. Part of why I'd wanted to travel so far away and for so long was to erase those blurred lines. I'd never felt such freedom.

Ronit and I both benefited physically from resting in Pokhara. My knees improved, and though Ronit awoke with back pain each morning, it wore off during the day. We also became friends with a group of Nepalis who were in a nameless local cover band. They would play in open-air tourist bars, so I called them "Live Music" since that's what was always written on the chalkboards outside. The guys were in their midtwenties and from Kathmandu. They didn't have day jobs and rode mopeds around Pokhara. Santosh was the shy, long-haired drummer, Rocky was the preppy and boisterous lead singer, and Dinesh was the slight bassist with shaggy hair and a smile that curled upward on the ends like *Batman*'s Joker. Their guitarist showed up only for the gigs.

One night after a show at the Himalayan Hard Rock Café, the boys from the band invited us to a Full Moon party across the lake. In a large wooden canoe, Rocky belted out song lyrics while Ronit spoke quietly with Dinesh.

Across the lake, a small crowd gathered in a forest. A DJ spun tunes and Ronit sat on a bench with Dinesh. When Rocky and Santosh went looking for girls, I stood alone, waiting for Ronit. The band members and I had smoked a joint on the boat and Dinesh's eyes had quickly glazed over. Ronit leaned toward him, coaxing him to talk. I walked away from them feeling jealous and wondering what she found so interesting about him.

The party crowd consisted mostly of backpackers like us, the light of the full moon reflecting on their pale faces. There were older travelers too, with tanned wrinkles tracing decades of sun and cigarettes. One of them offered me LSD, but I declined. He reminded me of characters in the parking lots of Grateful Dead shows—people who I could never imagine within mainstream society. I wasn't disobeying my family so that

I could become like *that*. I yearned for a long and interesting journey, not a neverending one.

Weeks passed and though we went on overnight excursions together, Ronit always wanted to return to Pokhara. I was ready to leave for India, but Ronit would avoid the topic when I brought it up.

One night while Live Music was playing at a place called Club Amsterdam, a tall fellow with silver spectacles invited me to play pool. Ramesh was a doctor from India who had studied in the United States. He kept his beer glass full and was equally comfortable speaking English to me and Nepali to the bartenders. We talked about Indian music and then when I mentioned that Ronit's back was still bothering her, he called the hospital from the bar's telephone and made her an appointment for the following day.

At the hospital the next morning, a doctor prescribed daily heat therapy sessions. Ramesh found us after the appointment and invited us to the local goat market for the upcoming festival of Dasain. We met him that afternoon and caught a taxi together to the market, where Nepali patriarchs entered pens to make their selections for sacrifice. Each of these goats would have their throats sliced as an offering to the gods and then be cooked and eaten.

Later that day, I observed the ritual slaughter from our guesthouse roof. Three generations of men restrained a goat while the eldest sliced its neck. Blood shot out across the patio. The scene was peaceful but disturbing. Once the task was complete and the carving began, the thirteen-year-old son held the goat's severed head by a horn in one hand.

That evening, I asked Ronit again when she thought she'd be ready to leave Nepal. In response, she asked, "Why do you always have to be *doing* something?"

"I want to explore, to experience new places."

"To *really* experience a place, you need to stay there for a while. You need to *live* there."

"Okay, but I don't want to live in Pokhara any longer. Don't you want to go to India?"

"I'm happy here."

It felt like we were moving backwards—or at least stuck in place. I'd spend the evenings walking Pokhara's main dirt road, popping my head into each of the lakefront bars looking for Ronit. She was always in one of them, until one night when I couldn't find her anywhere. The band wasn't playing and the bartenders hadn't seen her. None of us had cellphones and I didn't know any of our friends' home phone numbers. I went to our room, where I waited and worried.

I'd been up all night when Ronit called the guesthouse at six in the morning. She'd been "hanging out" with Ramesh at his home until late. When they prepared to leave, his moped had a flat tire. She apologized and said that she hadn't called because she didn't want to wake anyone up. The irony burned because I hadn't slept at all.

I couldn't understand why she would act like that. Was she just being insensitive or was she trying to end our relationship? It was infuriating and sad at the same time. In those early-morning hours, something between us died. I really had no idea what I was still doing in Pokhara. My only purpose there seemed to be keeping track of Ronit as she drifted around town. The night that I couldn't find her, not only was my trust broken, so was my identity.

By evening, everyone had resumed their positions at Club Amsterdam. Ramesh greeted me at the pool table with "I definitely owe you a beer, man," and clarified that he wasn't making a move on Ronit. They were talking and it got late. He glanced to the other end of the club, where she sat with Dinesh, and tried to explain about the flat tire. I appreciated his apology, but I was done hearing about it. I believed him and wanted to keep him as a friend, so I let it go.

Live Music was on stage. The guys had been inviting Ronit to sing with them every night and she would grab the attention of the room with a passionate rendition of U2's *One*. Until that night, I hadn't realized that it was a breakup song.

> "One love, you get to share it.
> Leaves you, darling, if you don't care for it."
> – *One* by U2

At age twenty-seven, Bono was on top of the world. The Joshua Tree had catapulted U2's record sales, and the Irishmen used their newfound artistic and financial freedom to celebrate the gospel and R&B traditions of the United States with a movie and an album, both titled Rattle and Hum. *The effort was widely panned by critics, who called the band presumptuous. The group fell into a crisis of confidence. It took them three years to release another record.*

The sessions that produced the follow-up album, titled Achtung Baby, *were ripe with conflict. The band disagreed on their musical direction and might have broken up had they not coalesced around an airing of grievances, the song* One.

> "Is it getting better, or do you feel the same?
> Will it make it easier on you, now you've got someone to blame?"
> – *One* by U2

I had someone to blame, but I didn't feel any better. Aside from the free beer, everything was the same. I didn't want to make a rash decision, but I needed a change.

A few days later, I was walking along the lake when I noticed the chiseled face of Ocal, a Nepali I'd previously bought marijuana from. His cheekbones rose as he smiled and approached me. He told me that he was taking three Dutch people on the Annapurna Skyline trek for four days, and he invited me to come along. The trek was short but known for its spectacular mountain views. My immediate reaction was to say no, but Ocal said that he'd be at Club Amsterdam later that night and I could let him know if I changed my mind.

I told Ronit about Ocal's offer. She couldn't trek because she was resting her back and visiting the hospital every day but she knew how restless I was feeling and encouraged me to go. We both agreed that four days apart would probably be good for us.

The hike was exhilarating. I spent most of it convincing myself that if I were more present with Ronit, her interest in me would rekindle. When I returned to Pokhara, she was glad to report that her mobility was improving. I didn't dare ask about leaving for India, but she seemed warmer, more welcoming. Had absence made her heart grow fonder?

That evening, we went to Club Amsterdam, where Ramesh was playing pool with some people we didn't know. My Dutch friends sat at a table, celebrating our hike with a toast. I joined in, and they invited me to the Full Moon party across the lake. I'd seen the full moon on the trek, but until they mentioned the party, I hadn't realized that Ronit and I had been in and around Pokhara for a full cycle of the moon. Ronit, who had detoured to another club, returned and said that the boys from the band were also going to the party but that she needed to get to sleep. I said goodnight to her and caught a boat with the Dutch hikers.

The next morning, Ronit and I went out for breakfast. She shocked me afterwards in our room by tugging at my belt, looking up at me, and saying with a mischievous smile, "I missed you." She undressed me, pushed me onto the single bed, and climbed on top of me. The bed itself spoke to the unlikeliness of this midday seduction. We originally accepted the room with its two twin beds with the intention of moving to one with a queen bed when it became available. After more than a month, we'd never bothered.

We connected in a way we hadn't in so long, looking in each other's eyes as we made love. We'd been apart for four days, but it felt more powerful than when we'd reunited after six months. It was the closest I'd felt to Ronit in at least that long. We stayed in bed that day and ignored the outside world. Eventually, we showered and went out to eat again. I shared stories from my trek and Ronit talked about India. I was so happy that she was thinking past Pokhara. Perhaps the days apart were just what we needed?

As we returned through the gate of our guesthouse courtyard, the owner came out of his office to tell us that we had a message. A traveler friend had left a note on a scrap of paper:

Ronit, Mark,
I couldn't find you guys.
Dinesh died last night.
Everyone is going to the Hard Rock for a memorial.

CHAPTER 4

Pokhara: Creep

I'd seen Live Music perform more than a dozen times. While the band played, I'd be chatting and only paying peripheral attention, but I knew the set. Usually, Rocky would jump around the stage for a few tunes and then yield the microphone to Ronit for her nightly rendition of *One*. Later on, Dinesh, the bassist, would take the mic. He always chose *Creep* by Radiohead. His singing was fine, but I hated the song. The fuzzy guitar was intrusive and I couldn't relate to the protagonist shouting that he wants to be *special*. I was always glad when the song ended, but on the day that Dinesh died, I wanted nothing more than to hear him sing it one more time.

"But I'm a creep. I'm a weirdo.
What the hell am I doing here? I don't belong here."
– *Creep* by Radiohead

Though Dinesh and I had both gone to the Full Moon party the previous night, I hadn't seen him since before my four-day trek, when we were on the back patio of the Himalayan Hard Rock Café after a Live Music show. We had talked as a group while Dinesh rolled joints of tobacco and hashish, silently lighting and passing them around, as he retreated into a stupor. Ronit had stared into his eyes as though she were searching for his soul. She wanted to help him. After we got up to leave, Ronit had said, "I don't know why he does that to himself every night." I reassured her that he would be better tomorrow. I'd hoped he would feel the joy of a clear mind in the morning light.

Now, on that same lakefront patio, at least fifty people gathered for the wake. Offerings grew organically into a colorful array of candles, incense, and flowers. I wished that Dinesh could see the love that the world was giving to him. I thought of his family wondering what they could have done to prevent losing their child and brother, so suddenly and forever.

It wasn't clear to me if his death was an accident or suicide. We knew that he had gone to the Full Moon party across the lake, and I learned at the memorial that he had taken LSD. At some point, Rocky and Santosh had lost track of him. His body was found in the lake, drowned and clothed, at 8 a.m. at Gauri Ghat, the dock near our guesthouse. His shoes were on.

I wanted to somehow turn the clock back twenty-four hours, find Dinesh, and steer him to safety. I knew the potency of LSD because I had taken it years earlier at Grateful Dead shows. It can drastically alter the user's perception, leading to euphoria or terror. Knowing of his tendency toward depression, Ronit had urged Dinesh not to take it. He'd ignored her and also broken a key rule: Stay with your friends. Hallucinogens can

make you do stupid things. Friends can keep you from going too far, even if they're also tripping. In normal circumstances, Dinesh would surely have taken his clothes and shoes off for swimming, but high on acid, it might have felt normal not to.

Ronit and I had gone for breakfast that morning near Gauri Ghat at 9 a.m., only an hour after Dinesh's body had been pulled from the lake. I recalled no sign of the incident. No police, no caution tape, no flowers. I may have missed something, but it's more likely that there was nothing to see. Death is accepted as a part of life in Nepal. Hindus believe that when a person dies, their spirit moves on to a higher plane. For that reason, bodies generally aren't buried. Instead, they're immediately incinerated, usually next to a river, where the ash flows away with the current. Dinesh's body had been taken away quickly and awaited his family, who would come from Kathmandu for its cremation.

The mystery of Dinesh's death bothered me, but it tore Ronit apart. Around midnight, she was still gathering information and crying near the abundance of flowers. I was tired and ready to leave the memorial, but Ronit insisted on staying and encouraged me to go back to the guesthouse. When some friends assured me that they were staying also, I walked down the lakeside road to my bed.

My sleep was interrupted at 3:40 a.m. when Ronit swept in and out of our room in a flourish. As she stuffed clothes and a sleeping bag into her backpack, she explained that she had been to the hospital and visited Dinesh's bloated and frozen corpse. She was leaving now to tend to his shrine at the Hard Rock Café. I was too exhausted to try to stop her. Doorknob in hand, she said, "He told me he was going to die." Then she closed the door and left.

As morning sun brightened the sky, Ronit returned, drained of energy. I closed the blinds and covered her in blankets. Before closing her eyes, she said, "He wanted to die young." I could feel her guilt, and I understood why she couldn't let it go. I wondered if I could have helped him, but Ronit had been warned. I hoped that sleep would bring her peace.

When she rose later in the day, Ronit said, "When you were on your hike, Dinesh came to visit me here every day. He would sit over there." She pointed at my bed. "We talked for hours." I wondered why I didn't know about these visits already, but the answer came quickly. "The night before you came back, he tried to kiss me. I told him no and asked him to leave. When he was out the door, I locked it."

The story was upsetting but not shocking until she said, "He pleaded with me at the door to let him back in. I refused. He was begging. It was... pathetic. I was trapped in here. Then he sat in a chair on the porch all night, crying. I couldn't sleep because I could hear him... for hours."

"When did you leave?"

"He eventually fell asleep, so I left after sunrise and stayed out all day. I didn't want to come back and see him. The next night at the café, we both acted like it hadn't happened."

"And then he went to the Full Moon party," I remembered, "... and we didn't see him again." His death made more sense now.

"Don't think that he's a bad person," Ronit said, still using the present tense.

All that time that Ronit had been searching for Dinesh's soul, it turned out that she'd stolen his heart. I was jealous that he'd hit on my girlfriend, but it felt strange to care what a dead man had done when he was alive. She'd refused him, and that felt like a thread keeping Ronit and me connected.

"Did you love him?"

"As a friend."

I realized then that we'd made love for the first time in so long in the aftermath of Ronit's rejecting Dinesh. I wondered if she'd been expressing rekindled feelings for me or repressed desire for him. Perhaps it was both, but I finally understood the full weight of her burden. In hindsight, his night of tears had been more than desperation. It was a warning.

So, it wasn't an accident?" I asked.

"Mark... he had stones in his pockets."

> "I don't care if it hurts, I want to have control.
> I want a perfect body, I want a perfect soul.
> I want you to notice when I'm not around."
> – *Creep* by Radiohead

Our time in Pokhara had felt bland, but it was also a break from the intensity of life back home. Though I'd grown tired of waiting for Ronit in that room, part of me enjoyed the repetitive simplicity. Not needing to *be* anywhere or *doing* anything put me in a kind of suspended animation. When Dinesh died, that feeling of comfort did too. It made things real—*too* real. We were suddenly dealing with life and death, and I knew what side of that equation I wanted to be on. I wanted to feel alive and that wasn't going to happen until we left town.

Ronit still wasn't ready, though. I found her the next day, rifling through her things, looking for a piece of paper with Dinesh's email address on it. She'd been wearing his sweatshirt for days and had a key to his apartment. She was desperately trying to turn back time.

> "Have you come here for forgiveness?
> Have you come to raise the dead?
> Have you come here to play Jesus,
>   to the lepers in your head?
>   – *One* by U2

I was still hesitant to ask Ronit about leaving Pokhara, but then she surprised me by saying, "Rocky and Santosh are going to Kathmandu. We can go, too, if you want." It was the day before my birthday and I couldn't have imagined a better gift. It had been months since we'd left Kathmandu, a city in mourning, in the monsoon. We brought the wake this time, but Dinesh's name remained unspoken when we met Rocky, Santosh, and some other friends for dinner to celebrate my turning twenty-seven.

We went to a club afterwards, where they all surprised me with a birthday celebration. Ronit brought a chocolate cake and our Nepali friends gave me presents: a journal for writing and a desk calendar that Rocky admitted to stealing from a gift shop on his way to dinner.

We drank and danced. It felt good to let loose, especially with people who loved Dinesh. Life had to go on, so we partied toward our next stages of mourning.

Ronit and I talked late that night about how to sustain our relationship. She suggested that perhaps we should see other people while remaining a couple. When I told her that plan didn't make sense to me, she said, "I don't want to lose my only real friend." We bought plane tickets to Varanasi, India and hoped once again for a fresh start.

I saw Dinesh's death as the premature loss of a kind but troubled soul. He wasn't a *creep*. He *was* special and right where he belonged, among friends and expressing himself through music. It's tragic that he couldn't see that truth through a cloud of drugs and despondency.

His death was a wake-up call for me. I looked ahead to India, not wanting to be a silent stoner resigned to a fate beyond my control. I wanted to feel aware of life's beauty and how to make the most of it.

CHAPTER 5

Varanasi: Divali

Buddha found enlightenment after traveling from Nepal to India. When I made the journey two thousand years later, all I wanted was a change of scenery.

As soon as our flight was in the air, Ronit's back pain returned in force. She laid across three airplane seats, biting her lip to keep from screaming. She felt cursed and kept repeating, "I shouldn't have left Pokhara…"

Stepping out of the airport in Varanasi, we navigated a chaotic wave of mustachioed men calling, "Rickshaw, Sir, Taxi, Taxi, Rickshaw, Sir!" They grabbed at us, blocked our path, and shouted in our faces. I hired the calmest-looking driver and asked him to take us to a hospital. In India, they drive on the left side of the road, but this driver, not so much. He spent more time on the right, weaving around oxcarts, brushing beside dented buses, and dodging oncoming three-wheeled auto-rickshaws.

At the hospital, a security guard directed us past scores of people awaiting attention and toward a young Indian woman in a white coat who asked first if we had insurance (yes), if we were married (no), and then about Ronit's condition. The woman looked me in the eye and said, "A doctor will see your wife tomorrow." Then she waddled her head in a strange motion, as though her neck was a loose joint and she was drawing figure eights with her chin. I would later learn the affirmative intention of this common expression, but at that moment, I puzzled over it. It resembled the familiar shake of no, but her gaze was warm. She waddled her head again, raised her eyebrows, and looked to the door. I understood this time—we were done for the day.

When we returned to the hospital, the room Ronit stayed in was a sanitary oasis from restless Varanasi. It had a private bathroom and a television. A preteen boy visited hourly with a stack of small, white plastic cups in one hand and a silver pot of chai, traditional milky spiced tea, in the other. The infusions of caffeine calmed our uncertainty until an MRI revealed that Ronit had a herniated disc pressing on a nerve in her back. She was told to rest in bed indefinitely.

Ronit regretted leaving Nepal and I felt bad for pressuring her to travel. She felt trapped in the hospital and longed for the freedom she'd had in Pokhara. I reminded her that, because of Dinesh's death, nothing could be the same in Pokhara. She knew I was right but was upset nonetheless. She didn't want to return home, but being stuck in a hospital room in India without *seeing* India felt even worse.

A couple of days after we arrived, *Divali*, the annual festival of lights—a celebration of hope over despair—was beginning. The holiday is known for the colorful candles, flowers, and fruit that devotees offer to the Ganges River. As the sun set that evening, Ronit encouraged me to go for a walk to the river and experience the festival.

I left the hospital at dusk, found the river, and walked downstream. The Ganges, or Ganga, is wide and long. It flows from high in the Himalayas, down the northern Indian plains, through Varanasi, and eventually to the Bay of Bengal. Holy to Hindus, the river is used for commerce, prayer, and transporting the ashes of the dead. In Hinduism, the Ganga is the most auspicious place to die—an express lane to liberation of the soul.

The Ganga is lined with ghats, concrete platforms with steps, which serve as portals to the river. Each ghat has its own significance, including religious ritual, bathing, socializing, and cremation. As I walked in the dark, a foul stench indicated that some of the ghats were used as public toilets.

I eventually came upon a ghat where women and girls prepared paper bowls with tiny wicks, dollops of oil, and flowers for a religious offering to the Ganga called *puja*. A young girl in a pretty orange dress handed me

one of the paper bowls and silently offered to light the wick. I cradled the bowl with both hands and watched as her small fingers drew the match in focused dedication. She looked me in the eye, motioned to the Ganga, and waddled her head. I lowered the offering so it could join dozens of other lights on the plodding river.

The warmth of the candles served as a welcome to India for me. I had always felt most spiritually connected outdoors, and it was clear that the Ganga was a place of worship. The candles were a way of showing appreciation to the divinity in nature.

I moved on to Assi Ghat, where women in saris lit dozens of lamps at a Hindu goddess shrine. A mix of clean-cut and dreadlocked Indian men sat cross-legged, passing a conical hashish pipe called a *chillum* around a chanting circle, led by a singing holy man, or *sadhu*. The sadhu tapped a small drum while chanting, "Siga Ram paja kar bai. Siga Raaam…"

I kneeled outside the circle to observe, and was surprised when two white-shirted men shuffled to the sides, opening up to invite me in. I was hesitant to join the circle, but I told myself to keep an open mind. Growing up in a Jewish family, I'd been taught of the one God, nameless and faceless. I dismissed the ubiquitous Hindu gods of Nepal and India as impostors. Problem was, I didn't believe in the Jewish God either. He was too jealous and controlling for my taste, so I considered myself an atheist.

I sat among the men and watched the hundreds of lights floating down the Ganga. The chanting grew with an increasingly passionate rhythmic force. I closed my eyes and felt drenched in the devotion of my hosts. These men were pouring their hearts into the river.

I excused myself after a while, bowing with my palms together to exchange a blessing of namaste. Before walking on, I looked at the circle. I was back in the mundane world, but the men chanting were still climbing higher. I found their spirituality powerful and intriguing.

As I turned back toward the hospital, I learned that Divali's gentle feminine floating candles had a violent, male twin. Young boys lit small firecrackers that they called bombs along the riverside. Some would explode prematurely in their hands, causing the children to shout and laugh all at once. They intentionally exploded the bombs under stray dogs, and even tossed one in my path. I jumped in fear as the chuckling culprits ran away.

I knew I had a long walk ahead of me. The floating candles were gone and so were the people. I had to dodge feces and stray dogs, but I felt lighter than I had upon arriving in India. Though Ronit and I weren't yet rekindling the light between us, the holy Ganga had given me the change of scenery that I'd craved.

The lucid pulses of the chanters' worship had revealed Varanasi's spiritual power. I couldn't say if the power was inherent to the city or if the devotees created it. What I *could* see was that Varanasi was a lens that magnified life. Devotion and destruction cohabited along the Ganga, presenting challenges as immediate as a firecracker at my feet and opportunities as welcoming as a circle of prayer.

CHAPTER 6

Varanasi: Tabla

I spent the next few days in Ronit's hospital room and ventured outside only for errands. The three-story Heritage Hospital was on a dusty street cluttered with crooked signs overlapping on telephone poles. Students from a nearby university filled snack shops and internet cafés. In 2001, the internet was new and email and chatting online were billed by the minute, so I would send periodic emails to a mailing list of friends and family.

A message from a friend named Carrie caught my attention. After wishing Ronit a return to full strength, she wrote, "I studied tabla with Keshav Rao Nayak for a month in Varanasi. He teaches at the International Music Centre near Dasaswamedh Ghat. You should take lessons from him, or at least watch him perform."

Tabla is a set of two drums played with fingers and palms to create a wide range of beats. It's the rhythmic foundation for the mystical sounds of classical Indian music. I had a hand drum at home, but didn't think I could play something as challenging as the tabla. Still, Carrie's message stood out as an instruction to be followed. "Keshav Rao Nayak… International Music Centre… Dasaswamedh Ghat."

Dasaswamedh Ghat is at the heart of Varanasi's old city. The most efficient way to get there was by rickshaw, a bicycle pulling a two-seater carriage with a wooden bench covered by long-defeated padding. I held on as the driver, thin and shoeless, pedaled past taxis, cows, and oxcarts for a bone-jangling twenty minutes.

The driver eventually pulled over and indicated with hand motions that he couldn't take me all the way to the International Music Centre because the old city's maze of streets was too narrow. He waved his arm toward a road filled with pilgrims and said, "Dasaswamedh."

I joined the flow of humanity progressing toward the river and passed pillars with no structures to support, relics of a grander time. Beggars reached palms out from under plaintive faces. Many were missing limbs, and some held children. More than a different country, India felt like a different century.

At Dasaswamedh Ghat, pitchmen offered me boat rides, tours of the old city, and hashish. Their relentlessness made me wonder how Carrie could spend a month in such a place. But when I asked one of the pitchmen if he'd heard of the International Music Centre, his tone changed completely. He gave up on trying to convince me of what I wanted and, instead, provided exactly what I needed: directions.

The pitchman led me into a maze of narrow cobblestone streets littered with trash and cow dung. We'd jump aside when a motorcycle cruised around a corner, but when a cow took up the alley, we needed to reroute. The animals are sacred to Hindus and apparently have the right of way. Ancient buildings abutted one another in staggered structures of brick and cement. Each street twisted in disorienting directions, but my new friend eventually pointed me to the side of a building with a handpainted yellow rectangle with red letters above an arrow pointing toward the Music Centre.

"You will see more signs like this," he said, and then headed back to the ghat. He was correct. Matching red-on-yellow beacons with arrows appeared regularly, leading me to the knobby blue wooden door of the International Music Centre (Ashram). All of the signs included this last word, Ashram, in parentheses, suggesting  that the Centre could be a religious retreat if you wanted it to be. The brick building must have been hundreds of years old. I ducked to enter the doorway and arrived in a small performance space with wooden benches and a stage. I called "Hello?" and heard feet shuffling upstairs. A music stand held single-page flyers in the same red-on-yellow pattern as the signs on the street.

At the foot of a cement stairwell, a man said, "I am Keshav. Students call me Guruji." He remembered Carrie and gave me a quick tour of "this ashram," his barefoot steps and potbelly guiding us through the three-story building. He had the thick moustache that never seems to go out of style in India and a helmet of black hair covering his ears.

Keshav's cheeks were round like his belly, creating endless space for his smile.

The two upper floors of the ashram had balconies facing a square courtyard that was open to the sky. The third floor included living quarters and a kitchen for Keshav and his family. The second floor was the music school. I spotted a tall stringed instrument called a sitar in an open room where an elderly man sat as still as a statue. "My father," Keshav said, and the statue cracked a smile.

The tour concluded in a tiny room with loose carpet, cushions, and many tabla. Keshav assumed his spot across from the door. He sat under a black-and-white photo of a tabla player and next to a shrine for Saraswati, the goddess of the arts, who was joined by a statue of the elephant god Ganesh, and pictures of a divine couple, Shiva and Parvati. A burning pillar of putty-textured incense called *dhoop* filled the air with sweet smoke.

Keshav instinctively placed his hands on his tabla and began with the first question that every Indian person asked: "Which country?" After I responded, he said, "Many Canadians come to Varanasi to study Indian music. You want to study tabla?"

I had been so focused on finding the place that I hadn't considered the commitment involved in studying tabla. I told him that I loved to drum and he said that lessons were an hour per day and cost one hundred rupees (about two dollars) each. Keshav said I would also need to practice and that he had drums and space for that. As I nodded, he concluded, "Very good, you come tomorrow morning, ten o'clock." He wobbled his head and, as I rose to leave, he added, "You should also see me play. Come to our concert on Wednesday night."

It happened so fast, but I was enthusiastic about studying tabla. Ronit needed weeks to recover and we were in the heart of Indian music with nothing but time. I'd still spend most of my time at the hospital, but tabla would get me out for a couple of hours each day.

When I returned to the hospital and told Ronit, her reaction was flat. Her mind was still in Pokhara and, having not properly arrived in Varanasi, she didn't want to hear about it. She had the same reaction when I returned excited from my first lesson. Still, she encouraged me to stay in the old city for the evening concert the following day. In my second lesson, I was able to hold the proper hand position and was progressing on the basic rhythms, or *taals*, of the tabla. I wrote the taals in a notebook, but Keshav said, "You need the music in your head, not on paper. Listen to me and repeat:"

Dha Dhin Dhin Dha

Dha Dhin Dhin Dha

Dha Tin Tin Na

Na Dhin Dhin Dha

Each sound corresponds to a tap on the drums. Some are played with one hand, and others require both. To add to the challenge, the two drums are completely different. The left hand goes on the larger bass drum, called the *baya*. That side produces the instrument's familiar *whomp* sound as the player slides their hand up and down. The right side, also called tabla, requires a precise series of movements to produce distinct sounds. It was hard to move my hands simultaneously, but I stayed for a long time that day and eventually got the basic taal down.

While playing, it was impossible to think of anything else. It acted like a meditation—the longer I kept up the beat, the longer my mind was singularly focused. It felt wonderful, not only to correctly complete the taal, but also because I'd created peace in my mind. The aimlessness that I'd felt in Nepal was going away. Now I had a purpose. I was a music student. The mere act of playing was liberating.

When my fingers could handle no more, I walked to Dasaswamedh Ghat where, in a continuing celebration of Divali, hundreds of women in saris of every color created a kaleidoscope along the riverbank. They were offering puja to the Ganga by floating abundant fruit baskets and flowers

in the water, bringing grace to an area that had revealed so much poverty and desperation when I'd first seen it days before.

After a meal, I returned to Dasaswamedh in the early evening, where I saw another puja. This one, called *aarti*, involved young priests called Brahmins in white robes making a series of offerings to the river. A bell rang as five priests moved candelabras in synchronized circles from parallel platforms facing the Ganga. They repeated the ritual with smoking urns of dhoop. I learned that aarti is a nightly tradition in that spot. I didn't understand the ritual but appreciated the beauty of it. In that chaotic city, devotees created calm through the love of their gods and expressed it to the Ganga, a goddess herself.

I left aarti for the performance at the Music Centre, where I joined other travelers cross-legged on the floor in the small performance space. Sweet dhoop filled the air as Keshav took the stage. Rhythms rolled off of his fingers while he sat steady and cross-legged, smiling between red spits of *paan*. He plucked this mixture of betel leaf and areca nut from a daintily packed leaf next to his tabla and stuffed his cheeks with it. It seemed that most of the men in Varanasi indulged in chewing this tobacco-like substance and spit it through their teeth all over town. Red streaks of paan painted the outdoor walls of Varanasi.

Keshav was an amazing tabla player. His fingers moved like a hummingbird's wings and the music was entrancing. He accompanied a young Indian man on sitar. The music began slowly and built to points of climax where the two paused, looked at each other, and then began again with a laugh, matching each other's phrases and playing off of them.

I'd had a small taste of that elation with my own playing, but with their aptitude and the beauty of the music, they rose so much higher. The entire room caught the joyful wave. When it was over, I nearly floated out of the building.

CHAPTER 7

Varanasi: Shiva's City

When I come upon an elegantly built but dilapidated building, I like to imagine it on day one—with an optimistic owner inspecting fixtures and polishing floors. As I envision the history, I'm reminded that nothing lasts forever. As soon as the paint dries, that beautiful building begins to deteriorate. With sufficient maintenance, it may overcome the ravages of time. But neglected, it is destined to become an abandoned relic, like so many of the structures I saw in Varanasi.

By the time we arrived in India, Ronit and I were well beyond decorating our life together; still, we hoped to restore our ramshackle relationship. I did all I could to keep her spirits up in the hospital. I'd buy her magazines, look for better food options, and spend afternoons watching movies on TV with her. I'd offer to crawl into her bed, but she didn't want me that close, so I slept in a cot on the side of the room.

Sometimes she would cry at night out of desperation for her situation, but when I'd try to console her, she'd push me away and tell me that I didn't understand what she was going through.

She blamed me that we'd left Nepal, and I was frustrated with the implication that I'd caused her back to get worse. She needed to move forward after her experience with Dinesh, but she wasn't able to go anywhere, not even outside the hospital. She was morose when I'd leave for tabla lessons and no better when I returned.

After two weeks, Ronit was discharged with strict orders to rest all day and to avoid travel for at least another two weeks. I found us a room in a hotel near Dasaswamedh Ghat that had a rooftop restaurant overlooking the chaos of the city. I also bought us train tickets to Goa, a province known for its beautiful beaches. A month in Varanasi was long enough.

In celebration of our freedom, I bought my own set of tabla. I could now practice outside of the ashram, in our hotel room or on the rooftop. The drums were about twenty pounds combined, but I didn't mind carrying them in their soft blue case.

On Ronit's first day in the old city, I returned from my lesson expecting to find her resting on the hotel rooftop. She wasn't in the room either, so I practiced my drum on the roof while I waited for her. In the late afternoon, I went for a walk around the old city and saw that an Indian music festival was taking place at the Ganga. Upon my arrival, I was directed to a "Foreign Tourists" section facing the stage and the river. Only invited Indians could attend the festival, but carpeted terraces were available for foreigners to come and go at will. I felt uncomfortable being on the privileged side of the fence while hundreds of locals strained to enjoy the show from a distance. Uniformed army officers provided security. Their rifles were taller than the kids selling postcards.

In a different "Foreign Tourists" section next to the stage, I spotted Ronit in conversation with some other travelers. I was frustrated that she wasn't resting and hadn't told me that she was going out. After all of the efforts that the doctors, nurses, and I had made toward Ronit's recovery, she wasn't helping herself. I was too disappointed to get up and walk over to her. Instead, I focused on the performance.

Sitar and tabla sounds rose and descended as the orange light of sunset shimmered on the brown tributary. In that moment, I felt something shift. For so long, I'd thought of Ronit and me as intertwined. We had chemistry when we were together and I'd always believed that we'd rekindle our spark, but as the music flowed over my carpeted spot at the ghat, that conviction faded. Somehow, the stench and haze of Varanasi brought clarity. I had no vision of what I would do alone, but I knew that before the day was over, I would break up with Ronit.

By the time she returned to the hotel, I was already in bed. Faint moonlight shone through the solitary window of our wide, grey room. She was smiling and talked about moving to a hostel called the Yogi Lodge, where her exciting new friends were staying.

I asked her to join me on the bed. Speaking softly to change the tone of the conversation, I told Ronit that I thought India would be a great place for her to heal and grow, but that I would only hold her back from that growth. Her smile faded as I told her that it was too painful for me to be in a relationship that was gradually dissolving.

"But I need you…" she said. "I can't carry my backpack."

Insulted by my diminished job description, I said, "I think we need to break up."

Regardless of the logistics, I made it clear that we would no longer be a couple. She didn't disagree, but wanted to keep traveling together. I lowered my head and said, as though testing a new language, "That's not what's best for me."

She asked that we both move to the Yogi Lodge and that I still go with her to Goa in two weeks as planned. I agreed to do both, on the conditions that I would get a separate room at the lodge and then stay at a different beach in Goa after escorting her there. With those details sorted out, we went to sleep on the double bed turned away from each other.

When I arrived at the ashram a bit early the next morning, Keshav offered me chai in a tiny clay cup. These cups were used as vessels for the spiced milky brew all around Varanasi—at Keshav's ashram, at street carts, and in restaurants. They were Dixie cup-sized, but looked like tiny clay pots for plants, though textured on the outside with no lacquer. The clay began to dissolve as soon as the tea entered the cup. I drank fast to avoid ingesting the powder.

I never knew what to do with the cup because there were no trash cans in Varanasi. Keshav answered my question that morning when, without looking to see if anyone was walking by, he threw his cup out the third-story window of the ashram and it smashed on the narrow walking street outside. I followed suit and soon noticed that everyone did the same. The cups lasted only as long as the chai and then returned to dust.

As we went to the tabla room and sat behind our drums, I told Keshav the news about Ronit so that he would stop asking about my "wife." Marriages in Varanasi were arranged, so people didn't date. Because of that cultural difference, I wasn't sure how Keshav would respond. I was surprised when he said, "I have been teaching here for twenty years, and in that time, I have seen over a hundred couples come to Varanasi together…and leave the city apart." Seeing my stunned expression, he leaned forward for emphasis. "Yes, many times. It wasn't *you* who did this. Shiva made this happen. Do you know Shiva?"

I shrugged. I was familiar with the long-haired meditating god, but didn't know anything about him. Keshav pointed to the floor. "This is

Shiva's city." He then held his two index fingers toward the ceiling, separated them, and said, "It was Shiva who said, 'Okay, you two, not together now.'"

I squinted and he switched to a fatherly tone. "Shiva is the destroyer. Destruction is necessary for creation. Trees grow again after a fire and you too will grow from this."

I'd only known Keshav for about a week and a half, but I trusted him. His lecture short-circuited my belief in free will. I'd sensed Varanasi's intensity, but was floored by the idea that a place (or a god) could influence me. Keshav said that Ronit would be on my mind for a week or ten days, and that this phase, like everything, would pass. He predicted that I would find another "wife" when I was ready. As I placed my hands on the drums to begin our lesson, I almost believed him.

CHAPTER 8

Varanasi: George

"All things must pass. All things must pass away."
– *All Things Must Pass*, George Harrison

I made two trips to the Yogi Lodge the next morning, first with Ronit while I carried her backpack and then alone with my pack and tabla. I arrived feeling optimistic and liberated. The lodge was a haven for "westerners," as Indians call North Americans and Europeans. You could order pizza, watch a movie, smoke chillum, or just chill. Ronit chose a bed in a dorm with a couple of women and I rented a private room next door. That wall was important to me. My small piece of rented real estate represented a big step toward my independence.

As I helped Ronit unpack, one of her dormmates was packing for home. She was younger than us, Israeli, and wearing a sari. Her name was Galit and I was surprised when she asked no one in particular, "What eees thees enligh-ten-ment anyway?"

She had a pile of books on meditation, all with the same face on the cover, an Indian guru with a white beard named Osho. Galit had been at his ashram in Pune. She wore a string of beads with his face on a pendant and said, "I sat in that ashram for four weeks. And I mean *sat*, for hours and hours. I went to all the classes and I *still* don't know how to meditate."

In addition to the books, she had Osho CDs and portraits strewn across her bed. Galit scanned them with disdain and said, "I spent so much money in Pune and for what? Now I have to go home and I am no closer to enlightenment…"

I didn't know anything about meditation but felt that Galit was probably trying *too* hard to make it happen. I had also been sitting a lot—behind my new drums. My aspirations weren't as ambitious as enlightenment, but I'd found purpose in practicing tabla.

About a week before I was set to deliver Ronit to Goa, there was a buzz in the lodge because George Harrison of the Beatles had passed away and his cremated remains were rumored to be en route to Varanasi. Harrison's interest in Indian music had directly led to mine. When I was ten years old, I discovered the music of the Beatles in my friend William's basement. His older brother had all of their records, and William and I listened to them chronologically, tracing a path through the 1960s while we played ping-pong.

When the twang of the sitar introduced *Norwegian Wood* on 1965's *Rubber Soul*, I was struck by the new sound. Continuing onward to 1966's *Revolver*, the sitar on *Love You To* jumped out at me. The lyrics covered the Beatles' typical subject of love, but this time the sitar marched to the beat of a tabla through the ancient path of what I now understand to be a *raga* in a conveniently packaged three minutes. When the album rolled into the harmonized vocals of *Here, There and Everywhere*, I wondered what had just happened.

"Their music starts to get really psychedelic," William had said, leading me to believe that I must like psychedelic music. It would have been more accurate to say that I liked *Indian* music, but I didn't know then that the unique sounds that connected with me so viscerally were from a real place on the other side of the world. From the start, raga forged an opening to a fascinating purity for me. I think that even with all of the money and attention of the material world, George Harrison wanted to pass through that same portal—and India was the entryway.

Keshav had moved my tabla lessons to 11 a.m., allowing me the privilege of joining him and his family for lunch afterwards. We sat on the concrete floor with steel plates of rice and curry while his wife brought hot, fresh *chapatis* to us as they came off the stove. A long-haired sitar student named Otto, a "Bosnian refugee from France," would join us. I couldn't tell if Otto was a little bit crazy, just spiritual, or some of both. He would acknowledge the gods by chanting "Bom Shiva," "Hai Ram" or "Hare Krishna" at the end of every sentence while rocking back and forth from his cross-legged position. As we sat down to eat, he said, "Evvv-erybody go to Ganga when they die. Bom Siga Ram."

I understood Otto's cryptic comment as a reference to current events and said, "George Harrison had a special connection with India..."

"Yes," said Keshav through a mouthful of food. "Other Beatles came and left, but George Harrison was a son of India. I played music for him once, in Europe." Keshav then told us about a trip to Sweden where he played tabla for forty-eight hours straight to promote world peace. He took in only liquids and urinated in a hose. "No shitting."

I laughed out loud at the double meaning and Otto nodded, "Bom Siga Ram..."

That afternoon, down at Dasaswamedh Ghat, I spotted an English bloke from the Yogi Lodge. He asked, "Do you know if George, I mean, *when* George is showing up today?" I smiled and wondered if all Britons were on a first name basis with "George." I speculated that the family would prefer a private ceremony far from the crowds of Dasaswamedh Ghat.

I enjoyed Keshav's performance that night, but felt troubled when I returned to see Ronit in the lodge, lying on the bed of Yaron, an Israeli guy in an open dorm. Odd-smelling smoke billowed from the room and I declined when a traveler offered me a joint of opium and hashish. Instead, I sped upstairs and brooded alone in my room. Unable to sleep, I scrawled feelings into my journal. Did Ronit have to hook up with another guy already? Couldn't she wait a week for us to be in separate places?

Then there was a knock on the door, timid, but heavy enough that I knew that it wasn't Ronit. It was Yaron; I was seeing his scraggly beard and long, wavy brown hair up close for the first time. He seemed as uneager to approach me as I was to receive him. He asked me to locate a tube of back-relieving ointment from Ronit's bag in her room because her back was spasming and she couldn't move. I had applied that ointment many times. This time, though, I was only being asked to find it. Yaron would rub it in.

The next morning, I still felt jealous and humiliated, so I went walking along the Ganga to clear my head. I inadvertently climbed the steps of a tiny temple. It was framed by trees in open air and had an amazing view of the river. A young Indian man and an older gentleman sat together in silence, meditating. As my hiking boots turned back toward the entrance, the younger man smiled at me and said, "No, stay. Please…"

I accepted the invitation, sat cross-legged, and closed my eyes. I had never meditated before. Then the young man asked, "Which country?"

Meditation was no longer happening.

The older man opened his eyes but stayed completely still. I told the young man that I was a tabla student from Canada, visiting Varanasi for a month. He introduced himself as Rajesh and told me that the older man was his guru. Rajesh invited me for a walk and before leaving, he knelt to the ground and touched the bare feet of his guru, a sign of respect that I had seen from some of Keshav's students at the ashram.

As we walked together, Rajesh asked, "Have you seen the burning ghats?"

I had not. I had seen billows of smoke along the river from a distance, but hadn't considered visiting where the bodies were cremated. Rajesh said that it was important that I see these ghats before leaving Varanasi, but that I should go with him—there were protocols that he would guide me through. "Many people come to Banaras to die," he said, echoing what Otto had said the day before and using Varanasi's historical name. When I asked why, he said, "Ganga liberates the soul. My guru, who you met—he is enlightened. It is difficult to reach this while you are living."

At the burning ghats, soot-covered workers piled wood on platforms where bodies burned. The ashes were then swept into the Ganges. The smell was strong—like a macabre barbeque. Smoke filled my lungs and I covered my face with my shirt. Rajesh advised me to not look anyone in the eyes out of respect. He explained that poorer families could not afford much wood, so their loved ones' corpses would only be charred before being pushed into the Ganga. That explained the bodies I'd occasionally seen floating downstream. Then he pointed out a wealthier family sweating in their dress clothes. A shrouded body rested on a tall pile of logs within a flame that had to be ten feet high. It made the area as hot as a boiler room. The corpse would return to dust, like the clay teacups.

In the searing heat, I thought of Dinesh in Nepal. Had his soul been saved? I couldn't find redemption in his shortened life—it only felt tragic to me. I'd never know if Ronit's rejection had precipitated his suicide, but what did it matter? Liberated or not, he was gone. Rajesh directed me away from the fire and I wiped the sweat and soot from my forehead. My clothes and hair carried the smell of death for the rest of the day.

When the Beatles broke up in 1970, George Harrison was twenty-seven and ready for change. He was already an excellent songwriter, but within the group, his work was considered secondary to Lennon and McCartney's; he contributed two or three songs at most to a Beatles record. When he released his first solo effort that same year—an exploration of impermanence and renewal titled All Things Must Pass—*he had enough material to fill three records. The album was hailed as a triumph by critics and fans. No longer a supporting player, and unburdened from the expectations of others, Harrison thrived on his own.*

That afternoon, I saw Ronit alone on a couch in the lodge. Yaron had left town—off to find his ex-girlfriend elsewhere in India. She wanted me to know that they hadn't hooked up, out of *his* concern for how it would make me feel. I was glad that one of them had considered it.

That night, I returned to Dasaswamedh Ghat as the Varanasi sunset sky turned from burnt orange to brilliant blue and then black. The spectrum of colors reflected my experience in Varanasi. From the hospital to the ashram and the burning ghats, I'd certainly found a change of scenery.

Once the sun was down, the Hindu Brahmins of Dasaswamedh began the nightly ritual of evening aarti. The priest waved a candelabra in the dark air to bells and drumbeats. A clean-cut White fellow approached me and asked in a Scottish accent, "What is happening?"

"It's evening aarti. The priest is making offerings to the Ganga."

A moment later, he looked at the Brahmin pouring smoke into the air, forming circles with a steel urn of burning dhoop. He asked me, "What is he holding?"

"Incense."

After another long pause, he finally got to the point. "Is this George Harrison's funeral?"

"No...they do this every night."

Varanasi was so vivid that a routine prayer ritual could be mistaken for the funeral of one of the world's most famous rock stars.

When I closed my eyes in bed that night, I could still see the blazing fires of the burning ghats. I thought of George Harrison, of Dinesh, and of the bodies I'd seen on funeral pyres. I was mourning the end of a relationship that had meant everything to me, but as I prepared to travel alone in India, I knew that tabla would be my starting point. When I played my drums, all of the frustration and jealousy of the past few months dissolved. The rhythms of raga made me believe that things weren't always going to be this grey.

CHAPTER 9

Palolem: Home

Home takes on a different meaning when you're traveling. Ronit made a home in Pokhara's bars and then with a new crew in the Yogi Lodge. The ashram was where I felt most comfortable in Varanasi, arriving daily to Keshav asking if I had mastered the previous day's lesson. I became accustomed to the drone of sitars and intermingled aromas of incense and curry. Lunch on the floor with Keshav's family made me feel at home with them.

Home could also be a person. Though Ronit and I lived separate lives for our last ten days in Varanasi, she was still my strongest connection. Even when I was angry with her, I felt grounded by her presence in the lodge. It was only as we prepared to leave Varanasi that I started to feel alone. Like Wile E. Coyote in the old cartoons, so focused on catching the Road Runner that he would run right off the edge of a cliff before noticing that there was no ground beneath his feet, I had spent weeks looking forward to dropping Ronit's backpack and our figurative baggage off in Goa, but I had no plan for what I would do next.

On the train, Ronit and I chatted for a little while but quickly ran out of things to talk about. We had no shared future to discuss and the recent past wasn't ripe for revisiting. With our silence broken only by the rattling railcar, we both gazed out the window at the countryside. I sat and wondered where my next home would be.

At a stop in Mumbai, Ronit, a health-conscious vegetarian, shocked me by walking into a McDonald's restaurant. In three and a half years together, we had never eaten at a McDonald's. Ronit ordered fries and I snapped a final photo of her. But for the Indian *salwar kameez* she was wearing, the picture could be from a North American road trip. I eventually understood why she wanted to eat there. The location and taste were a connection to our home country. Ronit was also approaching a cliff, and McDonald's was a familiar stop before that leap.

Goa is a small state by Indian standards—a former Portuguese colony with ancient churches and gorgeous beaches. Ronit picked Arambol Beach at the northern top of Goa as her destination. Arambol was known for a huge banyan tree where holy men and travelers converged to share chillums and wisdom, sheltered from Goa's bright sunlight.

I delivered Ronit to Arambol as promised and she said, "What's the rush? Stay for at least a night. I have a double bed. We can share it. It's beautiful here."

It *was* beautiful at Arambol, a long and wide sandy beach with gentle waves and a slow pace, but I wasn't going to be tempted by Ronit's renewed interest in me. I told her, "I'm not worried about you. You'll make new friends in five minutes."

She walked me toward the bus stop for southern Goa. Before I crossed the road to get to the stop, we had a long hug of closure. As I waited for the bus, a Paul Simon song played in my head.

> "Hop on the bus, Gus
> You don't need to discuss much
> Just drop off the key, Lee
> And get yourself free."
>
> – *50 Ways to Leave Your Lover*, Paul Simon

But the bus wasn't coming. I could see Ronit on the other side of the road. She'd entered an outdoor restaurant and was already talking with people. She didn't look over to see if the bus had come or to give me a comforting look. My prediction that she'd make friends in five minutes turned out to be an overestimate. At the bus stop, my only company were

chickens and goats wandering aimlessly on the dirt road. The uncertainty of my destiny crept in as I waited. Instead of getting on with *my* new life, I was watching the first moments of Ronit's.

    The bus finally came and, a few hours later, I arrived at Palolem Beach, on the southern tip of Goa. It was the most stunning beach I had ever seen. Rocks jutted out on the water's edges, framing a postcard of beige sand and forgiving waves. The bus deposited me in the middle of the beach, and I instinctively turned to the south, farther away from Ronit in the north. Travelers sat under umbrellas drinking midday cocktails and reading books. The lodgings were simple—some small concrete buildings, but most were thatched huts, crammed too close together for privacy.

    Over rocks and around a bend, I followed a narrow walking path to where the huts were more spread out. Slowing my pace to pick out a place to land, I was greeted by Povi Pagi, a young, diminutive Goan fellow with a plan for both me and him. His family's guesthouse, named the Ocean Breeze, was perfect for me, Povi said. I couldn't disagree with the smiley Indian fellow. He set me up in a ten-by-ten-foot bamboo hut with a thatched roof, a bamboo bed, and a floor of sand. I took the key for the padlock on the door, laid my bags on the sandy ground, sat on the bed, and knew I had found a new home.

The guesthouse was at Colomb Beach, a cove that fishing boats departed from early each morning. It had a beachfront restaurant with white plastic tables in the sand and was sandwiched between beautiful, busy Palolem and its quieter sibling to the south, Patnam Beach. Patnam was remarkably sparse and also gorgeous.

Feeling fantastic when I awoke the next morning, I walked on stepping stones to the outdoor washing facilities. A small mirror framed in blue plastic hung from a nail in a palm tree, with a small sink below. The outdoor shower had a curtain for privacy that I could peek over the top of and see the ocean. I had breakfast at the guesthouse restaurant and then walked a few steps to practice tabla in the shade of a large tree. The tabla sounded different in a spot that was quieter than anywhere in Varanasi. Povi helped me to feel at home by bringing me a straw mat to sit on.

The sun moved across the sky and when the tree no longer gave shade, I took off my shirt. Unlike in conservative Varanasi, it was fine to be shirtless or in a bikini in Goa. Cross-legged at the drums in only my bathing suit, with no plans or connections other than my friendly host, I glowed in the afternoon sun.

Then a young blonde woman arrived alone to the Ocean Breeze. She sat down at one of the tables, opened a book, ordered coffee, and smiled at me while I continued to play. I wondered if she had chosen the restaurant because of the tabla music.

I watched her read while I played. She was graceful and gorgeous, casual and comfortable. When I stopped to stretch my legs and drink water, she put down the book and her blue eyes invited me to come and sit. Still shirtless and a little sweaty from the sun's heat, I introduced myself and learned that she was Angela from the U.S. She was traveling alone and had been in Goa for a couple of days. I can't remember what else she told me because it wasn't her words that I was focusing on. I was savoring the experience of chatting in the sun with a pretty stranger. It all felt new.

I eventually went back to my drums. Her coffee done, Angela disrobed to a bikini and went for a dip in the cove. The tide was out and the water sparkled in the lowering sunlight. As she floated in the shimmering sea, I played a rhythm that felt like a fitting soundtrack for her swim.

A short time later, Angela came out of the water in movie-like slow motion, flipping her hair back and smiling at me. I watched her glide up the cove to retrieve her towel. *Keep playing*, I told myself. *This would be an embarrassing time to mess up the rhythm.*

Once she was dry and reading again, I took another break at Angela's table. She and I were chatting when Povi approached and asked in his Indian schoolboy English, "Will you be having dinner with us tonight?" Angela nodded and we ordered food. I went to my hut for a clean shirt.

While we waited for dinner, the sun descended toward the ocean, lighting the sky in a purple and blue glow. The traditional Indian food from the Pagi family kitchen was filling and delicious. Angela and I learned that we were both traveling alone for the same reason—she had just come out of a tough relationship as well. After divulging our fragile states, we left the subject on the table like a cold, untouched dish.

I watched her hair lighten in color as it dried in the warm evening air and I enjoyed the lively sound of her voice as it filled the darkening night. I put dinner on my tab and she spoke of all-night dance parties at Anjuna in the north of Goa. I observed my inner resistance to anything in that area—my personal compass was pointing south, away from Ronit. I told Angela that I had just arrived at Palolem and planned to stay for a while. I nodded as she named DJs and beaches and then, seemingly from out of nowhere, she said, "I have to pack."

I was stunned. She meant now—she was going to Anjuna in the morning. I wanted to follow her there, but I hadn't been invited and I'd just said that I planned to stay put. Angela packed her book into her bag, thanked me for dinner, and stood. We hugged like old friends and I asked, "Do you want me to walk you back to Palolem?"

"No thanks, I'm good."

She slipped out the back, Jack! Her departure felt like another breakup, somehow more painful than the last. I returned to my hut feeling confused. I'd felt reborn that morning, but like a newborn baby, I'd looked to attach right away. After creating a fantasy of being with Angela and then watching it be destroyed, I was disappointed to be alone in a hut with two drums and a borrowed straw mat to play them on. Earlier that day, I'd been satisfied with just that. I decided that I'd better be careful about what I attached to next.

CHAPTER 10

Palolem: Choose Your Own Adventure

Early the next morning, I walked to Palolem and recalled telling Keshav that Ronit and I were breaking up. After describing Shiva's serial relationship sabotage, Keshav had said, "God has written this already." He held his palms open over his tabla, as if he were holding something. "There is this big book. God has written your story—everyone's story—in this book already." He waddled his head and said, "So, it is no problem."

Though I appreciated his support, I couldn't accept the theory. If God *had* written my story, maybe it was an outline, or one of those *Choose Your Own Adventure* books where each chapter ended with two choices leading to other sections that would reveal the decision's implications. I wondered, though, could it be that God was placing signs on my path? If so, my part was to recognize them and choose the right adventure.

The beach was quiet at that time of the morning. Cigarettes burned and coffee brewed, but most travelers slept while locals set up their businesses for the day. I kept an eye out for Angela, hoping to see her blue eyes one last time. I didn't see her, but I did see a sign.

The information was written in white chalk outside a sandy establishment with bamboo huts called the Rendez Vous Café. Yoga class was winding up as I arrived. I sat down in a green plastic chair to wait for the class to finish and to meet the teacher.

Did God intend for me to stop there, or did I choose to? Either way, I felt compelled. I'd vowed to be cautious with what I attached to next, and yoga seemed like a choice that would lead my story in a positive direction. I had tried it a few times at the gym back home. It felt good, but I hardly knew what I was doing. I did notice something different about the teacher, though: She had a calm and peaceful glow about her. I wondered what that glow was about, particularly when I noticed it again in Krishna, the yoga teacher at the Rendez Vous Café.

In the Hindu pantheon, the god Krishna is a model citizen. He is worshipped as a sweet baby, a mischievous toddler, a flute player wise beyond his years, and as a compassionate guru. Krishna the yoga teacher was a small fellow from the state of Kerala in the south of India. His short black hair formed in a peak on his round forehead. He was unshaven and wore red cotton pants and a white T-shirt adorned with yoga's ubiquitous *Om* symbol. Krishna was quick to smile and had a gentle voice. I liked him right away and felt that I could learn from him. "Come tomorrow, 8:30 a.m.," he said to me. "That is the beginner class. We will do the breathing exercises, the sun salutations, the *asanas,* and then final relaxation." From what I'd seen of his class that morning, yoga seemed calming. I knew that my old routines were no longer working, so I was motivated and optimistic about yoga.

I arrived early the next morning and sat on one of the straw mats that were laid in a circle under tall palm trees. Looking past the teacher's spot in the front, I noticed that each hut of the café was labeled with an Indian god or goddess. I was facing a poster of Shiva, the change agent that Keshav had taught me about. As I waited for Krishna and the other students to arrive, I said to myself, "Everything changes, whether you want it to or not."

First, we controlled our breath in exercises called *pranayama* that involved forcefully exhaling and then holding the breath for a long time. Krishna said that we could control *prana*, an energy within us, through our breath. Then we performed sun salutations, a series of twelve postures completed in quick succession. I broke a sweat in the morning sun.

After a moment to rest, Krishna led us in a series of poses, the asanas. Some were easy—standing like a tree—while others seemed impossible—standing on your head. We laid on our chests and raised our feet as high as we could. I lifted mine a few inches and couldn't believe my eyes as I watched Krishna's feet elevate over his back until he was bent backwards in a human C, with his feet nearly touching his head. I didn't know that bodies moved that way.

I was open to trying anything and often surprised when I held a pose, if only for a moment. I felt both drained and invigorated when we laid on our mats for a final relaxation.

The ocean waves provided background music while Krishna guided us through our bodies in his soothing voice. He began at the toes and went upward. "Your toes are re…laxed, your feet are re…laxed. Your toes and feet are to…tal…ly re…laxed…"

The journey continued to the top of the head. "Your mind and spirit are com…plete…ly re…laxed… You are to…tally free person… You are fresh born."

Opening my eyes, I *did* feel fresh born. I *did* feel totally free. I felt fantastic. The yoga class gave me a buzz that lasted throughout the day. I practiced tabla, floated in the warm ocean, and, after setting my alarm for the next morning's class, slept well. By the end of my first day as a yogi, I had fully bought into the program.

I began attending Krishna's classes daily. Other travelers came and went, but I focused on the teachings, holding poses for as long as I could. I saw my sweat dripping on the straw mat as an indication that I was pushing myself. I desperately wanted to not feel stuck anymore, and drop by drop, I was releasing from all of it. From the pressure of work, the expectations of my parents, my dysfunctional relationship…

After what ended up being a private lesson on my fourth day, Krishna declared that I was ready for his 7 a.m. advanced class. I thought it was too soon for me to jump up a level, but he said that I would enjoy the group of experienced yogis, and that he thought I could keep up. I was honored by his confidence in me and quickly adjusted my watch alarm for the earlier wake-up time.

That evening, I sat at the Ocean Breeze, writing. As the restaurant closed down and the Pagi family went off to bed, Lina from Switzerland was the only other person around. She was in her thirties and had shoulder-length light brown hair. Her hut was next to mine. Now she swung in the hammock next to my tabla practice spot, facing the water. We hadn't spoken before. She asked what I was writing about. I looked up and said, "About yoga…"

She asked if I practiced yoga. I moved my chair closer to the hammock and spoke of my recent experiences. I said, "My body feels stretched out and loose."

"Like a massage…" she said with a smile that might have been mischievous.

"Almost…" I said. I saw a choice ahead of me: I could wrap up the conversation and return to my hut or take a riskier path. In the darkness, I felt confident enough to ask, "Do you want a massage?" Lina suggested that we meet in her hut in a few minutes. I returned to mine to "change," but all I did was put a condom in my pocket. When I arrived at Lina's hut, she had candles lit. I didn't know if she was thinking what I was thinking, but when I entered her room, my doubt dropped to the floor along with Lina's clothes.

I'd been single for less than a month, but I felt like a teenager as I explored her unfamiliar body. I was nervous and it felt strange to be with someone new—someone I'd just met. My body wanted her, but my mind was running interference. The whole experience didn't last very long, but Lina was kind. By being with me, she pushed my relationship troubles from the present into the past. When I got up to leave, she thanked me and asked me to be honest about what I wanted from her. I told her that I would, just as soon as I figured it out for myself. I returned to my hut to sleep before my now-earlier yoga alarm.

It was cooler at 7 a.m. and the advanced class included a nice group of students. I was dragging a bit from the night before, but I made it through. After class, I had breakfast with two young Slovenian women who had both worn red tank tops to class. I called them the "red team" and they didn't mind. They asked if I was traveling alone, and I explained that I had begun the trip with a girlfriend and that we were now on different paths.

One of them said that she had split from her boyfriend of four years, but that she was happy now. The way Elsa said it, I assumed that the breakup was recent, but it had happened more than two years ago. She was beautiful with blonde hair and an athletic body. Her being happily single didn't make sense to me. I asked if she'd seen other people since then and she said that she hadn't.

I took Elsa's experience as a lesson that being alone was okay, and perhaps even ideal. I'd been working for so long to cultivate a relationship that replacing it seemed like the logical next step. I wondered, though, could a relationship with a woman be replaced by a renewed relationship with myself? This Slovenian yogini was pointing out a chapter in my story that I was skipping past: I had to learn how to be alone before I could relearn how to be with someone else.

When I returned to the Ocean Breeze that morning, Lina smiled at me from the hammock. I sat with her and we talked for a little while. She'd asked me to be honest with her, so I told her that I was coming out of a long relationship and needed some time alone. She said that she could wait for me, but I asked her not to. She looked at me as quizzically as I had at Elsa, wondering why someone would want to be alone. She was on vacation and wanted to have fun. I wasn't on her wavelength, though. I had things to figure out.

As I sat down to practice tabla, Lina watched me from the hammock. I realized that I'd ruined my own favorite spot by sleeping with my next-door neighbor. Wanting a break from the awkwardness, I packed up my drums and walked toward Palolem.

Not far from the Ocean Breeze, an Englishman called to me from his concrete beachfront porch. He was shirtless, tattooed, and wearing leather pants with a spiked belt. A tattooed buxom woman with long dark hair and wearing a black bikini swung on a hammock next to him. As I approached, the fellow said, "Do you want to smoke a joint?"

I hadn't smoked much pot since leaving Nepal, but it was still one of my favorite things to do. When I was high, music sounded better, food tasted better, and jokes were funnier. I hesitated for a moment at the invitation, knowing that my decision would impact the rest of my day. In the end, I was happy for an escape after my interaction with Lina.

The couple chatted about the impressive quality of Indian hashish and the country's comparatively mundane marijuana. They had both, so we rolled up a few joints and puffed billows of smoke off of the porch. When we were done, they gave me a small bag of pot and returned to their room.

My routine immediately lost its structure. My tabla stayed in its bag and I swung in the hammock at the Ocean Breeze, listening to music and writing in my journal. With my motivation dimmed from the pot, I savored the sensation of having nowhere to be and nothing in particular to do.

I caught up with Krishna that night and enjoyed hearing more about his life. He'd become a yoga instructor in a monthlong teacher training course at an ashram. I lit up a joint while he said that he wanted to start an evening meditation group. Some of his yoga students were interested and he thought it would be perfect on the beach at sunset.

I told him about my travels and the recent encounter with Lina. Krishna said, "Shiva made love to Parvati atop Mt. Kailash for ten thousand years. After that, he meditated in a cave for ten thousand years." Though my few minutes on the mountain with Lina fell well short of Shiva's record, I felt that it was time to find a cave and meditate.

Then Krishna told me that yogis don't smoke. "When you are smoking, focus on the taste and, over time, your body will reject it."

And just as things were starting to make sense, Krishna asked for a puff and did yogic breathing exercises with the pot smoke. The contradiction reminded me that Palolem was a part of India, after all, a place where anything is possible and we each have to write our own story.

CHAPTER 11

Palolem: Free Person

Krishna's meditation group began the following night. I wanted to have a clear head for it, so I held off from smoking pot all day and rolled a joint for afterwards. The sun was about to set when we gathered on a section of sand between the Rendez Vous Café and the ocean. The red team took part along with a few other travelers. Krishna advised us to focus on our breath with our eyes closed. I followed most of what he said, but couldn't resist watching the sun lower into the sea. The sky was a brilliant orange that turned to pink before fading finally to dark blue.

Krishna's voice was calm. "Any thoughts… let them float away. And when another thought comes, let it float away also… Then focus again on your breath…" Everyone remained silent and still. My eyes were fixed on the horizon as I tried to ignore thoughts and observe my breathing. It was hard to do, but I felt empowered by the group. They were all looking inward for something deeper and I was inspired by that. Each meditator felt like a pillar of support under the darkening sky. I didn't even know them all, but I could feel their intention.

Krishna concluded the session under deep blue dusk and few words were spoken as the participants dispersed. I walked to my hut in silence. I had planned to light the joint, but I was content and decided that there was no need to. Besides, I had a yoga class to wake up early for.

I maintained my new routine for three days—advanced yoga with the red team at dawn and meditation at sunset. In between, I practiced tabla under the tree at the Ocean Breeze. Walking at Palolem one hot afternoon, I met a group of Canadian travelers playing didgeridoo and a hand drum. I grabbed my tabla and jammed with them for a few hours.

They passed a hash pipe around, but I declined. I hadn't smoked since the meditation group started, wanting to see if my new routine felt better than the old one. It wasn't easy to say no. I craved pot, but I didn't want to burn out in the daytime. As I meditated in the evening, I'd noticed how frequently I thought about getting high. I enjoyed a beer once in a while, but I never thought about drinking. Pot was different. It probably didn't help that I was still carrying that same joint I'd rolled before our first meditation group in my pocket. I decided that as long as I waited until after meditation, I'd finally light it that night.

There were some new faces at meditation that evening. As I observed the kaleidoscope sky, I saw that I wasn't the only one who'd ignored the instructions to keep our eyes closed. A tall brown-haired woman was also staring out to sea. When I noticed her, I closed my eyes so I'd look like I belonged. I wasn't the new kid anymore.

I felt the ocean breeze on my face. Meditation was harder without the sunset to focus on, but I was reveling in the joy of a perfect day, augmented by playing music with new friends in the afternoon. When the session was done, I stargazed, in no rush to leave. The new brunette was asking Krishna a few questions. He answered but didn't stay to chat. Then she turned to me and asked, "How long have you been meditating?"

Her white blouse and khaki shorts would have fit in at a country club. She was Swedish and I could tell that she hadn't been sitting on Indian floors for long. She had parachuted into a spiritual energy that she was struggling to grasp. I said, "I'm probably not doing it right. But I've been trying for about four days. It's hard to *not* think."

She tilted her head and asked, "Are you always this happy?"

I laughed and told her no. I said that I'd had a great day and that I found the evening sessions uplifting even if I couldn't really dismiss my thoughts like a proper meditator. She'd caught on to the glow of the group and was probably also feeling some benefit from her first meditation. She was asking a rookie, though—I didn't have any guidance for her.

I lit the joint from my pocket and offered her some. She declined and excused herself. Enjoying my first buzz in a while, I reconsidered the purpose of my journey. No, I wasn't always this happy, but could I be? Sure, traveling was fun, but I sought sustainable solutions. After only a week on my own, I didn't have answers yet, but the lightness I'd gained from yoga with Krishna told me that I was finally pointed in the right direction.

I always set an alarm for yoga class, but a rooster perched near the thin walls of my hut rendered it redundant. After his call, I would brush my teeth and walk the ten minutes to Palolem under moonlight. Cross-legged on a straw mat, I'd close my eyes for pranayama and see daylight's beginning when it was time for the asanas.

I kept that routine up for a few more days until December 26th, when the red team told us that it would be their last class. The musical Canadian friends were heading out also. My community was dwindling, but updates on email helped to soften the blow. My college friend Josh was coming in a couple of weeks. He mentioned yoga and an interest in "easing" himself into India, so I suggested that he begin his trip at Palolem with Krishna and me. I also received a message from Robin, an acquaintance from Edmonton who was working with eunuchs in Tamil Nadu in India's south. She had time off and was heading to Goa. She asked where to find me and I gave her my coordinates.

On a break from tabla practice, I sat in the hammock to write in my journal. For the first time that I could recall, I had no thoughts. Normally, I'd ruminate on relationship struggles and life-balance questions, but it was refreshing to have none. I'd been working to let my thoughts float away in meditation, and I started to think that I might be making progress.

Afterwards, I jogged over to nearby Patnam Beach. I was doing cartwheels in the sand when a tanned brunette in a black bikini appeared. Her name was Lisa and she practiced capoeira. She taught me some kicks and we spun around in synchronicity. I was invigorated by the movement and dripping with sweat. Lisa suggested that we jump in the ocean to cool off.

As we floated in the cerulean sea, I noticed that I still didn't have any thoughts. I felt supported by the ocean and by my gurus, Keshav and Krishna. I looked over at Lisa and we both swam back to shore. She said goodbye with a hug and turned to walk on. I wanted to say something to her—to cling to the magic of our interaction—but I bit my lip. I knew that allowing a beautiful moment to pass was as much a part of my learning as dismissing unwanted thoughts.

The next day, the advanced yoga class was a private lesson because I was the only student. Krishna urged me to stay for the beginner class that followed. No one else came to evening meditation either, so Krishna and I just hung out. I mentioned how it was easier to focus in a group and he explained, "It is called *satsanga*. More people make a meditation more powerful." It made sense that a group of like-minded truth seekers could raise the collective vibration of a space. I'd noticed it during the ashram concerts in Varanasi, and that was why Krishna had started the group. He knew that it would magnify the effect.

The next morning, I returned from my double yoga class and found Robin from Edmonton waiting for me at the Ocean Breeze. I ordered breakfast and she rolled cigarettes from a pouch of loose tobacco. We knew each other a little bit from parties back home. She had straight black hair and sea-blue eyes. Her broad smile broke frequently into a chuckle. She was self-deprecating when referring to the community service work she was doing in "that town I'm living in." After a few months there, she still couldn't pronounce Oddanchatram.

Robin relaxed while I played tabla and then we chatted from afternoon until sunset. She smoked her handrolled cigarettes and I lit up a joint. It was a warm night. When the sky became filled with stars, Robin said, "You should come with me to Om Beach for New Year's."

I didn't like the idea of leaving Palolem. After two weeks there, I was feeling better than ever. I said so and Robin said, "You can come back. Besides, can't you be happy anywhere?"

There was that question again. I honestly didn't know. My time at Palolem had been almost perfect and I didn't want to change a thing. Still, I told Robin I'd consider her invitation. We walked back to the Ocean Breeze. She hadn't inquired about a hut and when I opened the door to mine, she walked in, climbed into my bed, and said, "We both fit." I laid down by her side and gave her hand a friendly squeeze to say goodnight. She looked over with inviting eyes and kissed me.

She was pretty, but I hadn't been thinking about being with her—Robin wasn't quick to reveal her desires, and we had a lot of friends in common. I just assumed she wasn't looking at me that way. Besides, my experience with Lina had revealed that I had a lot to learn, particularly in matters of the heart. Robin and I made love, and it felt natural and unburdened—as though home was checking up on me and telling me I was doing alright.

After Robin fell asleep, I looked at the stars through my hut's bamboo roof. I could tell then that Robin was not only *from* home, she *was* home, for at least that one night. As she slept on my shoulder, I realized that I was the same for her. Robin wasn't just passing through Goa—she had traveled across India on a hunch that I could be a temporary home for her also. On a break from her community service work and the intensity of India, my voice took her back to the familiar, if only for a few hours.

Would we have even hooked up back in Canada? It's hard to know—I had a girlfriend then. But months and miles away from home, we seemed to have so much in common. I appreciated her companionship and thought about Om Beach. Lina was still at the Ocean Breeze. If she saw me with Robin after my assertions that I needed to be alone, things would get awkward in a hurry. Maybe I didn't need to be alone after all, but I did want to feel free of my relationship errors, distant *and* recent. I decided to go south with Robin. I trusted that I'd be back in my thatched hut soon enough.

I awoke to the rooster the next morning and left Robin a note asking her to wait for me to return from yoga so that we could leave together. When Krishna said that I was a "to-tal-ly … free … person" at the end of class, I believed it. I was choosing to try something new and I believed that I could bring some of my experience at Palolem with me.

I told Krishna that I planned to return with my friend, Josh. He advised me to keep practicing yoga every morning, and I promised that I would. I already craved it. It was opening me, and I had felt closed for a very long time.

The bus stop was on Palolem's main road, a strip of black pavement perpendicular to the beach and lined with T-shirt stores and smoothie stands. Across from the bus stop was a tiny standalone *chaat* shop with Indian fast food, in this case, fried dough called *puri* with *chana masala*. The place was so small that you could easily miss its pale blue painted concrete walls with no sign at all. It marketed with smell. The aroma drew us in—especially me, hungry after yoga and the long walk with our bags. After we'd ordered and gotten our food, I said to Robin, "Back to India."

"Back to India," she replied, toasting the decision with a piece of puri. Of course, Goa is a part of India, but the little shop reminded us that we were leaving the tourist bubble of Palolem and joining the masses of humanity and exhaust fumes. The bus came by and we got on, but all of the seats were taken. We stood in the back with the chickens.

CHAPTER 12

Om Beach: Shiva's Eye

"Om" is a mantra used not only by yogis and Hindus, but by many traditions to bring inner peace. A mantra is a sound that can be repeated vocally, or silently in the mind, to create calm. Both methods lift the spirit. Buddhists chant "Om mani padme hum," Christians and Jews say "Amen" at the end of a prayer, and children around the world call their mothers Mom, Mama, and Oma. Om is universally soothing.

At the end of each yoga class at Palolem, the students joined in Krishna's guttural Om. The mantra was enveloping when we chanted it in satsanga.

The Om symbol is from Sanskrit, the ancient Hindu language, but is commonly known. Om Beach was so named because of its resemblance to the three-shaped symbol, with one small beach connected to a larger one, both curved and meeting in the middle. It even had the dot. An island of boulders offshore was named after the destroyer god himself: Shiva Rocks.

As December 31, 2001 approached, my resolutions were simply to continue with yoga and tabla. I was hopeful that Om Beach would lift my vibrations like its namesake. Our landing spot, the Namaste Café, was one of only two establishments on the beach and was as mellow as could be. It was filled with Israeli travelers and had an Indian waiter who spoke Hebrew. Robin and I shared a room behind the restaurant.

The reason I kept meeting young Israelis across India had to do with mandatory conscription in their country. After high school, all Israelis were required to join the military. It was a three-year commitment for men and two years for women. These young soldiers were forced to grow up fast, often on patrols in dangerous areas. Once their service was completed, the twenty- or twenty-one-year-olds had money in their pockets and time to decompress. Many came to India because it was exotic and inexpensive. I met some Israelis who were interested in music and yoga, but not at the Namaste Café. This group's mantra was "puff, puff, pass" with the chillum, morning, noon, and night.

I would complain to Robin, "No one *does* anything here," but she didn't mind it. She was resting from her work with the eunuchs, and had a good book and her tobacco to roll. I'd wake up early for yoga and then practice tabla for an hour or two.

New Year's Eve featured a small party with a DJ, but I was hit with a round of Delhi Belly from something I ate and turned in before midnight. I woke up late on New Year's Day to Robin's sensual touch. "I think you're better," she said. I noticed a tattoo of an eagle flying through antlers on Robin's hip and asked about it. She said, "It's from an indigenous folk tale. My sister tells the story in a dance. The symbol represents strength and endurance."

Robin had both qualities in ample supply. Hers was a quiet strength. She'd seen a lot in Tamil Nadu but didn't talk about it much. Also, her physical endurance exceeded mine. Despite my yoga and exercise, I couldn't keep up with her in bed. After our lovemaking, I would feel like I needed to come out of our concrete room for air.

The following day, I felt a lot better and was able to practice yoga at sunrise. Pink clouds reflected on the water as fishermen set out from the flat bay of Om Beach. Restaurant staff slept on the cement floor of the café.

Cows sauntered along the empty beach while I practiced with Krishna's voice in my head, guiding me through the asanas, final relaxation, and a private, quiet chant of Om three times.

After breakfast, I perched in the corner of the restaurant facing the sandy bay for tabla practice. A young Israeli woman named Miriam sat next to me, listening and knitting. She joked that she was my first tabla fan and told me about her military service. She'd been required to have an M-16 by her side at all times. She called hers "Mickey" and though she'd been a civilian for months, she still reached for the rifle all of the time.

Miriam was cute. Her sandy blonde hair flipped at her shoulders and she was sarcastic. She seemed strong but had baby fat in her cheeks. It was hard to imagine her as a rifle-toting soldier. She was decompressing like the rest of the Israelis—not by getting high but, on this day, by watching the ocean and listening to some amateur Indian music. I enjoyed her company.

Robin sat in the café, smoking cigarettes and drinking coffee. I was turned off by the stoner scene and a bit more restless than either of my female friends. I got to talking about yoga with a French fellow named Oscar who was with a French *baba*, or holy man. The baba wore the robes of a Hindu priest and had dreadlocks tied around his head like a turban. Oscar invited me to visit them at Paradise Beach, a further oasis that could be reached only by boat or on foot.

That night, the tide was low. I walked with Robin and Miriam to sit and watch the sunset from Shiva Rocks. As the sun dropped past the ocean, Robin returned to the café. I stayed and laid down for the spectacular colors that were sure to follow. Miriam slid over, cradled my head in her lap, and tousled my hair. The sky turned brilliant orange through cotton candy clouds. I sat up, looked at her, and said, "I can't…"

She tilted her head toward the café and Robin. "I couldn't tell if you two were together…" I explained that we were friends but also intimate. Miriam understood. I held her tight for a while, feeling our affection and unfulfilled desire. Afterwards, I wondered why I seemed to be attracting so much female attention. That didn't usually happen. Perhaps my new routine made me seem a bit more alive than everyone else at the Namaste Café.

When we're seeking direction, vibrant people are appealing. Sexuality is one way of connecting with the life force of another person, but I was starting to see that it wasn't the ideal way for me at that time. Passion was taking energy away from me rather than adding it. My yoga glow was fading and I didn't want it to. That was why I took a break from the café and hiked to Paradise Beach the next morning.

I found Oscar barefoot among pebbles in the water, wearing only a loin cloth and collecting Shiva's eyes. The dime-sized, swirled half circles were eroded shells, smoothed from being tossed repeatedly over round rocks by waves. I found a few and was happy to have a portable reminder from Shiva that everything is always changing, that I shouldn't become too attached to one place, one person, or one routine. I didn't regret leaving Palolem. Robin had helped me with the transition, but now things were heating up at the Namaste Café and I needed the opposite. As the ocean cooled my feet, I yearned for simplicity.

The French baba sat nearby, captivating the attention of a bikini-clad blonde woman squatting in the grass. I couldn't hear a word, but assumed he was spouting platitudes just to hold the pretty woman's attention. As though he could tell what I was thinking, Oscar said of the baba, "Ee knows things… Ee has been to the other side."

I gave a skeptical look and Oscar said, "Ee is enlightened."

As Oscar walked away, I sat on the beach and wondered why I mistrusted gurus even though I'd gained so much from Keshav and Krishna. When I got up to begin my walk back to Om Beach, the baba and the blonde got up at the same time. I crossed paths with them and the baba asked me, "'Ave you been to Hampi?"

I was surprised by the question and shook my head no.

"You should go."

The young woman's blue eyes widened, implying that I should do as the holy man said. They walked on and I stood alone on Paradise Beach for a moment, wondering where Hampi was and if this directive was a sign I should follow. It felt as though he knew something, as Oscar had said. I suddenly felt bad for thinking he was a fraud because he spoke very kindly to me. I wasn't sure what to think, but I had a twenty-minute walk back to mull it over.

I was feeling ready to move on anyway. In two days, Robin would begin her journey back to that town she was living in. In addition to acceptance and friendship, she had given me something else that helped me to move on from Ronit: guilt-free, sweaty pleasure—more of it than I could handle. The cork was definitely off of the bottle. I felt satisfied and ready to be alone again, largely because of the one thing that Robin hadn't given me: her heart.

I was glad that Robin wasn't affectionate. She had given me an opportunity to feel without *feelings*. My wounds were still too fresh to get into anything real. As I considered following the baba's suggestion to move on to Hampi, I realized how much Robin was protecting her own heart also. She wasn't open about her feelings and I wasn't about to ask why.

My simultaneous passion for Miriam told me that I wasn't feeling love for either of them. Flat-out desire was only helpful to a point. It was like the Israeli boys and their chillum. It might take them to a deeper place if they treated it as a sacrament, but they were overindulging by getting high all day in the café. I felt that I was falling into the same kind of pattern with sex. I wanted a break from it in hopes that, next time, it would be for something more than a release.

Back at the Namaste Café, it was easy to learn about Hampi. All of the Israelis had been there and even Robin had heard of it. It was in Karnataka, where we were already, but a long bus or train ride away. Hearing about its temples, boulders, and sunsets, the place sounded lovely. I had a bit more than a week before I would meet Josh back at Palolem, so I decided to head to Hampi the following morning.

Om Beach had not raised my spirits like its mantra namesake, but I still appreciated my time there. Robin's companionship had given me the confidence to travel alone without feeling that I needed a woman to make me happy. I gave her a Shiva's eye as a gift and I packed up. It was time to get back on the solo trip.

CHAPTER 13

Hampi: Ravi Chandra

Arriving in Hampi felt like pulling into a movie set. Grey morning light shone on ornate temples overlooking rice fields along a winding river. The Vijanayagar empire had chosen the spot in the fourteenth century for its unique beauty and I could see why. Massive boulders dotted the landscape like marbles strewn by giant-handed gods. I pulled my bags off of the overnight bus and saw carvings climbing to the sky on pyramid-shaped temples.

I had budgeted during the bus ride and determined that two hundred and fifty rupees (about five Canadian dollars) a day would get me past the expiration of my six-month Indian visa in May. I would have enough money for another adventure before I had to return home in late June for my sister's wedding. Ronit and I had talked about going to Thailand after India, but my latest idea was to return to Nepal for a springtime trek in the Himalayas.

I'd heard that affordable accommodations were on the other side of Hampi's plodding river. I wound my way down to the riverbank and past

a ghat where women in saris were up to their knees in laundry and soapy river water. Big woven baskets called *corracles* ferried ten to fifteen people across the river at a time. One basket had a motorcycle in it, but a car would have been too big.

Across the river and down a dirt road, I noticed the handpainted sign of the Ravi Chandra guesthouse. It was a single-story row of ground-level rooms run by a jovial fellow named Bhima. He offered me a room with a mattress atop a cement platform built into the wall. Concrete tables and plastic patio chairs placed outside the rooms created a communal feel. Bhima's wife cooked for the guests, and in order to maximize the available accommodations, Bhima and his wife slept on the kitchen floor with the guesthouse's namesakes, their young son Ravi and baby girl Chandra.

On my first morning there, I practiced yoga near a small tributary of the river on the property. I had a view of the sunrise over boulders on the horizon, but Bhima advised me that a better place for yoga would be at the ashram down the road. I agreed to check it out the next day.

When I opened the door to my room after the yoga session, a chicken scampered past me and out the door. I was startled at first, but laughed when I found a warm, single egg next to my pillow. Bhima confirmed that the head of the bed was her laying spot and he took the egg and put it in the fridge. The hen visited daily, so I began delivering the egg on my own.

As the town's low-budget lodging option, the Ravi Chandra attracted some interesting characters. One was Thomas from Holland, whom I found in the midst of building a raft out of bamboo. He and a friend intended to float down Hampi's river just to see where it would take them. They had attempted to launch, but the vessel sank under their weight. Their new plan was to tie empty water jugs to the bottom of the raft. I found the two men to be funny but also cheered them on. After all, like their raft, I had an unstable foundation but was being built with the best intentions.

Another character was an Indian baba who visited frequently. These holy men, also called sadhus, could be easily recognized by their loincloths and dreadlocked hair, often wound around the top of their heads. They would commonly walk barefoot with a cane in one hand and a begging bowl in the other. I recalled Keshav putting food in a sadhu's bowl outside the Music Centre in Varanasi.

The sadhus were also high most of the time. They smoked *manali*, a type of hashish named for a city in northern India, from the conical chillum at all hours of the day. They looked like stoned, homeless beggars to me, but Indians treated them as important members of society. Sadhus weren't expected to work. Their job was to connect with God and, in doing so, bring spiritual benefit to their community. It was hard to understand that perspective and this particular sadhu didn't make it any easier. His first words as he held out his bowl were, "Do you have manali?"

I said no and he quickly pivoted. "Do you want? I have some."

He was a beggar *and* a pusher. I told him that I didn't smoke manali, but that I did like *charras* (marijuana). He sold me some and hung around for a while. When I mentioned yoga, he showed off his skills by putting both feet behind his head. He was old and wrinkly, but sat with a proud smile, balancing on his bony buttocks, toes popping up behind his dreadlocks. If I hadn't just put a hundred rupees in his bowl, I might have tipped him for that maneuver alone.

That night, I climbed up to the Achutaraya Temple and gazed at an orange sunset, sitting among sadhus and other travelers while young boys sold chai from aluminum teakettles. Next to me, two Indian guys were cuddling. Public displays of affection are acceptable in India, but only between males, which I found amusing and sweet at the same time. I felt thankful that I had followed the French baba's advice to go to Hampi. It was another place where most people didn't *do* anything—except for the boys building the raft—but I was enjoying traveling on my own.

A young Indian girl approached me and asked, "Helicopter ride?" She didn't speak much English, but those two words were clear. The problem was that I didn't understand what she meant. She grabbed my hands and started to run in a circle to demonstrate. She wanted me to spin her around in the air like the propeller of a helicopter. The thrill seeker took flight as I held her wrists and twirled. With her dress flapping in the breeze, she found a way to make the most of that moment—to be exhilarated, joyful, and alive. In hiring me as her pilot, she did the same for me.

The next day, I followed Bhima's advice and walked on the muddy paths between rice paddies to a nearby, white-tiled ashram for yoga. The building was mostly underground with a courtyard elevated above the rice fields and fenced in by a low wall. The temple was closed, so I chose a spot on the deck facing the sunrise and unrolled a borrowed straw mat. I went through Krishna's full hour-and-a-half routine, his voice still fresh in my mind.

Later that morning, I recruited Cliff from Australia for a mountain bike ride to visit ancient temples on Hampi's dirt roads. I wouldn't call them ruins, because the structures were so well preserved. We had an awesome time, but on the way back, I was reminded again that everything changes. This time the messenger wasn't Shiva.

As Cliff and I climbed into our coracle back across the river, I found myself face to face with Yaron, Ronit's Varanasi cuddle buddy. It felt like so long ago that I'd seen him, but it had only been a month. Jealousy rose quickly in my chest and fell just as fast. As painful as those days at the Yogi Lodge had been, I wasn't angry anymore. Yaron froze, allowing me to decide how this encounter was going to go. I nodded my head to acknowledge him and he did the same.

While avoiding any further eye contact, I thought about what had changed in the past month. Yoga was helping me to feel strong and focused. Meditation was showing me how to dismiss unhelpful thoughts. Also, as silly as it may sound, by getting high only once a day, I was pretty sober by the standards of my current peers and my own recent past.

I *did* feel different from how I had in Varanasi, but it wasn't all progress. In breaking up with Ronit, I had been emotionally honest and that openness had set me free. After a few days away from Ronit and my brief emotional roller-coaster ride when Angela left Palolem, I'd boxed up my feelings and put them in storage like all of my possessions back home. That was partly why I had had no time for Lina and hadn't connected deeply with Robin. I wasn't ready to trust anyone. Being alone was safer.

The next morning in Hampi, I noticed two unusual-looking backpacks planted in the courtyard of the Ravi Chandra guesthouse. It was rare to see bags left unattended, but I chuckled that the packs didn't look too enticing anyway. They were small, dirt-covered, and seemed to be almost empty. Most of the backpacks around were like mine—tightly packed bundles of worldly possessions. The bags in the courtyard were of a different sort and I assumed that their owners must be as well.

That evening I sat in my underwear in bed, listening to music and reading. Then I heard a knock and got up to find two attractive and well-traveled-looking young women outside my door. They were trying to find the guesthouse owners so that they could sort out their accommodations. They wore salwar kameez, indicating that they had probably been in the country for a while. I was interested in hearing their story, but focused instead on helping them. I gave an Indian arm wave and said, "The family sleeps in the kitchen, over there."

They peeked into my room. One of them was tall and outgoing—a leader with short blond hair. Her friend had curly brown hair and soft features. Both had radiant smiles. I saw that this pair went with the two backpacks I'd seen earlier that day.

The leader blurted with American exuberance, "You have music!"

I nodded and looked over at my mini-speakers, currently playing something mellow. Then she asked, "Want to have a dance party?" Despite the clock ticking closer to my bedtime, I felt that it would be a mistake to turn them down. I tidied up the room and put on some clothes.

The two women returned a few minutes later for the "dance party." I put on the liveliest music I had in my CD case, James Brown's *Funk Power*. The blonde leader was Fran, her brown-haired friend was Liz, and they were both from California. Fran and I sat at opposite ends of the bed and got acquainted while Liz sat in the middle and browsed through my CDs. Fran said, "That's impressive… Traveling with so many CDs and even speakers."

Apple's iPods weren't released until after my trip had begun, so the big CD book felt like a necessity. I responded, "Yep, it was tough to choose, but I settled on those eighty (CDs)."

Fran laughed at me, but I didn't mind. "Why so many?"

"It's a long trip."

Fran laughed again. Liz pointed at *The Best of Leonard Cohen*. "My friend says that I'm Suzanne," the title and subject of the first song on that album. I was intrigued to hear that she emulated Cohen's rag-wearing, free-spirited muse.

Liz and Fran had recently graduated from UC Berkeley and "the co-ops," a living arrangement they described as utopian. Work shifts were assigned according to skill and everyone cooked vegetarian meals for each other. Their parties inevitably concluded with everyone naked in the hot tub.

Since then, the two had volunteered for three months at a hospital in Tamil Nadu. That commitment complete, they were traveling the country. Their first stop had been at Anjuna, Goa, where they danced a lot and slept on the beach. In that same spirit, they planned to sleep in the Ravi Chandra's treehouse that night. When I asked them if the guesthouse had any rooms available, Fran said she didn't know. I chuckled at that. My room had cost less than two dollars, so I wondered what motivated their desire to sleep outdoors.

Then Fran asked me, "So, what are you doing in India?"

"Oh...just seeking the meaning of life. You guys, too?"

Fran answered, "Oh, we found that already. Now we're just having fun."

Talking with them felt surprisingly comfortable. I admired their spirit of exploration. We didn't actually dance, but when they left, I felt that I had two new friends. They were both attractive but, having recently sworn off women, I tried not to notice. It would be easier that way.

CHAPTER 14

Hampi: Treehouse

At dawn, I walked the rice paddy path to the ashram's outdoor platform for yoga. The air was fresh but warm. The space was silent and I remained focused, guided by my memory of Krishna's teaching. After the session, I stopped for a croissant and returned to the Ravi Chandra to wash up before moving on to tabla practice. Walking to the washroom carrying my toothbrush, I saw Liz, the quiet brunette from the night before. She was sitting in a sunbeam, looking pensive and graceful in a purple batik blouse. She seemed troubled, so I asked how she was doing.

"I'm okay…"

I told her that didn't sound too convincing and asked what was on her mind. She said that at breakfast in the guesthouse courtyard, another traveler had declared India a "third-world wonderland" and a "Disneyland for travelers." He'd elaborated that with such low costs for everything, visitors could do whatever they wanted. So soon after working with malnourished children in farming communities in Tamil Nadu, Liz found the comment disturbing.

The closest I had come to humanitarian work in India was my ongoing mission to save myself, but I could still sense what Liz was feeling. I appreciated India's rich culture and I'd already learned so much from Keshav and Krishna. I said to Liz, "The conversation made you wonder if you're in the wrong place."

She asked how I could tell and I said, "I've had that feeling a lot on this trip." She asked why and I said, "Long story... But I haven't had that feeling here." She asked why not and I said, "Hampi has been great. You can do whatever you want." I smiled to show that I was joking and Liz finally released the crinkles in her forehead.

Then she asked, "What's the long story?"

I sat down on the concrete floor next to her. "Well... I didn't start this trip on my own. I left home with a girlfriend, but she is no longer my girlfriend. Nepal was lovely, but I felt like I was in the wrong place. It took me a long time to figure out why." Liz wanted to know what I'd learned, so I told her about finally realizing that I needed be on my own. "And once I took that time for myself, I started to discover new things."

I was embarrassed to be talking so much about myself, but Liz seemed to be right there with me, feeling the journey. I told her about tabla and about yoga. She said that she had been practicing yoga since she was fifteen and that they did "naked yoga" at their co-op house in Berkeley. I invited her to join me at the ashram the next morning, "but I think you'd better wear clothes." I then told her about Palolem and my trip to Om Beach with "a friend from home." I concluded with "...and that's how things worked out for me."

"No," she said, "that's how *you* worked things out."

It was *that* kind of a conversation. Our trains of thought kept converging and we built on each other's ideas. Then she observed, "There's a newness about you."

"Can I keep it?"

"No. Savor it. Watch it grow. You'll keep on changing."

I knew that she was correct, but in that moment, I didn't want *anything* to change. I felt loose from yoga and was basking in Liz's beauty and wisdom. Then I noticed the sun high in the sky. With my toothbrush still in hand, I got up and finally went to shower.

Reflecting on those hours, I can only describe it as love at first sight. Ringo is certain that it happens all the time, but to me it was a revelation. I'd been in love before, but it had evolved slowly. This time it was like a sun shower. It struck when I least expected it.

Walking back from the washroom and still glowing from the conversation, I heard a voice calling to me from above. I looked up to see Liz in the treehouse. "Someone gave me a papaya. Want to help me finish it?"

I climbed the handmade ladder to the thatched platform to join her. I could see the ashram, rice paddies, and massive boulders from there. We finished the fruit and Liz was about to climb down to wash her hands when I said, "Just rub it in." I demonstrated, rubbing some papaya juice into her gentle palm. It was silly advice, but I wanted her to stay up there with me. Our hands were sticky, but we didn't care. I asked, "Did you sleep up here last night?"

"No, the family didn't want us to. They put us in the storage room."

I looked up. "Stars would be amazing from here at night."

She agreed and I asked why they wanted to sleep outside.

"We slept on the beach the whole time in Goa."

I asked if many people had done that.

"No, just us."

I asked if it was safe.

"Stray dogs kept guard over us."

Then Liz talked about her adjustment from working in Tamil Nadu to the expatriate party scene in Anjuna. She and Fran were among longtime wanderers—westerners who sought refuge in Goa's low cost of living, beautiful beaches, and party scene. They'd been sent there by some "old hippies" from Berkeley who were board members for the organization that Liz and Fran volunteered for, the Seva Foundation.

"I know Seva." I said. "The Grateful Dead used to do benefit concerts for them."

"We heard about Anjuna from a woman named Jahanara and her husband, Wavy Gravy."

I was impressed. Wavy Gravy is a counterculture icon, initially famous for being the Master of Ceremonies at Woodstock. He and his wife had visited the hospital in India while Liz and Fran were volunteering. Upon his arrival from a long journey, Liz asked Mr. Gravy if she could get him anything. He replied, "Just an end to world hunger."

Jahanara suggested visiting her friends in Anjuna as a friendly start to Liz and Fran's India travels. There, Liz had been drawn to Hampi by a *National Geographic* magazine with pictures of the area's incredible temples. I told her that I'd biked to them the other day.

"Will you take us?"

I told her I'd be happy to. "Where is Fran?"

"Still sleeping."

"Wow, it's late." I said.

"She did a lot of drugs in Goa."

"I see...and you?"

"I don't do drugs. I'm tripped out enough without them." I was tripping too—on how this girl was making me feel. I climbed carefully out of the treehouse.

By mid-afternoon, we had finally moved on to separate activities. Aside from the croissant and papaya, I had forgotten to eat or drink. Liz went to shower and I sat at my tabla. Notes raced off my drums, tapping beats of release.

In our four-hour conversation, it felt like Liz was speaking directly to my soul. Through brown eyes that sparkled green in the sunlight, there was honesty and understanding. She accepted the damaged, developing, rebounder for what I was. I saw someone with a kind heart and a curious spirit, who also happened to be gorgeous.

After getting dressed, Liz sat down across from me while I played, scrubbing her foot with a sock. She wondered aloud if she had a skin disease as she scraped layers of brown from her foot. I stopped and had a closer look. "Were you barefoot in Goa?"

"The whole time."

"Then my medical assessment is that you have dirt caked into your skin."

Liz smiled and scrubbed harder.

That evening, I sat in the courtyard of the Ravi Chandra with Liz and Fran. Watching the two women interact, I wondered about their respective heritages. "So, your full names aren't Liz and Fran … what are they and where do they come from?"

"Francine is French and my parents are from Romania."

"I see, and … Elizabeth?"

"Ee-lees-a-bet. My mom is Cuban."

"Ah ha!" I was proud of my investigation. "Who calls you Elizabeth?"

"Only my parents, and only when I'm in trouble."

We all laughed and I asked, "And when you're not in trouble?"

"They call me Lizzie."

"Well, Lizzie," Fran said, "I'm going for a walk."

Liz headed to the treehouse to stargaze and I followed. We laid on our backs and admired the sparkling sky. The stream bubbling below us made it feel like we were floating on the straw platform. I reached for her hand. We sat up and looked in each other's eyes. Feeling the warmth of our newfound connection, I leaned forward and kissed her.

"I knew that would be amazing," I exclaimed before I could catch myself.

"Really?" she asked, and I answered with a big hug. We laughed nervously, glad to have cleared the hurdle of our first kiss. We returned to our backs and the blanket of stars.

When the night air cooled, I led Liz to my room. I put on some classical Indian music and slowly undressed her. Slowly and gently, I admired her beauty until the early-morning hours. We didn't make love, but it somehow felt even more intimate. I was oblivious to time and didn't recall falling asleep.

I awoke to the sound of a grumpy chicken scratching at my wooden door. Sun blazed into the room, indicating that it was long past the chicken's usual egg-laying time. Every other morning, when I had been out early for yoga, the chicken would squeeze under the door. But she wouldn't do that with us inside—we were interfering with her schedule.

I got up and opened the door. The chicken marched over to the bed, jumped up, and conducted her delayed morning ritual with no interest in Liz or me. Then she hopped down and walked out, seemingly still peeved. I picked up the warm egg and handed it to Liz. Surprised and amused, she held it up and said, "I guess that's a good omen."

CHAPTER 15

Hampi: Little Wing

A square window deep in the concrete wall of my room faced the Ravi Chandra's outdoor tables. That morning, sunbeams burst through every crack in its wooden shades. I had already closed the door behind the chicken, but chatter penetrated our sanctum and I felt exposed. I usually passed through the courtyard before anyone else, but this time it was already mid-morning. At some point, Liz and I would have to step into a scene already in progress.

We exited separately to maintain modesty. No one at the tables noticed or cared.

Meeting up with Fran and Cliff at breakfast, we planned a day of biking together, but Liz was acting distant. I wondered if her feelings for me

were already receding. On the ride, we all shared laughs and took pictures, but Liz avoided eye contact with me. It would have been a perfect day if doubt hadn't traveled with me to every stop.

I'd recently declared my independence, but Liz was special. If Robin was home for me, Liz was family. She almost felt like a little sister. Not like *that*, but it's the best way I can describe the feeling. What I wanted the most for her was to be well, but as we biked from temple to temple, I also wanted an indication of how she was feeling.

I didn't get it, not until that evening when she and Fran returned from dinner in their salwar kameez with two Israeli guys in tow. I wasn't sure if they were invited, but the fellows were clearly enchanted with the American women. I was playing tabla when they arrived, and Liz sat next to me on the concrete ground and asked, "Will you show me how to play?"

After hardly hearing from her all day, I was happy to be her escape. I guided her hands on the drums and she was surprisingly good at it. I guessed correctly that she played piano. The Israeli boys tried to make small talk, saying things like, "So, you're *really* from California…" and "You wear Indian clothes…" When Fran eventually responded, they saw an opening and offered to massage Liz and Fran. They were persistent and I laughed to myself—*I know that line…*

Fran said no a couple of times but eventually accepted on the condition that Liz go, too. I was left alone at my drums as the four of them retreated to Liz and Fran's storage room. I looked up into the starry sky and wondered if Liz would emerge before the end of the night. I believed that she would but had to also laugh at the absurd situation. Our moment at the tabla was reassuring. I wanted to be close to her, to *know* her. Somewhere below my self-doubt, I sensed that Liz was also having powerful feelings and wasn't sure what to do about them.

I drummed to break the night's silence and after a *long* thirty minutes, the women emerged unruffled from their massages. Happy beats bounced off of my tabla as Liz and Fran hugged the Israelis, dismissing them for the night.

Liz invited me on a walk. Under a dome of stars, she thanked me for being patient with her and said that the following day would be her last in Hampi. She planned to leave for a Buddhist monastery nearby. She was "on the hunt" for a Tibetan monk, a friend of a friend. I told her that I would be off soon as well, to meet my friend Josh at Palolem. Happy to be alone with her and talking again, I asked why she'd been silent all day.

"I was tired."

It felt like a partial answer. We walked back on the dark road and Liz stopped in starlight at the entrance of the guesthouse property. She said, "Fran is going home in April and I'll be in Thailand for a month after that. Do you want to travel with me?"

I'd spent all day wondering if Liz would ever talk with me again and now she was discussing "us" in the future. I hadn't even known that there was an "us." I said that I'd consider her invitation, but that I was thinking about hiking in Nepal after India. As pleased as I was to be connecting with Liz again, the idea of waiting for her to be available felt eerily familiar. I didn't want to chase a feeling or be hurt when I couldn't catch it. I asked if we could meet again sooner and she said that she planned to visit Kerala (in the south) soon. While I rambled about my travel options, she interrupted me with a kiss.

I looked in Liz's beautiful but tired eyes and said, "You should get some rest. Sleep in your room tonight." She was perplexed that I wasn't asking her to come to mine, but I said, "I'd probably keep you up all night again."

She knew that I was right and asked me to wake her for yoga. I was surprised with myself. It was our second-to-last night together in Hampi, but I wanted what was best for Liz.

Lying in bed, I could see her face. Her kaleidoscope eyes sparked my curiosity and her gentle touch warmed my heart. Time together strengthened our connection and seemed to also bring me closer to myself.

The next morning, I led Liz to the ashram's white-tile platform under the glow of sunrise. She noticed a sign at the gate that declared, "The search for self is essential. Life without this realization is a waste." We shared a smile and were glad that we weren't wasting our lives.

A rice farmer was walking by as we began our yoga session. Each of his ribs was visible above the dirty white *lungi* (cloth) around his waist. Noticing that I was sipping water, he guided me, "Don't take water before yoga—little bit okay." He waddled his head and I thanked him for the

advice. I was impressed to see how ingrained the practice of yoga was in Indian culture.

Liz followed my instructions. Halfway through our two-hour session, I lifted my torso from near the ground, suddenly felt light-headed, and nearly passed out. Everything went black and I lost my sense of place. After a few seconds, the setting faded back in and I could feel my feet on the ground. I looked over at Liz. She was holding the pose, awaiting my next cue.

When I told her about it later, Liz said, "The point of yoga is to transcend your conscious mind…" Neither of us thought that meant fainting, but the experience *had* been mind-altering. I'd stepped away from time and space for a few seconds. When the lights came back on, joy rushed in along with the image of Liz in a warrior pose, facing Hampi's boulders in the morning sun. I was right where I wanted to be.

Later on, at the guesthouse, Liz joined Bhima's wife to wash clothes on a rock at the stream that ran through the property. When our host was done, I joined Liz at the water with some laundry of my own. Jasmine flowers fell into the stream and floated by, scenting the creek.

I was impressed with how little Liz was traveling with. She had shed things along the way and most of her clothes were in the local style. Liz and Fran weren't trying to prove anything by dressing like Indian women. They were only trying to make Indian people comfortable by covering their bodies. And I could now understand why Liz's bag had looked almost empty: She and Fran wanted to be nimble enough to walk all day with their packs on and choose their lodging, or suitable patch of ground, when it suited them.

I set up my CD player with Jimi Hendrix's *Axis: Bold as Love* as Liz and I continued to wash clothes. I'd been thinking of the album's Indian-style cover. On it, the band members are incarnations of the Hindu god Vishnu. Where Shiva is known for destruction, Vishnu is the preserver of all that is good in our world. Liz knew the album and smiled as we listened to *Little Wing*. Hendrix's muse walks through the clouds and rides with the wind. She offers him everything, but he urges her to fly on. He's not ready.

That evening, Fran invited me to an outdoor café, saying that Liz would be there soon. Fran asked a lot of questions and I realized that she was checking me out, as any loyal friend would. She said that it had been over a year since Liz last had a boyfriend. Liz had been hesitant to open up to anyone since, but Fran thought it seemed different with me. She could see our strong connection. She asked what I thought of Liz.

"She's made a profound impression on me."

"She seems to have that effect." I recalled the Israelis from the previous night.

"What do *you* think about us?"

"I think you'd be good for her."

I was basking in Fran's endorsement when Liz arrived, talking about the evening's beautiful sunset. We all shared a bowl of hummus and Liz invited me for dinner. She chose a small restaurant around a bend. We sat on cushions on the ground in a concrete alcove and, over candlelight, Liz began to ask me about my hometown, my friends, and my family. I attempted to bounce some questions back at her and chuckled when she kept circling back to me. It felt like the second in a series of interviews. I must have passed the screening, because we returned to my room after our meal. It was another beautiful night. We continued to take things slowly and I felt so comfortable falling asleep and waking up by her side.

After practicing yoga together and packing up, Liz invited me into the treehouse. She opened her journal to tell me a story about a crystal healer from Goa who she had met two weeks earlier. Liz described laying on a sheet on the ground wearing only her underwear and a faded, tie-dyed T-shirt from the Salvation Army. Her brown locks were spread out around her head and the healer placed crystals on and around her body. The healer told Liz that she was *the* goddess—a being separate from her physical body. She led Goddess Liz on a swim through her body's *chakras* (energy centers). Each one felt different—some beautiful and others resistant. Goddess Liz moved freely until she reached the throat, where she perceived a boulder slowing her passage.

Liz wasn't sure what it all meant, but I appreciated her sharing something so personal with me. I think it was her way of showing me what her journey was really about. She wasn't just dancing and sleeping on the ground in Goa. She was searching for her true self.

Liz mentioned Thailand and I asked again if I could see her sooner. Two months felt too far away to plan for. She said she'd keep me posted on the monk hunt and let me know when she was heading to Kerala. There was no social media in those days—no following, no friending. We had each other's email addresses, but that was all. If her feelings changed, she might not write back. I took her picture so I'd have something to hold onto in case I never saw her smile again.

Then Liz, Fran, and I rode in a corracle across the river. On the raft was a drum salesman who sauntered regularly through Hampi with over a dozen drums hanging off of him. I asked if I could try a drum. When I began to play, he handed drums out to others on the small boat. We jammed while locals who were bathing in the river started to dance. Liz, Fran, and I were sharing our good feeling with everyone around us.

On the other side of the river, Liz and I stopped at a used bookstore. She recommended that I pick up a guide to the ashrams of India, called *From Here to Nirvana*. Months ago, I would never have considered visiting an ashram, but Keshav's music school was an ashram and our yoga spot in Hampi was an ashram. I was finally accepting that ashrams weren't only for weak-minded followers. Liz also gave me a book that she'd planned to trade in, called *What Buddhists Believe,* and I bought *The Favourite Game* by Leonard Cohen.

We hiked uphill past boulders and piles of human and animal feces for one last view of Hampi's temples. A group of well-dressed Indian kids asked to take their picture with us. It was common for Indian tourists to ask for a picture with a White person that they didn't know. I wasn't sure why, but would oblige when it happened. This group of kids was particularly charming, so I asked them to take one with my camera as well.

After that, I piled my bags into a three-wheeled auto-rickshaw and said to Liz, "I'm surprised that I *want to* do this." I expected to feel more conflicted about leaving her. I knew I didn't want to rush into a new relationship, but it still felt strange. I needed time to process it all and I hoped that by meeting up with my yoga teacher and an old friend, I'd find clarity.

Liz said, "It must be what's right ... for now."

Then she said goodbye with a wave and no hug (only acceptable in public if it's two guys, remember?) Then she flew on, like Little Wing.

CHAPTER 16

Palolem: Suzanne

The bus ejected me to the side of the road sometime between late night and early morning. It was almost too dark to see, but the sound of the ocean confirmed my proximity to Palolem. It was a long walk—an hour at least—to the Ocean Breeze and there were no vehicles on the road. Fortunately, I wasn't alone. A couple of Spaniards I'd met in Hampi—tall, balding Oscar, and dark, scraggly-haired Pio—were with me. It was their first time in Goa.

I'd played music at the Ravi Chandra with Oscar, a flamenco guitarist. As we began to walk toward the beach, Pio asked where I had learned tabla. Recalling Varanasi and Keshav helped distract me from the weight of my bags. Pio mused about going to Varanasi to study tabla later on his trip.

We arrived sweaty at the Ocean Breeze and I woke Povi. He greeted me like an old friend and led me back to hut number four. He settled the Spaniards into huts of their own while I sat on the bed and unpacked. My new Leonard Cohen book reminded me of one of the first things I'd heard Liz say—that a friend of hers thought that she was *Suzanne*. I flipped to the Leonard Cohen CD I had and put on my headphones.

Leonard Cohen grew up Jewish in Montreal in the 1940s and 50s. He dropped out of graduate school twice before achieving critical acclaim as a poet at the age of twenty-seven. It was around that time that he wrote The

Favourite Game, *an autobiographical novel about a young man who falls in love and doesn't know what to do about it.*

It was another five years before Cohen realized that his poems could be songs. Judy Collins recorded *Suzanne* in 1966, and a year later, she urged Cohen to perform it. That night changed the course of his life. The tale of a mystical lover became the opening track on the first of fourteen albums he would record over a forty-nine-year career as a singer-songwriter.

I appreciated Cohen's music, but his moods were powerful and I'd only listen in an appropriate time and space. My sandy hut before sunrise felt right for revisiting *Suzanne*. Cohen's tranquil voice wasn't through the first line before my eyes began to leak. Liz's friend was right. The song *was* about her.

It was also about me.

I knew the song, but it had new meaning to me now. Liz *had* taken my hand and led me to a place near the river. I *was* about to tell her that I had no love to give her, but she got me on her wavelength and let the jasmine-scented river answer a question that I hadn't even been asking. I had "always been her lover."

In the song, "Suzanne holds the mirror." When I spoke with Liz, I saw deeper into myself. She helped to reveal who I wanted to be. I wasn't crying because she was gone. It was because she existed at all. I hadn't cried during my separation from Ronit or when Dinesh died. I'd closed off my heart and let my analytical mind take charge. *Suzanne* breached the dam and it was a relief. The tears rested on my cheeks like welcome raindrops in a desert.

Unable to sleep, I walked out to the rocks above Palolem. Sunrise blessed the ocean with pink highlights on blue ripples as I headed down the beach for Krishna's advanced yoga class. It had been more than two weeks since I'd rushed out to go to Om Beach with Robin. Krishna was eager for updates, so we made plans to meet up in the evening. After class, I learned on email that Josh had landed in Mumbai but needed a couple of days to rest from his flights before traveling south to Goa.

It was wonderful to be back at the beach. I jammed with Oscar at the Ocean Breeze and savored the Pagi family's hospitality and food. It felt different from when I'd first landed at the Ocean Breeze damaged but determined to find purpose. I had looked through the eyes of a newborn when I started in Krishna's class. On this second visit, I felt like a sponge in the ocean of India, prepared to soak up all of the wisdom that it could offer.

I met up with Krishna at sunset. Meditation group wasn't happening and I hadn't smoked pot since meeting Liz, so I rolled up a joint and passed it to the yogi. I told him about Om Beach and Hampi, drumming and biking, Robin and, especially, Liz. He said, "Some women have good energy and can help us with the spiritual life."

"And some don't?"

"Women are also *Maya*."

"Who?"

"This world," he said. "The world where we live is called Maya. Some women can help us with the higher consciousness, but they also keep us in Maya."

I nodded and he continued the lesson. Maya, the reality we live in, magnifies the separation between Brahman and Atman, the God without and the God within, respectively. Brahman is the divine nature of the universe and Atman is the spark of divinity within us that we work to get closer to. It made sense to me that these two concepts of God had their own names.

"Connect with the Atman through yoga and you will see that Brahman is everywhere."

Those sounded like instructions to follow. I was releasing an anguish I'd traveled with for a long time and I was eager to fill that space with goodness. After allowing me a moment to digest the teaching, Krishna held the joint and started to repeat the old story.

"Shiva made love to Parvati on Mount Kailash for ten thousand years...."

"I remember," I said. "And then he left her to go and meditate for ten thousand more."

Krishna drew in a huge puff of smoke, held it in with a serious face, and then exhaled slowly with a smile. He wasn't going to tell me which stage I was in—that was for me to figure out. Every man (and god) needs to decide when it's time to express devotion or to turn inward. Liz was on her monk hunt, so I didn't need an answer yet. I also didn't know what choices I'd face in the future. One thing was clear, though: there was only one goddess I wanted to be on the mountaintop with.

CHAPTER 17

Palolem: Grateful

In 1993, I was entering my second year of university in Ontario, Canada, and moving in with friends. We had met in our dorm the previous year, and had now found a house off campus where eight of us could live. When my mom dropped me off, I was greeted by my friend Josh. School didn't start for another week and the house was almost empty. As my mom's car pulled away, Josh said, "I'm going to Ohio tomorrow to see the Grateful Dead. You should come."

"I just got here." I hadn't even started unpacking.

"Lucky for you!" His friend was coming in the morning and had an open seat in the car. Josh assured me that I could find tickets on site and that I wouldn't regret it.

Though he was only a year older than the rest of us, we called Josh "Grandpa" because of his penchant for musical education. In our first year, we would smoke a joint outside and then gather in his dorm room, three or four friends sitting on each of the twin beds. Josh would turn out the lights and crank the stereo for an inspiring piece by the Grateful Dead or someone unexpected like Supertramp or Steely Dan. We would close our eyes and become attuned to the force of a jam that was new to us but already familiar to Josh.

Josh was a Deadhead. He knew every song and had collected hundreds of live cassettes. After a year of hearing about the unique phenomenon of a Dead show, I now suddenly had the opportunity to experience one for myself. I was told to expect a transformative experience, unlike any other concert. The band was playing in the Richfield Coliseum near Cleveland for three consecutive nights. Josh and company planned to attend them all. I was skeptical about making such a commitment, but Josh assured me that after the first show, I'd be in for all three.

The border crossing went smoothly from what I could tell out the back window of the two-door sports car. Because of the band's well-known associations with drugs, we didn't mention to the customs agent that we were going to see the Grateful Dead. After checking into our hotel room, I was surprised to observe our driver taking a tiny screwdriver to his Grateful Dead tapes. They were packed with doses of LSD and rolled joints. He inventoried the drugs and replaced the tiny screws. I was glad that he hadn't told me in advance. That knowledge would have made me nervous about the border crossing.

Outside the show, vendors sold T-shirts, beer, and grilled cheese sandwiches. Many fans were looking for tickets, but I managed to buy one, paying a little bit over face value. Once we were inside, security was tight and I had to stay in my section, much higher up than my travel partners. Alone with no one I knew, the opening lyrics of *Feel Like a Stranger* were apt. The band promised that things would get stranger and I was ready for it, but it still felt like someone else's party.

The Deadheads were dancing and I was waiting for my transformative experience. Flower dresses twirled in the patchouli- and pot-scented arena. When the opening song ended with "gonna be long, long crazy, crazy night," I wanted to believe it. When would I not just hear the show, but feel it?

The first set sounded great, but it was… a rock concert. I wanted to understand why Deadheads would see consecutive shows, or even an entire tour, but I wasn't getting it. At set break, I sat down and people-watched. I saw women in tiny tops that barely covered their torsos. Some men had "hair so long they got to calling it home" like the protagonist in the Dead's *Saint Stephen*. Attendees connected as old friends, talking about what shows they would be seeing on the tour.

Then I felt a tap on my shoulder. It was Josh. He'd trekked up with two ticket stubs, and I would use a borrowed one to get into their section. I squeezed into their row as the lights dimmed for the second set. Our driver lit one of his smuggled joints and passed it on. I took a drag as the band tuned up and the crowd's anticipation bubbled. When the first notes of *Foolish Heart* filled the building, the atmosphere felt completely different than when I was alone in the stands. This show *wasn't* a regular concert. My senses were enhanced by a fresh buzz, the company of friends, and an improved vantage point, but apart from all of that, there was something about the band's sound in the second set. The songs lengthened, Jerry Garcia's guitar painted sonic circles, and the building rocked to the beat of the two drummers. My mind danced in the swirling images of the music and I loosened up enough to enjoy it all. It felt transformative.

At one point, Josh grabbed my shoulders and shouted, "Marky, you've arrived!"

Josh arrived in Palolem as I played tabla under my favorite tree at the Ocean Breeze. We hadn't seen each other in four years but had kept in touch. Glasses framed his thin face and his short brown hair had receded a little since I'd last seen him. Still, having just traveled across the world, he looked as healthy as ever. He was happy to find me. We had a long lunch and caught up on everything from the past few years to the past couple of days.

As Josh had predicted, I *did* end up going to all three concerts in Ohio. After that, I saw the Grateful Dead as often as possible. I didn't drop out of school or anything, but I did see them twenty times in their last three years as a band—frequently with Josh. We would drive long distances and then drop acid or eat psychedelic mushrooms for the shows. The difference between listening to a bootleg cassette in a dorm room and attending a show on acid was like jumping from black and white to three-dimensional technicolor. The drugs and songs led my mind to unchartered dimensions while Garcia's guitar dripped liquid gold in my ears.

When Jerry Garcia died, we shifted our attention to the next great improvisational band, Phish. I had last seen Josh in New York City for three Phish concerts over New Year's 1997 at Madison Square Garden.

Since then, I had dialed back on hallucinogenic drugs and apparently, he had also.

Josh had completed law school, but like me, he wasn't feeling satisfied on the professional path. In a vigorous search for clarity, he had found meditation. The practice had led him to yoga and yoga had led him to India. He was happy to start his journey in the paradise of Goa and he was looking forward to Krishna's classes.

Josh's backpack was stuffed with books on yoga and meditation. He made them as available to me as his Dead tapes had been back at school. If I was a sponge, soaking up the knowledge of India, Josh was a meditation database. He couldn't stop thinking about the practice of not thinking.

When I told him that I was drawn to yoga for how it made me feel physically, but that it was also bringing contentment, Josh said, "That means it's working." He was teaching just as before, only this time it wasn't on the difference between a 1972 Dead show and one from 1977, it was about life. Then he said, "Don't worry, I'll give you direction."

"I think I'm going in the right direction, but I could use more focus."

"I'll give you that, too." He handed me a yoga book by Donna Farhi called *Yoga: Mind, Body and Spirit* and said, "There are eight limbs of yoga. You've only done two of them."

The next morning, we walked in glowing moonlight to Krishna's early advanced class. Josh demonstrated his yoga experience by standing on his head, something I hadn't yet attempted. It motivated me to test my own physical limits in the class. He and Krishna hit it off right away and the two gurus quickly agreed that we should meditate together at sunset.

Back at the Ocean Breeze, I practiced tabla while Oscar jammed along on guitar, Pio watched, and Josh read a book. To keep track of each guest and our tabs at the restaurant, Povi identified each of us by the number of the hut we were staying in. I had always been number four and Josh was now number five. Pio was in Lina's old hut number two and Oscar was number three.

On a tabla break, I opened *Yoga: Mind, Body and Spirit*. In the introduction, Farhi writes that the vast beauty we find in nature also exists within ourselves, explaining that it can be found through yoga. As Krishna had said, Brahman is all around us and Atman is within. I had that in

mind later when I sat with Josh and Krishna for meditation at sunset. As the pink-purple glow dimmed over the shimmering water, I closed my eyes, observed my breath, and worked on letting my thoughts drift away. Meditation was so much harder than playing tabla, where I could tap the thoughts out of my mind. With my body inactive, my mind ran in circles.

After what felt like forever, I rolled onto my chest in the sand. I found it hard to accept that nature's beauty was within me. The ocean felt separate—stronger and timeless. I listened to my breath and the waves rolling onto the beach. I closed my eyes and let my thoughts flow.

My imagination brought me back to the creek at the Ravi Chandra in Hampi, washing clothes while jasmine floated downstream. I recalled the sweet smell and cool rush of water on my hands, while Jimi Hendrix sang about sandcastles slipping into the sea. In my mind's etching of that moment by the river, Liz was a part of nature's beauty. So was I.

When Josh and Krishna finished meditating, I lit up a joint, the last of the pot I'd bought from the baba in Hampi. Krishna smoked with me but Josh abstained, explaining that his journey no longer included drugs. I was surprised at first—we had smoked together so many times—but

I quickly understood, knowing that clouds of smoke might impede his search for clarity. I was starting to feel the same way as my reality became sharper by the day.

After meditation, Josh told Krishna about the concerts that he and I had attended together. He described each show as a satsanga of thousands, collectively aiming toward higher consciousness. "We all have different realms to explore and ways of navigating them. We may explore some of the same realms and we may even explore them together, but we do it as individuals, each having our own experience."

He was right. I explored other realms every chance that I could. Be it in a smoke-filled coliseum, in Keshav's tiny music room, or on a yoga mat on the beach, I altered my reality in a continuing quest for liberation from the mundane. The drugs and music served a common purpose: to venture into the beauty without and hopefully find my way to the beauty within.

On the walk back to the Ocean Breeze, I considered if pot was holding me back from reaching my potential. I wondered if I could stop smoking it and be just as happy. Inspired by Josh's abstention, I vowed that night to no longer carry my own stash. I might accept a joint, but I would no longer be the one rolling them. Like my earlier decision to only smoke at night, this would be a step toward separating from one of my last big attachments. When I told Josh, he said, "There's that *focus*. It's a step on your *spiritual* journey."

"Is *that* what this is called?"

Josh's ticket to India had "spiritual journey" stamped on it, but I'd stumbled onto one. Josh explained that I wasn't exploring a *new* realm; my trip was a continuation of a path I had started on years earlier. Just as the immersive music of a Grateful Dead concert could bring my focus to the present, yoga allowed me to stop searching, if only for moments at a time. It brought a wonderful feeling that I couldn't explain. If that feeling was Atman, the God within, that was a definition that I could get behind. Something wonderful that you can't explain—it is divine, it is grace.

CHAPTER 18

Palolem: Ashtanga

Josh had suggested that I learn about *ashtanga*, the eight limbs of yoga. Ashtanga is a path that includes asanas and meditation, but begins with precepts called the *yamas* and *niyamas*. Donna Farhi, the author of the book that Josh had handed me, encourages her readers to consider the relevance of each precept in their lives. Like ten commandments of yoga, the yamas and niyamas focus on issues of honesty and property, but they also contain spiritual and practical guidance. Farhi describes them as "vehicles for getting to the essence of who we are." I was interested to see how I measured up against the ancient wisdom of the yogis.

The precept of *ahimsa*, or nonviolence, includes having compassion for all living beings. At the Ocean Breeze, the rooster outside hut number four was still preempting my yoga alarm by half an hour every morning with his signature "cock-a-doodle!" When I complained about it to Josh, he said, "Put yourself in the rooster's shoes. Try to feel the joy of his call." That level of ahimsa was a stretch for me, but I *did* get halfway there and stopped getting angry when the rooster crowed.

That same day, our Spanish friend Pio had rented a motorbike. He was late returning from his jaunt around Goa, and Oscar feared that he'd been in an accident. He'd been right to worry. Pio had slid on a patch of gravel and crashed the bike. He returned with road rash on his head, one arm broken, and the other stitched up. We were thankful he wasn't more badly hurt, but needless to say, Pio would not be studying tabla with Keshav in Varanasi.

The next day, Pio scowled from under his bandage and smoked a lot of pot and cigarettes. He looked irritated when I played my drums. His dour demeanor caused me to avoid interacting with him. The accident had impacted his outer shell, but wasn't he still the same guy inside? I was amazed at how someone's personality could change so quickly and drastically.

Another one of the ashtanga precepts is contentment, or *santosha*. Farhi suggests feeling satisfied with your experience and finding hopefulness even when it feels scarce. When I saw Pio the next morning, the lights were back on. He looked like himself and I could tell that he was ready for the world again. He told me, "I've crashed bikes four times, but this time, it's finished. No more motorbikes." Touring his body, he said, "This arm is okay; just these stitches. This one (in a cast); it's getting better. So now I stay longer in India. I am not able to work yet, so I'll take a longer vacation." After just a day, Pio had found satisfaction amidst disappointment. Santosha had pulled him through. It's a lesson I still try to remember when times are hard.

Regarding *ishvarapranidhana* (celebration of the spiritual), Farhi writes that "Yoga tells us that the spiritual suffuses everything—it is simply that we are too busy, too distracted, or too insensitive to notice the extraordinary omnipresence that dwells in all things…" Before leaving home, I would have scoffed at the idea of a "spiritual journey." It wasn't that I had strong religious beliefs. On the contrary, I had none. My perspective was limited to what I could see and understand. I probably *was* too busy or too stoned to feel any kind of spiritual connection. But thanks to India, by the time I read about ishvarapranidhana, that perspective had completely changed—the pursuit of extraordinary omnipresence was my new hobby.

The precept of *tapas* (burning enthusiasm) is about focusing our energy in a disciplined way. Krishna was full of tapas. In one of our classes he said, "We generate prana through pranayama so that we can awaken the *kundalini*." I asked what that was and he said, "The kundalini is a coil of energy, like a snake at the base of the spine. We raise it with yoga and pranayama. It brings great spiritual power."

"Have you awakened the kundalini?"

He waddled his head. "Trying trying...little, little, every day."

I was generating tapas from my new activities. When I first met Keshav in Varanasi, I knew that I wanted to study tabla with him. I had the same reaction when I met Krishna. Now I was on to the precept of *swadhyaya*, the study of yogic philosophy. Donna Farhi clarifies that swadhyaya consists of any activity that causes us to reflect on who we really are. I saw a parallel to the precept of *shaucha*, or purity, where Farhi encourages readers to be conscious of what they include in their lives. Like Pio's decision about motorbikes, I could finally see what was nourishing me and what wasn't. I felt more like a student than a traveler. If swadhyaya was a process that reveals who we really are, I was peeling layers off of that onion every day.

A few days after Josh arrived, I was practicing tabla under the tree when I heard a drum approaching on the beach path. I stopped playing to listen. Seconds later, a familiar-looking drum salesman appeared at the Ocean Breeze. He was draped in a dozen drums and playing one to attract attention. He smiled when he saw my tabla and asked if I wanted to buy a drum. I recognized him from our drum jam in the corracle in Hampi and asked if he remembered it. He smiled blankly for a moment and then said, "With the girls? Pretty girls..."

I nodded and smiled. "Yes, with the girls."

I asked how much he wanted for his smallest drum. It was made of soft wood with simple carved patterns and twin drum heads. It hung from a long shoulder string and would come in handy when the tabla was too unwieldy to carry. Though prices were always negotiable in India, I was too pleased to share in a memory of Liz to bother to haggle.

Regarding another precept, *aparigraha* (not grasping), Donna Farhi warns that holding onto things and being free are mutually exclusive. I had begun my journey grasping a vision that could never manifest. I believed so strongly in a stable future with Ronit that I was willing to leave everything else behind when we left for Nepal. Varanasi had taught me that everything changes and in Palolem, I could feel it. *I* was changing. Rather than grasping at a planned future, I was opening myself to an uncertain one. I was rewarded as it unfolded before my eyes.

But my "just right" days at Palolem were impermanent also. Josh was making plans to visit Hampi and then travel north to Osho's ashram in Pune. I felt pulled to the south. To me, continuing south represented going deeper into India. It would be even warmer there and to get to the bottom of this yoga thing, I wanted to go to the bottom of the country. Also, Liz had talked about heading to Kerala after Mysore. That may have had something to do with it.

I checked email later that day, but Liz still hadn't written. I tried to be patient—I knew that she was traveling to a remote area that probably didn't have internet access. I did have a message from Robin, though. She was planning to visit a beach called Varkala in Kerala and asked if I would be nearby. I wrote that I might be going that way and would let her know.

Farhi describes *brahmacharya* (celibacy) as the most feared and least understood precept by westerners. She encourages her readers to look at how they express themselves sexually and ask if it brings "you closer to or farther away from your spiritual self." This westerner was wary. All I knew about celibates was that they often couldn't keep their pants on. I didn't understand sexuality's connection to spirituality, but I could see how it could be distracting. When Robin had arrived at Palolem, it became difficult to maintain my routine. We stayed up late that night and then she slept in. I still practiced yoga at sunrise, but it took a lot more discipline. At Om Beach, I had to be my own guru.

I opened *From Here to Nirvana* and read about an ashram in Kerala called Sivananda. When I asked Krishna about it, he told me that it was where he'd become a certified yoga teacher. The connection felt serendipitous and he encouraged me to go. Josh was also supportive, but worried that I was letting Liz get away. As even-keeled as he was about most things, he would insist every day that I email her again. I resisted because I'd written to her multiple times since leaving Hampi and I didn't want to be grasping.

A couple of days later, I was walking on Palolem's main road with Josh when he saw an internet café and implored me to write to Liz again. I capitulated as Shiva's mantra, "Om Namah Sivaya," emanated from a shop nearby. Following the signs, I not only emailed her, but also put a plan in writing. I told Liz that I would go to the Sivananda Ashram for a "yoga vacation" starting February 1st and I invited her to meet me there.

After yoga the next day, I had a message from her.

Hi Mark,

Beautiful to hear from you. You did not hear from me because I was hot on the trail of Lobsang Tsering, a Tibetan monk. I got an email response from him that he was in Bodhgaya (in Northern India), but we went to his monastery anyway, taking public buses through the countryside.

Another monk named Sherap Lama picked us up from the bus stand and took us into his home. We slept in monk bed and ate monk food. Most of the monks were away for a teaching with the Dalai Lama but we saw the burning of an eighty-four-year-old dead monk that Sherap Lama had been caring for. We rode on a tractor with the funeral pyre wood to get to the site. It was really… something.

Unfortunately, a yoga vacation is not in the cards for me. Nevertheless, I would LOVE to see you. Fran and I are sweaty in Kerala at the bottom of a backwater trip in Kollam. We ride on the boat tomorrow and then we're off to Kochin sometime in the next 3-7 days. Lemme know your plans and we can arrange.

WHAT ARE YOU DOING? How's your beautiful life going?

You offered me a great big hug at the end of the email and that's exactly what I want, a big warm teddy bear hug.

Kiss the sea for me.

Love, Liz

My heart started pounding as soon as I saw the message. I wiped sweat from my forehead with my wrist and told Josh. "She wrote… Liz."

"I told you!" he said, still looking at his monitor. I allowed him the satisfaction of believing that his urging had made a difference. My plan put me at the Sivananda Ashram in Kerala in eight days. Liz would be in Kochin in around three. The distances in India were huge. It would take over a day to get to Kochin by train.

After rereading the message, I heard the voice of Yoda from *The Empire Strikes Back* in my head: "But you *must* complete your training…" I loved being at Palolem with Krishna and Josh, but I had already decided to go to the ashram. It was the idea of leaving *right away* that gave me pause.

My review of the yamas and niyamas had indicated that I was on the right path. I wanted to trust that I could stay on it without my gurus. I stared at my un-composed reply with fingers on the keyboard. Then, still facing his screen, Josh asked, "What did she say?"

"She wants to meet me in Kochin… in three days. She would *love* to…"

Josh turned and looked at me. "Marky! I guess you're going to Kochin."

CHAPTER 19

Palolem: This Has All Been Wonderful

Josh and I were housemates at university for just one year. The year of my first Grateful Dead shows, I was accepted into the business program. I was relieved—it had been hard to stay focused on academics in a house with eight guys. Drugs and alcohol were always on tap late into the evening. I couldn't avoid the festivities because I'd drawn the shortest straw and my bedroom was right next to the kitchen *and* the living room—which was next to the hot tub.

Soon after being accepted into the program, I had an opportunity to move into a much quieter apartment with my friend Matt. It seemed perfect. I would be going to class at 8 a.m. five days a week, and I didn't want to be dragging myself through business school hung over and exhausted.

Problem was, I'd been with my housemates since we met in our dorm the first year and I knew that if I left, things wouldn't be the same. Also, I didn't want to leave them in a lurch, needing a housemate. That gap would change the whole dynamic of the house.

While I internally debated the decision, Matt and I had a chance to see the band Phish for the first time in a small concert hall in Toronto. It was April, 1994. Fans of the Grateful Dead raved about Phish. We were excited to see them. At the concert, we found our spots on a narrow balcony above a dance floor.

Many of the songs' lyrics were goofy, but these guys could *play*. They ripped through material from their first three albums in the first set, but it was the beginning of the second set that I remember the most. Thoughts on my living situation rolled in my mind when the band played a pop-tinged number from an album that they had released that week.

"And I keep waiting for the time when I can finally say,
That this has all been wonderful and now I'm on my way."
– *Down with Disease*, Phish

The balcony bounced with the fans' enthusiasm. As the lyrics merged with the driving rhythm, I stopped ruminating on my decision. The answer emerged from the thick air of the packed concert hall: it *had* been wonderful and I was on my way.

Some of the housemates were upset with me, but Josh was supportive. He told me that I was making the right decision—that meant a lot.

Eight years later and on my way again, I savored every moment of my last day at Palolem. Krishna convinced Josh and me to do both morning yoga classes. In the advanced class, I tried a headstand for the first time. I fell over, but I didn't mind. I was pushing myself and it felt good. The day warmed during the beginner class, and I sweated through our second round of sun salutations. I sunk deeper into the postures and felt rubbery. After three hours of yoga, we rested on our straw mats as Krishna said, "You are to-tal-ly re-laxed."

I was to-tal-ly ready for breakfast.

After eating, I walked to the train station to buy my tickets, starting with an overnight train leaving in twelve hours. Along the way, I saw Krishna riding a bicycle into town. When I asked what he was going for, he smiled and kept on riding.

Unlike the massive station in Mumbai, the Canacona train station consists of a ticket booth, a tea stall, and a single platform. The track emerges from jungle next to a bright yellow sign with black handpainted English and Hindi letters displaying the location and elevation. I found it remarkable that I could hop on board and trace a seven-hundred-mile path down India's west coast over two nights and a day.

I walked back to the Ocean Breeze, feeling every step on Palolem's sand. I gathered my things and checked out of hut number four. Josh would remain in hut number five for another day or two before going to Hampi. I told Povi that I was traveling south and might be back.

I walked slowly to pristine Patnam Beach. I said hello to everyone who smiled at me, but I really meant goodbye. I'd put the yoga books away and wasn't pressuring myself to do anything—not even practice my drums. The natural beauty of Patnam was meditative. The sand felt as soft as the baby powder I used to keep my palms dry when playing tabla. With crashing surf as my soundtrack, I surrendered to the flow.

I dove into the ocean and swam past the waves. I filled my lungs with sea air and floated on my back, gazing at clouds in the divided sky. Salt water dried on my lips as I considered my plans. Was I falling into an old pattern of planning my life around a woman? It was at least partially true. At the same time, I knew that, until I found an ideal partner, I would always be looking for her. I could fill my time with activities—even spiritual practices—but I was not cut out to be alone. As much as I appreciated solitude, I knew that being single wasn't my destiny.

Still floating, I asked the universe when I would know if Liz was diverting from my path of growth. The sea lapped along my hairline and covered my ears, creating an enveloping silence while I waited for an answer. I closed my eyes and sunlight glowed through my eyelids. Then a voice in my head responded, "You'll know. Just go... You'll know."

I wanted to ask the voice why I hadn't known earlier with Ronit, but I already sensed the answer. I *had* known on some level that I was on the wrong path before I came to India. Problem was, I hadn't slowed down enough to see the light between me and my mind.

That night, Krishna held an impromptu goodbye party for me. He took Josh and me on a short walk inland to his humble concrete room. Before going inside, he made sure to show us the unique plumbing of his "pig toilet." It was an outhouse attached to a pigpen. He would use the toilet and the pigs would immediately eat the results. Krishna laughed at our jaw-dropped shock.

Inside his room, Krishna handed me a going-away present: a bag of pot. I scrambled to find meaning in a gift that seemed so inappropriate for a yoga teacher to give his student.

"It's for your enjoying. On the train..."

It hadn't felt important to tell him of my vow to no longer carry pot, so he wasn't aware of it. Josh knew, though, and said with a nod, "It's a test..."

I asked Krishna if the bag was what his errand into town was for, and he smiled. I put off deciding how to approach the "test" and pulled out my gift for Krishna, a card that I had written on the back of a photograph of me biking on the rocks in Hampi. It said:

Krishna Yogi,

> *I first arrived here in Palolem five weeks ago, looking for a fresh start. When I first met you, I thought, "I want to be like THIS GUY." I appreciated your ability to savor the moment. Now I feel that I have that ability. I realize how much yoga has to do with bringing assurance, appreciation, and clarity. For this lesson, I am thankful to you.*

You have entertained, trained, and inspired me, all by just being you. I guess it's easy when you are a yogi.

I look forward to seeing you next time and until then, I will continue to hear your voice in my head, guiding me through my yoga practice. Keep in touch… May all good things come to you. Best of luck in your quest to awaken the kundalini.

With lots of love and appreciation,
Tabla Yogi, Mark

With an hour until my train, I rolled up a couple of joints. Josh had loosened up and even started talking in a funny voice that I knew from late nights at school. He thanked me for easing him into India at Palolem and decided to liven up the party with music. He put *Mike's Song* by Phish on my mini-speakers and called it "spiritual music." Josh waited for a reaction from Krishna, but the yogi only sat and smiled. I think he was more interested in our glee than the sound emanating from the little black speakers.

The music reminded Josh of our most recent farewell a few years earlier. "Remember at Madison Square Garden, New Years? After the countdown, you said to me 'I took ecstasy tonight, man, it was incredible!'"

I finished the story. "You grabbed me by the shoulders…"—Josh smiled, knowing what was coming next— "…looked me in the eyes, and said, 'It's not the drugs, man. It's the music!'"

We both laughed and Josh shook his head. "You were flying…"

It felt fitting to be flying again with the same wingman, but this time it wasn't the drugs, it was the yoga. It was a new kind of high, a more sustainable transformation. My ecstasy wasn't coming from a white pill, but from the beauty of nature and the rhythms of my breath. It also came from the small satsanga that had developed among the three of us. I was so joyful that I forgot to light a joint before it was time to leave for the train.

My two friends took me to the station in a taxi. I sat in the front and to magnify my anticipation, Josh chimed from the back seat, "You're off to see the wizard, the wonderful wizard of Liz, because, because, because, because, because of the wonderful things she is!"

I was embarrassed but didn't mind being teased; I could feel their support. It had been wonderful at Palolem with Josh and Krishna, but I was ready to be on my way.

At the train station, a five-year-old English girl with wavy blonde hair ventured away from her parents to ask me about the small drum over my shoulder—the one from the Hampi drum man. I handed it to her and showed her how to tap both sides. She was surprised when I then opened my tabla bag and began playing the two larger drums along with her. Her parents took pictures as we jammed on the train platform. Then suddenly, the train appeared out of the trees. I rushed to repack my tabla and jump into the nearest railcar.

That moment of panic was an abrupt return to "India." Of course, I hadn't left the country, but Palolem had been an oasis for me, a tiny universe of wonder. The train felt immediately different. Nothing was left of the beach except the sand between my toes. I could call it a perfect vacation, but those "just right" days felt like an example of how life *could* be. I wanted to recall the beauty and simplicity. In moments of despair, I would need that kind of hope.

My fortunate feeling was magnified on the train by the raw reality of India. Shirtless *untouchables* averted eye contact as they crawled underfoot to clean the floor. Untouchables were in the lowest caste of society and for centuries their ancestors had performed similar jobs. My heart hurt to see them. There were also blind beggars and chai vendors. I checked my pockets for rupees to give to each of them. The taste of the chai brought me back to Varanasi. Hot, milky, and sweet, a full plastic cup perked me up before a long night on my top bunk, where green vinyl covered a thin layer of padding on wood.

Darkness fell on the Karnataka plains and passengers settled in for the night. Once everyone else had stopped moving around, I visited the narrow space outdoors between the railcars. We were moving quickly through trees and I could smell the ocean again. I pulled out a joint and lit it. I heard Krishna's voice in my head: "For your enjoying…on the train."

I rationalized to myself that I was only following my teacher's instructions and that, though I was carrying pot again, I hadn't paid for it. But then my body indicated that a few puffs were enough. Instead of trying to save the smelly roach, I put it out and tossed it on the tracks.

Back on my bunk, I asked myself if I was seeing greener grass where I shouldn't be. I decided that I was simply following the signs laid out for me and choosing the adventure that felt most right. I reasoned that it would be easier to get back into a yoga zone than it would be to find someone like Liz again. She supported my journey and I wanted her to be a part of it.

I'd loaded the top bunk with all of my possessions. My backpack was under my head, an overstuffed, too-hard pillow. My tabla bag was under my calves, elevating my feet. I'd been told that it was best not to leave anything loose because of thieves, so I even had my shoes tied to my bag. I put on my headphones and continued the live Phish CD that Josh had chosen earlier that night.

The next song begins under the "cool shade of a banana tree." It is the story of *Fee*, a "child of the twentieth century" and "Buddhist prodigy," who happens to be a weasel. Fee yearns for a faraway lover and "a life that's completely free." After a journey from Peru to Quebec, the weasel must fight an angry chimpanzee for his love. Fee emerges victorious with help from his lover, and they presumably live happily ever after.

I closed my eyes, hoping my journey would also lead to true love *and* a "life that's completely free." I didn't know if I could have both, but I stopped worrying as the piano denouement of the song merged with the rattling railcar and soothed me into sleep.

CHAPTER 20

Kochin: Jew Town

My train pulled into Kochin during the afternoon rush hour. When I disembarked, I was surrounded by people. The men's round faces and short black hair reminded me of Krishna. More women wore skirts than saris. I had expected an environment more like ancient Varanasi or rural Hampi, but Kochin was calm, charming, and modern. There weren't beggars at every turn and where were the cows?

I rode a ferry to an area called Fort Kochin. I was anxious to rinse myself off after two consecutive nights on a train, but my first priority was to write to Liz and tell her that I'd arrived. I hadn't seen my email since telling her from Palolem that I was coming. With the uncertainty of Indian travel, she could have been a day or two ahead of or behind me.

I had many emails, including from my family and Robin, but I only clicked on the most recent one—a message from Liz that she'd sent minutes before. She was at an internet café in Fort Kochin. I spun in my chair and scanned the empty room—it had to be a different café. I suggested a hotel where we could meet and my heart beat faster when she instantly responded. She and Fran would head right over. I left my other emails unopened and went to the hotel to clean myself up before they arrived.

Before I was out of the shower, there was a knock at my door. I wrapped a towel around my waist and answered it. It was delightful to see Liz and Fran. They immediately made themselves comfortable in the

room. It wasn't much—a double bed on tattered rugs with undecorated, red-painted walls and a window facing another building. It had a private bathroom, though, with a big open shower and was luxurious compared to where Liz and Fran had been staying. Straight from their backwater boat ride, they too hadn't bathed in days. Fran asked to use the shower, tossed her clothes on the bed, and danced naked into the bathroom.

I sat on the edge of the bed next to Liz and held her hands in mine. Her eyes felt like a familiar place. I didn't know what to say and she was quiet. Fran was not. She sang in the shower and then laid nude on the bed to dry off.

I decided to give them some privacy and took my tabla to the hotel rooftop to practice. As I was setting up, I reasoned that Fran wasn't putting on a show—she was simply comfortable with me. After being among monks and hot on a riverboat in her salwar kameez, she saw my room as a haven—the first place in a while where she could stretch out and be herself.

After a long time, Liz and Fran appeared at the stairwell wet-haired and dressed. They took a moment to admire the view of Fort Kochin's old buildings and then Liz flipped through my India guidebook. A moment later she said, "We should go to Jew Town."

I had read about it—an area of Kochin that used to have a thriving Jewish community, something unique in that part of the world.

Liz added, "It's Friday night."

I said, "Shabbat." Friday night is the beginning of the Jewish sabbath, something that my family celebrates every week.

Fran said, "Let's do it." She meant now. I hadn't been sightseeing in a while, so it took a moment to register. They stood and I packed up my drums.

Jews have lived in Kochin for hundreds of years. Their community grew when Jews in Europe were oppressed, such as during the Spanish Inquisition (fifteenth century) and the reign of the Ottoman Empire (sixteenth century). When Israel was founded in 1948, many of the Jews moved there and the Jewish population of Kochin dwindled. By the time we arrived, there were only fourteen left.

The guidebook led us to the 450-year-old Paradesi synagogue. We arrived at dusk and sounds emanated from inside. The thick wooden door was locked, so we knocked. An elderly White man with an Indian accent asked through a crack in the door, "Are you Jewish?"

Taken aback by the blunt question, Liz and I nodded, then we all looked at Fran. She shook her head and smiled. Ignoring Fran, the man invited Liz and me to enter, warning us that the evening's service had already started. I nodded at Fran and said, "She's with us."

"This is not for tourists. It is a religious service."

The exclusion didn't feel right to me. The man appeared anxious for our answer when Liz said, "Thank you. We'll leave."

As he began to close the heavy door, Fran said, "Wait." He stopped and Fran, turning to us, said, "You guys go in. I'll be fine. I'll see you back at the hotel."

I gave Fran the room key and the man welcomed Liz and me in. I took a yarmulke from a basket and put it on my head. There was a pile of shoes near the door like at a Hindu temple but unlike any synagogue I'd visited. We kicked off our sandals and walked barefoot onto the temple's blue and white tiled floor where a service was in progress.

There were less than two dozen people there. I guessed that the well-dressed older participants were local and the casually dressed younger people were visitors like us. Rows of chandeliers illuminated a pulpit in the middle of the floor where a white-haired rabbi recited familiar Hebrew prayers. I opened a prayer book and saw that it had been "Made in Palestine." That was Israel's name from the era of the British Empire. The book was more than fifty years old.

I had gone to synagogue with my parents every week as a child. I found the services' repetition boring and would take long bathroom breaks that involved wandering the hallways outside of the sanctuary. At thirteen, I completed my bar mitzvah, a ritual that included chanting in Hebrew and giving a speech in front of my entire community of family and friends.

When I wasn't walking around the building, I would read the English translations of the Torah and prayers. That reading was what turned me into a skeptic about religion. In story after story, God came across as blameful and reactionary. He wanted praise and loyalty, but I wasn't willing to give it. He didn't seem kind or forgiving, so I didn't want to follow him.

I believed that I was in control of my life and couldn't accept that God was a decision-maker. That disillusionment caused my aversion to divinity—until I arrived in Palolem and started to feel wonderful things that I couldn't explain.

When the Kochin service ended, the congregants were invited to bless sweet homemade red wine served in tiny plastic cups and a braided challah that was then torn apart by hand. The rituals and the flavors were just the same as at home.

Though Liz hadn't said much to me about being Jewish, it was in conversation with the senior community members that I found out that, like me, Liz had gone to her local reform synagogue. She'd had a bat mitzvah and had many friends who were Jewish.

The elderly Jews of Kochin looked familiar in their yarmulkes and tallit, but they had Indian accents and mannerisms. The serious faces they'd worn in the sanctuary gave way to smiles as we asked questions about their community. Though their progeny had moved away, mostly to Israel, they were proud to carry on the legacy of their ancestors. Liz and I wished them "Shabbat shalom," put on our sandals, and left to find Fran.

We walked in darkness down streets named Jews Street and Synagogue Lane, and then soon passed Hindu temples and a tabla player practicing in an open-air studio. It was still India, but my mind was elsewhere. I told Liz, "I once went to a synagogue that looked a lot like that. When I was fifteen, I went to Poland and Israel on a trip called *The March of the Living*. We went to Poland for one week to visit the concentration camps, and then spent a week in Israel."

Liz had also been to Israel as a teenager, but not to Eastern Europe.

"We went to Auschwitz. Everything is still there except the bodies. We saw rooms filled to the ceiling with shoes, glasses, and children's toys."

Being only two generations removed from the horrors of that time, all Jews our age were exposed to the awful details of the Holocaust. Our parents wanted us to know what had happened, remember our identity, and work to prevent such atrocities from recurring.

"The synagogue I visited was in Krakow, Poland. Their city had tens of thousands of Jews before the war, but when we arrived in 1990, only a few elders remained.

"The next day they took us to see the Jewish cemetery. At first, I didn't understand why we would go—it pre-dated the Holocaust and it was overgrown with trees and vines. But once we started walking, I saw how vast it was. The headstones bore the last names of families we knew and first names that some of us shared. It was the only remaining evidence of the people who had lived there—*our* people. And they had been wiped out."

Liz asked how that trip to the cemetery had made me feel.

"More Jewish than I ever had in synagogue. Our group shed a lot of tears in Poland. Sometimes one of us would want to stay on the bus and not see *another* concentration camp, but we supported each other and bore witness—together. It was a lot for fifteen-year-old kids to take in, but I'm glad I did it."

"And then you went to Israel for the first time?"

"Immediately. It was incredible."

"It was a propaganda tour."

"Yeah, they were grooming us into Israel supporters. It worked for me—for a while."

For years, Israel has maintained oppressive policies toward the country's native Arabs, now called Palestinians. The irony of the situation isn't lost on many who have studied the Holocaust. In conversation, Liz and

I found that we both valued Israel as a homeland for Jews but not at the cost of human rights. As we approached our hotel, we talked about how Fran had been identified as an outsider that night. We were both sensitive to being excluded, but back at the hotel, Fran said that she didn't mind at all—she'd had a nice time exploring.

I thought that Fran might have gotten her own room, but it was clear that she was staying put when she undressed—noting that, "It's too hot for clothes"—and laid on one side of the bed. Liz did the same, lying down on the other side. Not wanting to be the prude of the group, I took off my underwear and crawled between the two of them.

At their college co-op, being naked was a ritual. Coeds revealed their bodies, accepting all shapes and colors. On that humid night in Kochin, Fran used her experience to invite me into the circle that she shared with Liz. And though she was in the company of two people from the same tribe who were falling in love, I think that she was done with being excluded.

Fran rolled onto her side and turned her back to us. I placed a hand on Liz's abdomen and looked into her eyes. We fell asleep holding each other in the warm night air.

CHAPTER 21

Kochin: Attachment

Fran always slept late. The next morning, Liz was happy that she didn't have to wait for her and could join me on the rooftop for yoga. The streets were quiet and the air was warm. We moved in silent synchronicity for well over an hour. By the time we rested on our mats in savasana, equatorial sunshine blazed through the haze. Sweat poured from my forehead on to the concrete floor. It felt like the perfect start to a day.

While Fran still slept, Liz left to explore town. I chose to practice tabla before midday heat took over the rooftop. Rhythms came easily and I felt that I was where I belonged. After about an hour, I returned to the room to find Fran packing up for a move to another room. I got in the shower and as I was drying off, I could hear her haggling over price with the hotel manager. When that negotiating was done, Fran invited me to breakfast.

In what felt like a continuation of our conversation in Hampi two weeks prior, Fran wanted to talk about my relationship with Liz. "There's something special there. I can tell by the way she talks about you." She said that since her last boyfriend, Liz had sabotaged all relationship opportunities out of a fear of being hurt again.

"How do I avoid relationship sabotage?" I asked.

"Well, that depends. What are your intentions?"

As in any effective second interview, we had reached the crux of the matter. Though I'd spent less than a week with Liz, I *had* thought about whether we might have a future together.

"I'd be lucky to be with her."

"In California?"

I smiled, noting that no one was suggesting that Liz move to the Great White North. "I was thinking about looking for work in Australia or New Zealand after this trip, but California sounds great."

"You would move there?"

"You suggested it!"

My exclamation broke the tension and our conversation transitioned to the short term. Fran seemed relieved that I was heading to the Sivananda Ashram in a matter of days. I could tell that her argument with the hotel manager had come from frustration—getting a room of her own wasn't what she'd signed up for. She welcomed my cameo appearance on their trip, but her courtesy would have a limit.

I returned to the hotel, hoping that Liz would be there. After so much talk about a future together, I wanted to experience her in the present. She was still out, so I did all I could to fill my time while I waited for her to return. I read, wrote, and tried to practice tabla some more. I lacked the focus of the early morning and struggled with familiar drum patterns. Distracted by Liz's absence, I couldn't keep the beat.

Since drumming wasn't going well, I picked up *What Buddhists Believe* by K. Sri Dhammananda, the book that Liz had given to me as we were leaving Hampi. I hadn't opened it yet as I'd been soaking up Josh's library in Palolem, but Liz mentioned the book frequently and I hoped that it would provide some insight into what was going on in her mind.

The book begins with the story of the Buddha. Then known as Prince Siddhartha, he had renounced his royal lineage and abandoned his wife and child on his twenty-ninth birthday in order to embark on his spiritual journey. Dhammananda explains that were it not for those detachments,

Buddha would never have discovered the remedy for the suffering of mankind. He writes that Siddhartha "had to sacrifice everything including worldly pleasures in order to have a concentrated mind free from any distractions, in order to find the truth..."

I could relate to Siddhartha's desire to leave home, but not to leaving his young family. As great as I was finding yoga to be, I just couldn't relate to that level of commitment to a spiritual life. I wanted meaningful and loving relationships more than enlightenment.

Still, the book offered helpful perspective. Less than twenty-four hours after arriving in Kochin, I was attached to being with Liz. I no longer had a "concentrated mind free from any distractions" because I had expected to spend the day with her. When that didn't happen, I was disappointed or, as Buddha might say, I was suffering. It was a familiar feeling from when I would walk the streets of Pokhara looking for Ronit. I decided to stop waiting for Liz, because there was really no difference between looking and waiting.

I packed up my tabla and went to the internet café to catch up on my emails. Robin wrote, "Did you know that the *Lonely Planet* lists the three most beautiful beaches in India as Palolem, Om Beach, and Varkala?" She was inviting me to Varkala. Liz and Fran planned to leave Kochin in a couple of days, once a friend arrived. I'd still have a few days before my yoga course at the ashram. Varkala was on the way, so I wrote that I might stop by. Sure, I'd have to tell her about Liz, but as a "friend with benefits," Robin would understand.

Josh wrote from Palolem. He was now running at Patnam Beach in the afternoons. I missed it. Liz still seemed worth passing up Palolem for, but I wasn't *with* Liz. It was late afternoon and she still hadn't returned. I walked out of the café intending to explore, but I hadn't walked more than a block when I spotted Liz gliding down the road and smiling. She had returned to Jew Town and met a Jewish woman who guided her through the art galleries while they talked about their families. It was odd to me that Liz had connected so deeply with a stranger while I was in town at her invitation and not for very long.

After the galleries, Liz had seen a traditional Keralan silent dance performance called *Kathakali*. Now I felt foolish for not having ventured out at all. Liz was glowing, but she could see that I wasn't feeling as high about the day. "I'm sorry that I didn't come and get you for the Kathakali show. I wanted to, but it was about to start, so I went in. It was amazing. You should really see it."

I said, "I want to see *you*."

Liz tilted her head and said, "I did a lot of thinking during the show…"

I wondered if she would express regret about us meeting up in Kochin. I was feeling that it might have been a mistake, but she said, "I'm feeling *desire*…"

That was *not* what I expected her to say, standing on the street with Indians and tourists passing by.

"But I worry about becoming attached to you."

And now I felt like a student who had done the reading before class. "Because attachment leads to suffering…"

Liz looked pleased that I understood. I continued, "I read some of *What Buddhists Believe* and it made me realize that I was creating suffering for myself. When you were gone, I was filled with disappointment. It was all because I'd created an expectation of what today would be like. It tells me that I might not be ready…"

"Me neither," she interrupted. "Have you thought about Thailand?"

I *had* thought about her invitation to travel together. "Two months feels really far away, but if it still feels right to both of us by then, I'd like to do it."

Liz seemed relieved and suggested that we stop talking about *us*. I thought about what Fran had said earlier about sabotage, but this wasn't that. It was just that the time was wrong.

Though we were in traditional India, she took my hand. We strolled along the paved shoreline admiring Kochin's enormous fishing nets. The nets were suspended by logs more than twenty meters tall and looked like gigantic spiderwebs hanging over the water. The fishing nets framed a reddish-orange sunset glow.

Recalling her conversation with the woman in Jew Town, Liz said, "My ancestors also left Spain during the Inquisition…"

"Like the Jews of Kochin…"

"Yeah, on my mom's side. They moved from Spain to Turkey, lived there for a few hundred years, and then migrated to Cuba in the early 1900s. And then they went to America when the Cuban Revolution happened."

"Wow, that's a lot of exile. Why did they leave Cuba?"

"Communism. My grandpa was a businessman. My uncle met Fidel Castro at a casino after Castro had taken power. Castro shook my uncle's hand and commented that it felt uncalloused. Then Castro said to him, 'You'll be leaving (Cuba).' Castro knew that once they started taking people's property, those who *could* leave, would."

"And Castro was right?"

"They left within a year. My mom was fifteen. She came to the U.S. alone, with five dollars in her pocket."

It was another story of what you can find when you leave it all behind. Her mom had done well in America and, unlike Siddhartha's, her family had reunited.

Eventually, Liz's thoughts turned to Fran and she wanted to find her. I told her that we'd eaten together and that Fran had a separate room. Knowing that Liz now had a choice, I hoped that she would stay with me for the night. In the spirit of detachment, I didn't mention it.

Later in the evening, I went to the rooftop to look at the stars and *not* wait for Liz. Of course, I was waiting for her and I asked the starry sky for clarity. I didn't regret coming to Kochin, but it wasn't turning out like I had expected. I wanted to be with Liz, but maybe she was right: traveling together in Thailand without Fran was the only way for us to truly see if this relationship was going to work.

The full moon rose and so did Liz—from the stairwell, with brown curls relaxing on her shoulders. She looked magnificent in the moonlight.

She said that she'd had a good conversation with Fran and then she took my hand and said, "Thank you for being so patient with me."

I leaned over and kissed her. "You're worth waiting for."

"Fran told me that you were thinking of moving to California…"

"Is that what she said? She asked if I would. I've thought about looking for work abroad… California is pretty exotic for a boy from Edmonton."

"I was telling one of the Tibetan monks about my trip and he said, 'Sometimes you need to run away.' He was speaking from experience. He left Tibet as a young man and he will probably never go back. He doesn't regret it, but *home* is a lot to give up."

"I thought I'd feel liberated when I packed up all of my stuff, moved out, and quit my job, but I didn't get to that point until I was on my own. And now I don't know if I can feel that way with someone else. I don't know if I can balance it all."

It was ironic to me that as we both sought to shake ourselves free of attachment, our greatest support was coming from each other—another attachment.

We returned to what was now *our* room and held each other in the warm night. When I plucked a fallen eyelash off of Liz's cheek, she said, "Make a wish."

"I don't have one," I said, because I felt fulfilled in that moment. "You wish."

"I don't have one either."

We blew the eyelash off of my fingertip together. It had no wishes attached to it.

CHAPTER 22

Kochin: Full Moon

A Jewish boy officially becomes a man at his bar mitzvah, but for me it happened ten months later. My childhood ended on August 9, 1988. I was thirteen and a half.

It was the last day of summer camp in the foothills of the Rocky Mountains. My group had just returned from a week-long canoe trip. We delighted in showering and eating in a clean dining room. We ate s'mores and loaded into an assembly hall for a sleepover with boys on one side and girls on the other. As I laid down near the center where teenage counselors established the boundary, I noticed that I was near one of the female counselors, a sixteen-year-old named Melanie. She had wavy brown hair and a bright smile. I'd always found her to be lovely.

Late in the moonlit hall, I couldn't sleep and, apparently, neither could Melanie. I caught her smile peeking out from inside her sleeping bag across the wooden floor. When she didn't look away, I wormed my wrapped-up body closer to hers. When I arrived, she didn't tell me to slither right back to where I came from. She actually inched closer to me. Of course, counselors were required to keep a distance from the campers, but it was the final night of the session and everyone else seemed to be asleep.

On our sides on the wooden floor, we stared into each other's eyes. Careful to be quiet, Melanie touched her forehead to mine and closed her eyes. I did the same, submitting to the mystery of the darkness until our lips found each other. I was nervous that we would be seen, but that thought was interrupted by the realization that this kiss was a *real* kiss. I'd had a few fumbling pecks on the lips before, mostly while playing games like "spin the bottle," but this time was completely different. A young *woman* was kissing me, for real.

I laid one arm across the floor and Melanie rested her head on it. She held me tight and we kissed again. In the quiet darkness, my embrace gave Melanie enough comfort to sleep. I laid awake, basking in her glow. I wanted to deserve her trust, so at the first sounds of morning, I rested her head back on the floor and wiggled my way back to the boys' side.

The room began to stir and Melanie acknowledged me with a smile before resuming her duties. Before boarding the yellow bus with my peers, I waited as Melanie wished farewell to her girls. Keeping our unspoken vow of silence intact, I hugged her goodbye and reluctantly let go. From a window seat near the back of the bus, I could see her standing and waving. I put on my headphones as the bus pulled away and rolled through forest toward home.

I was tired when we returned to the city. My mom hugged me and then rushed me to the car—it was in a loading zone. She wanted to hear all about camp, but first she had something to tell me. Once I was sitting in the front seat, she said, "They traded Wayne Gretzky."

She handed me that morning's sports pages and turned on the radio. Sports writers analyzed the poorly kept secret and radio reporters prepared for a press conference to announce the trade that they called a "sale." I'd been out of touch for over a week and knew nothing about it. I checked to be sure that it wasn't April Fool's Day. No, it was really happening.

In August 1988, Wayne Gretzky was twenty-seven and on pace to be the most prolific hockey player in history. He was a four-time Stanley Cup champion and until that day, he was ours. Gretzky had brought glory and relevance to our northern city. I was a huge fan. When the Edmonton Oilers first won the Stanley Cup in 1984, I cried because I was so happy.

In the car now with my mom, I was furious. "We didn't even get their best player? Pocklington (the owner) got fifteen million dollars?"

The Oilers' owner was in financial trouble and decided to sell high on Gretzky's contract. Wayne was off to California, and though I wasn't leaving Edmonton, my life had also turned.

The press conference was a mess. Gretzky could hardly speak from the tears. I hoped that Glen Sather, the team's coach and general manager, could explain. Instead, he said, "I don't want to try and philosophize on what's happened… because I don't think we can justify the reasons why this has happened…"

What?

If the architect couldn't justify why greed should triumph over loyalty, I couldn't either. If that was what adult success looked like, I wanted nothing of it.

I went to bed early that night. In the sanctuary of my bedroom, I resolved to stop being angry about the hockey trade that I couldn't control, and my thoughts turned to Melanie. I realized that I might never see her again (I didn't), but I was okay with that. She had already given me something more important than hope for a future *with her*. With silent kisses in the moonlight, she had shown me how it felt to be accepted—even desired—by a beautiful woman. On a night when I was desperate for something to believe in, I resolved to follow that feeling—a feeling that was pure and powerful enough to bring hope in the face of disaster.

That night was one example of something I've often noticed: People act differently on the last day of school or summer camp. Without concern for the fluorescent lights of Monday, people say what they really feel about each other. Young lovers make the last day count. I often wonder if life can feel like that all of the time, if I can be more unfiltered in my interactions with people, particularly those whom I want to be closer to.

My last days with Liz in Kochin felt unfiltered like that. Once we decided that we weren't going to travel together for at least a while, we relaxed and actually traveled together. We walked to sights and told each other stories from our pasts. We didn't discuss the future and I saw a playful side of Liz.

When Fran would emerge from her room around noon, I'd retreat to the rooftop. She and Liz would go out to eat and I would play tabla and write. On the rooftop on our last full day in Kochin, I flipped through

my journal and read something I'd written after first arriving at Palolem, about a month earlier: "If I had a love interest, I'd have no worries."

I was embarrassed to read it, but considered that I *did* have both a love interest *and* no worries. Thinking of aparigraha, I asked myself if I had moved past reflexive grasping or if I had simply satisfied it. I'd only be able to judge that difference after parting ways with Liz.

On that last day, Liz returned late in the afternoon and we walked along the seawall near the fishing nets. Liz noticed signs for a local group who were gathered to clean the beach, and she suggested that we join them. The young locals were surprised to see foreign travelers getting their hands dirty. Though I wouldn't have thought to do it on my own, it felt great to help out.

As the sky darkened, Liz and I walked back to the fishing nets and stopped on one of the platforms to watch a brilliant orange sunset. No one else was around. I gently touched the sunlight glow on her cheek with my fingertips and then kissed her.

"I feel an opening," she said, and put her hands to her heart. The last sunlight of the day felt pure and revealing. I was trusting her and on this last night before who knows when, I had to say *something*.

I mumbled, "I feel it, too. I…"

She mercifully kissed me while I searched for words. She already knew what I meant. That was how we were at dusk: in sync, just as when we practiced yoga at dawn. It was in the light of day that we both pulled back. We weren't ready for prime time, but we also couldn't deny the connection forged by our shared sunrises and sunsets.

We had gone down a path that neither of us expected and we agreed that it was time to turn back. We both wanted to explore and learn. We didn't want to be distracted by desire, but hoped that we could balance desire with freedom, eventually. We would run away from our feelings this time because, as the monk had said, sometimes that's what you have to do.

We returned to the hotel rooftop as a huge full moon crept over the horizon and lit up the sky to a dark blue. Thinking back to our trash cleanup, I said, "Thank you for showing me where to look among the garbage and the flowers."

Liz looked confused as there were no flowers in our day.

I said, "Oh, you know that song, *Suzanne?* Your friend said that you're Suzanne… That's a line from the song."

"I actually haven't heard it."

I went downstairs and returned with my mini-speakers. We held hands and listened.

In reference to *Suzanne's* wardrobe of "rags and feathers from Salvation Army counters," Liz said, "My tie-dyed shirt is from the Salvation Army." Then she pursued a deeper analysis. "Do you think he's talking about universal consciousness when he sings about the river?"

"I hadn't thought of that. The river answers… You may be right."

"Another thing about that song: Susan is my mom's name."

"Mine too." It was a coincidence but still emblematic of our familiarity.

Suzanne brought back memories of our first meeting in my "chicken room" in Hampi. Liz said that when she met me, I was "bubbling with joy." I said that meeting her felt like a second chance. Then she pulled out her journal and read something that she'd written about our time in Hampi together:

The essence of our relationship:
Him admiring the Goddess strength that I see in myself,
    us loving each other a little,
      and he discovering love's abundance in himself.
Salutation of a rebirthing, moving with our entire body and begin.
Nature speaks for us.
Re-creation.
Namaste

I thanked her, she said, "I appreciate you so much," and we kissed.

I opened my eyes to see the full moon bathing Fort Kochin in light and words spilled from my mouth before I could catch them. "I'll see you in a month, at the next full moon."

Despite our plan to not meet again until Thailand, Liz looked pleasantly surprised. It wasn't my nature to follow the moon or the stars, but once I had a moment to think about the words, I trusted them. She and Fran were leaving in the morning to see the palaces of Rajasthan. Then they would go further north to a Tibetan enclave called Dharamsala where they'd registered for a ten-day silent Buddhist meditation retreat. Without counting the actual days, I guessed their retreat would be over about the same time as the twenty-eight days of the lunar cycle. I knew that Liz would leave India soon after that and I wanted to see her before then.

I also thought it sounded romantic.

CHAPTER 23

Varkala: Leaf in the Wind

On our last day in Kochin, Fran got up early. When Liz and I returned from yoga on the rooftop, she was packed and dressed. She was ready to have her travel partner back and I knew that it was best for all if I gave the two of them space. Liz and I packed up and we all hugged goodbye in the hotel foyer. They went to check for an email from a friend they were meeting and I walked to the bus stand. It was the right thing to do. Three was a crowd, and for me at that stage, two might even have been as well.

En route to the bus, I was surprised to see Liz and Fran's familiar salwar kameez drifting up the road. Their friend had been delayed and wouldn't be there for another day yet. They weren't leaving, but Liz didn't ask me to stay. I felt ready to go anyway—my emotions were safely packed away like my clothes and drums. But she walked with me to the bus stand and we called it "bonus time."

On our way, she suggested, "See what you can learn about *tantra*." When I asked what that was, she said, "I heard about it in the co-op. It's an ancient Indian tradition that has something to do with making love."

She had my attention. "Like the Kama Sutra?"

"I don't really know, but see what you can find out and report back."

I laughed. "I'm going to miss you."

Then the Buddhist prodigy advised me *not* to miss her. There's no reason to be attached, she said. "I'm a leaf in the wind. The breeze is taking me away."

I wanted to hug her, but we had arrived at the bus and a bunch of young Indian men were watching us from the vehicle's back window. In keeping with our culturally sensitive tradition, we shared a touchless goodbye. Before I knew it was over, Liz tested my attachment by walking backwards, emulating the metaphorical leaf in the wind with her hands twirling in the air. I laughed and felt the pain of attachment in my heart as she became smaller in the distance.

I clambered to the back of the bus, where one of the Indian fellows asked, "She is leaving?" I nodded and with confused looks, they turned to look at Liz and then back at me, wondering why I would be parting ways with a beautiful girl. The same fellow asked, "She is going where?"

"Rajasthan."

The men looked shocked. Rajasthan is thousands of miles from Kochin and probably not somewhere that these fellows would go. The same one asked, "And you are going where?"

"Neyyar Dam." The Sivananda Ashram wasn't in a famous or unique city, just a town in central Kerala. They reacted as if I'd said I was planning to go swim in a toilet, shaking their heads in vocal disappointment. I tried to change the subject. "First, I'm going to Varkala…"

Mentioning the beautiful beach earned me a few head waddles, but they still wanted an explanation for my strange behavior. They pointed out that arranged marriages are the standard tradition in their culture, and one is extremely fortunate to find "real love." Another fellow asked, "Do you love this girl?" I laughed with embarrassment and that was enough of an answer for them. "You are lucky man."

I was. It was hard to leave Liz behind. I put on headphones and closed my eyes. In my mind, I could see the leaf in the wind, walking backwards and smiling. The image dissolved and I sought guidance in *What Buddhists Believe*. Dhammapada writes, "While there is every reason to feel glad when one experiences happiness, one should not cling to these happy states or be sidetracked and forget about working one's way to complete liberation."

I found it interesting that the Buddhists and yogis agreed that it's best not to be clingy. But what did that leave me to hold onto? As the bus began to roll past the now-familiar flow of paddy fields, oxcarts, and palm trees, I hoped that the ashram would provide me with answers.

I arrived in Varkala in the afternoon and walked to the edge of its grassy cliff overlooking the Arabian Sea. I had never seen anything like it. A long stairway led down to a gorgeous beach named Papanasham. Locals believe that the water there can wash away one's sins. I walked along the bluffs, enjoying the ocean breeze and looking for my friend Robin.

I found her having a long lunch with friends at a cliffside restaurant. Still carrying my bags, I said, "I'll go find a hotel." But Robin said that her room was huge and had plenty of space for me. She would be leaving in the morning and I could have the room after that.

I enjoyed catching up with her. Robin had loved her time in Varkala, and I told her of my glorious return to Palolem and awkwardly about the "American girl" I had met in Hampi. We talked until well past sunset and then walked carefully along the cliff in the dark to her guesthouse. I had wrongly assumed that her "huge" room had more than one bed, so instead I settled onto the far side of her king-sized mattress. The beach town was quiet and I was tired from travel. I fell asleep quickly.

At some point in the night, I awoke to find Robin touching me. It was disorienting and familiar at the same time. I didn't participate, but also didn't ask her to stop. Then, with only body language and no words, she asked me to make love to her—and I did.

In the morning, Robin slept in, so I practiced yoga and then tabla on a concrete patio facing the grassy cliffs above the ocean. Sunshine was heating up the porch when Robin emerged, showered, dressed, and packed. She leaned against a railing and said that my tabla playing had improved a lot in the past month. She gave me a hug goodbye and whispered "thank you" in my ear. And then she was gone, back toward Tamil Nadu and the eunuchs.

I started packing my tabla, but couldn't complete the task as a flood of feelings flowed into me. I reentered the room in a ball of confusion, sat on the edge of the bed, and cried. I had been naive to share a room with Robin and was weak for not resisting her in the night. What did I really think was going to happen? I was shaken by the realization that I had been tested and failed. I hadn't been true to my feelings for Liz, but Robin couldn't tell. When she whispered "thank you" and walked away, she meant it sincerely. To me, though, "thank you" was an acknowledgement that what had happened in the dreamy darkness was real. I had said goodbye to Liz in the morning and made love to Robin in the night. I was a creep and an idiot, but Liz didn't know it yet. I was alone to pick up the pieces of what I had done.

Robin had suggested I stay in the room for my last night in Varkala, but as beautiful of a spot as it was, I needed to not be there anymore. I packed up and found a new hotel.

After settling in, I considered how many of the yamas and niyamas I'd violated in the night. I *had* been honest with Robin, but if I saw Liz again, I was going to have to tell her. I wanted release from my guilt by telling her right away, but an email on the topic would only ensure that I'd never see her again. I promised myself that I would tell her in person.

I now understood brahmacharya. I'd taken my spiritual growth two steps back en route to the ashram. I was disappointed in myself and didn't know what to do about it, so I decided to venture out of my new hotel room and into the world. I dropped a roll of film off for developing and then noticed a sign for Kerala's famous Ayurvedic massages. I went in.

The masseuse was an Indian woman whose shoulders were as straight as a coat hanger under a bright red sari that revealed her abdominal muscles. She greeted me with a warm Keralan smile and asked me to disrobe.

She draped a sheet over me and then pressed her firm belly against my head while she rubbed sweet-smelling oil into my chest. Her hands traveled up and down my body, rolling away the tightness while my mind floated away.

I still felt awful for betraying my feelings for Liz, but as I sunk deeper into the massage table, I dozed off. I awoke for the foot-massage finale and came out of the room shiny with oil. I then went to pick up my photos and immediately flipped to the ones of Liz from Hampi. One of the pictures showed her sitting cross-legged in the treehouse, smiling. As I sought refuge in the image, an Indian man standing outside the photo shop looked over my shoulder. I showed him the photo and he said, "Beautiful. Where is she?"

"Rajasthan."

He gave a look of disappointed confusion. I laughed at the consistency of Indian men's opinions on the matter and then walked to the long stairway from the bluffs down to the beach.

I swam in the ocean for the first time since leaving Palolem a week before. In the magnificent glow of sunset, massage oil dissolved into the salt water and I hoped that my sins would follow. Despite the beach's reputation, I could feel that they wouldn't. As much as I would have liked to turn back time, I knew that moving forward was my only option.

I inhaled deeply and rose to the surface. The sun was warm, the water was cool, and I floated in between, a leaf on the sea.

CHAPTER 24

Neyyar Dam: Decorate Time

I had no idea what to expect from a yoga ashram. I wanted to build on the bursts of clarity I'd experienced in Palolem, but I felt shaken after being with Robin in Varkala. Alone in a railcar on my way into the jungle, I began to wonder if I was making another bad decision.

I dug the photos of Liz out of my backpack. As I tried to imagine practicing yoga with her on a beach in Thailand, I began to doubt that I could give the best of myself to Liz if I did find her again. Then a vendor offered me chai and returned my mind to where my body was—on a green vinyl bench rolling toward the unknown.

Approaching the lakeside Sivananda Ashram by bus, dark clouds turned afternoon into night. Waves of rain soaked the cement path as I jogged through forest to meet my destiny at the gate. As droplets filled my eyes, I wanted to believe that the rain would rinse away my transgression in Varkala and give me a reset for my yoga immersion.

Once inside, I passed a pale-yellow open-air hall on my way to the front desk. There I met an ashram staffer, a young woman in a loose-fitting T-shirt the same shade of yellow as the hall. She spoke in a Canadian accent, but had an Indian name. When I asked Saraswati where I could use the internet, she said, "Being here is a good way to lose touch with the rest of the world." I smiled at her unhelpful response and wondered about her name—it felt like she was hiding something.

The ashram was named for Swami Sivananda, a tall, bald, paunchy yogi who lived in the mid-twentieth century. It was founded by his disciple, a Keralan named Swami Vishnu Devananda. His portrait reminded me of my teacher, Krishna. A smile filled his round face and he too had a sizeable belly. He'd established Sivananda yoga centers around the world, beginning in Quebec, Canada.

Swamis are the monks of yoga. There were a handful of them on site, easily identifiable by their orange robes. They seemed peaceful and…normal, speaking with ashram staff and walking around the grounds.

The ashram had a lengthy list of rules, promised two yoga classes per day, and rituals in the morning and night called *satsang*. From the same linguistic root as satsanga, satsang is a gathering that includes meditation and devotional chants. We "yoga vacationers" would attend lectures, do something called karma yoga, and eat *only* two meals per day.

When a bell went off at 5:30 a.m. the next morning, I tried to stay in my saggy cot, but a staffer stood in the dormitory doorway to remind us that "satsang is mandatory for everyone." The service began with half an hour of silent meditation in the still-dark open-air hall. Toward the end, forest birds chirped, we chanted a long prayer, and it felt like summer camp when a swami read announcements before dispatching us to our first sessions of the day.

The yoga classes were similar to Krishna's lessons on the beach. I was famished at 10:00 a.m. when we all lined up for our first meal of bland, lukewarm Indian food. The ashram rules had mentioned that onions and garlic were forbidden due to their stimulating nature. Also excluded were contact between men and women, drugs, alcohol, and "non-devotional" music. As I sought nourishment in the mushy meal, I wondered if the ashram's austerity could actually make me a better person.

I spent a rare break hiding from the rain in the bookstore. Liz had suggested that I learn about tantra, so I picked up Philip Rawson's *Tantra, The Indian Cult of Ecstasy*. The author explains that sensual enjoyment can serve as "spiritual rocket fuel." The *tantrika* is continually absorbed in the shining image of a beautiful goddess. As she lets her hair down, the goddess has the power to expand the world and wrap it up again. This image is more significant to the tantrika than "any actual woman." Sitting cross-legged on the bookstore floor, I thought about the photos of Liz in my backpack. I was absorbed in her shining image, but was the image more important to me than the actual woman?

Rawson explains that human acts of love are manifestations of the earth's creation. He encourages tantrikas to find the right partner and achieve spiritual fulfillment by rousing all of the senses in prolonged sessions of divine lovemaking. He also warns of wasting energy on "untransformed indulgence." I had experienced great joy from intimacy, but hadn't considered that I was inching closer to the earth's creation. I just thought it felt better than anything else. The idea of sex as a spiritual practice seemed to contradict brahmacharya, but tantra sounded like a lot more fun. The problem was, tantra involved something that I was trying desperately to move past: depending on someone else for my happiness.

My afternoon yoga class felt great. The rain had stopped and I was feeling strong and loose. I tried a headstand and actually balanced upside down for a few seconds. By the end of class, I stopped doubting my decision to come. I was where I wanted to be.

Then our group of yoga vacationers had a session where the hosts asked us to describe what brought us to the ashram. Most of the stories started with, "My *spiritual* journey began…"

Josh had said I was on such a journey, but I hesitated to call it that and kept my introduction brief. "Hi, I'm Mark from Canada and I'm here to surrender to the flow." Guests spoke of struggles with illness, injury, heartbreak, and mourning. I didn't know that people turned to yoga to fix things. We all seemed to believe that, by standing on our heads, we'd improve their operation.

The next morning, humid wind blew through the high arches of the yoga hall. I sat cross-legged while the ashram's head swami guided us to close our eyes and focus on our third-eye chakra while repeating "Om." I was better able to ignore my thoughts than I had been in our Palolem sunset meditations. Then we transitioned to the chant that was repeated at every satsang. It lasted for more than ten minutes and was exactly the same each time. Many gods and gurus were mentioned, including the swamis Sivananda and Vishnu Devananda. I looked at their portraits and wondered why they had big bellies. Had they stopped practicing yoga at a certain point? I learned only years later that their physical shape had changed as a result of their yoga practice evolving away from the physical and toward something called karma yoga.

I was introduced to karma yoga later that day. It means selfless service and translated into an hour a day of chores. I was handed an iron brush and told to scrape the moss off of terracotta pots lining a path to the entrance. There were at least twenty pots, all in a tropical shade of green. I don't mind manual labor, but I generally rely on music to get me through it. I didn't use my CD player because non-devotional music was forbidden. It also didn't help me to get through the hour when a staffer told me to slow down my scraping.

"But I want to finish this pot before the hour is up," I said.

"Accomplishment is not important. Karma yoga is about your experience." He sauntered off and I began to wonder why I was paying for the *experience* of scraping a pot that didn't need scraping. When the bell rang for our single hour of free time, I left the pot eighty-percent done.

For the break, I hauled my tabla down a long outdoor flight of stairs to a yoga platform where palm trees lined a reservoir. A handpainted sign announced:

But I saw a man in a bathing suit splashing alone in the water. I tapped on my drums, gazed at the lake, and eased into the rhythms of Varanasi. Thoughts dissipated as I focused on the taals that were now a part of me. After a few days in the conformist ashram, I could finally express myself. It was liberating to properly complete a taal, punctuating the ending with a climactic pattern called *chakradhar*, like in Keshav's performances.

On my breaks from playing, the space was silent. It was rare to be alone in the ashram and I was savoring the moment until the swimmer emerged on the shore. He headed toward the stairs and said without breaking stride, "You really shouldn't be playing that."

As he climbed the tall staircase, I followed him with angry eyes. I shouldn't play tabla, a classical Indian instrument? Isn't this *devotional* music? I hadn't seen anything in the rules about not playing instruments. I did read about not swimming or taking our shirts off, though.

That evening, I was able to laugh off the swimmer's complaint when I saw a tabla on the stage in the huge meditation hall, next to a wooden flute called a *bansuri* and a harmonium. The performer turned out to be a guest swami with a band of supporting musicians. The swami was a young, long-haired, bearded Indian man who performed chants in ancient Sanskrit. During instrumental interludes, he would elaborate in

English on the meaning of the chants. Supported by beating tabla and faint flute, the swami spoke of life as a trip down the river of consciousness, just as Liz had described it on the rooftop in Kochin. I closed my eyes and envisioned the creek at the Ravi Chandra guesthouse in Hampi, jasmine flowers floating like thoughts along its grass-fringed shore.

Then after more chanting, the music became faster and louder. People who had been soothed to sleep by the swami's storytelling sat up to listen. The swami spoke loudly over the rising beat, "Ask not how time will decorate us, but how can we decorate time?"

I knew. I'd been sober for days, but I felt a sudden sensation I'd only had on the most fortunate of drug trips: a feeling that everything was just exactly perfect. I knew what the swami was going to say before he said it. Not his exact words, but I knew how to decorate time.

"The decoration of the present moment is through the *divine*. Simplicity, freedom, the flow of the river, humbleness, being surrounded by loved ones…with *love*."

It made sense. No practice of yoga, tantra, or anything else would get me anywhere unless I started with *love*. Love of myself, love of others, love of *life*. The swami added, "Other decorations—food, thoughts, and things—will be eaten by time. The compassion your mother placed in you will *stay*."

He was describing our true nature: to be loving. Strip away the ego and that's what's left. Drums rumbled and flute fluttered. The swami chanted in Sanskrit and then said, "There is no difference between a spark of fire and a huge fire… There is no difference between a moment of love and a lifetime of love."

The spark is equivalent to the fire. Begin with love and you will find love. The music built toward a climax and the swami concluded to a roaring rhythm, "When you lack guidance…when you are in doubt…recall of a divine moment…a moment of love will evacuate you. Nothing else will."

Flute and tabla erupted toward a final peak. I swung my shoulders to the cycles of sound. I only stayed seated because everyone else was. Either there was a rule against dancing or I was just more into this than anyone else.

As the show concluded, I noticed the guest swami doling out a rare taste of fruit to everyone exiting. The fruit was *prasad*, a blessed offering to the gods. I bowed with hands together to say thank you for the performance and the swami smiled into my eyes as he scooped grapes and melon into my open palms. The juicy jolt tasted particularly sweet.

While savoring a grape outside the meditation hall, I saw a familiar face. It took me a moment to place him, but it was Ronan, one of the Israelis who had given Liz and Fran massages in Hampi. He was at the ashram for a yoga vacation like me and he'd just arrived.

I asked what he thought of the "amazing show" and he said that he enjoyed it, though his eyes seemed to question my enthusiasm. Maybe I *was* just more into it than anyone else.

We discussed our travels since Hampi and I asked Ronan if he remembered Liz. "Of course, the beautiful California girl!" He was impressed that I'd seen her again and he said, "Those two girls… They are…different." I knew he meant it as a compliment; they weren't like other travelers, with their salwar kameez, tiny backpacks, and general refusal to conform. Ronan seemed happy for me, but then his face took on the puzzled expression I'd become accustomed to as he asked, "But where is she now?"

I explained that Liz and Fran were on a sojourn together and that I didn't want to be the third wheel. He kept asking questions as we talked for a while on a bench outside the hall. He was such a good listener that I said something spontaneous that I might have otherwise filtered out—that my next challenge was to see if I could "love myself as much as I love Liz."

We were both surprised by the comment and agreed that it was time to return to the dorm to sleep. I laid on my cot and counted six hours until the morning bell. I found it odd that I'd seen Yaron in Hampi and Ronan in Kerala. We were chasing the same goddesses with mixed results. Was my pursuit a noble one or simply the repetition of a cycle?

As I closed my eyes in the silent darkness, I remembered the swami's suggestion that when in doubt, recall of a moment of love will *evacuate* you. I realized that I had been evacuating from my doubts every time that I reached into my backpack for the photo of Liz in the treehouse in Hampi—her shining image from the thatched treehouse floor. Was it blind devotion to an image or something more valuable, more important?

Still buzzing from the concert, the answer felt clear to me. The photo had captured a moment of love. Liz's eyes looked through the camera lens and told me so.

Before I could sleep, I thought about what I'd said to Ronan. For years, I'd been focused on finding and pleasing a woman. The singing swami was telling me that if I truly wanted to honor her, I needed to first connect with the divine inside of *me*. Whether I achieved it through yoga, music, solitude, or all of the above, I needed to accept myself, including my faults and failings. Without that acceptance, I'd never love a woman the way that she deserved—with an open heart.

CHAPTER 25

Varkala: Paradise Waits

Every backpacker in India knows Ganesh. He's the god of travelers, the remover of obstacles. His image is on every bus and train, encouraging perseverance through adversity. He'd know a little about that: His father lopped off his head and replaced it with an elephant's when Ganesh seemed too comfortable with his good looks. Who was his dad? Shiva, of course.

The ashram's twice-daily chant began with a salutation to Ganesh, but the morning after the singing swami, I was too tired to appreciate the recitations. The previous night's transcendence had vacated the yoga hall and I would have been happier in bed. I dragged myself through the morning yoga class. It didn't help that the teacher was new and the pacing was off.

Then after another unsatisfying meal, I returned to the bookstore. I wanted to read Swami Sivananda's thoughts on tantra. I learned that tantra is actually a general term used to describe many practices of channeling the divine energy within humans. While Sivananda didn't have anything to say about sex or goddess worship in his book on tantra, he did share that, "Everything in the world is a passage to perfection, the visible is not an obstacle." And, "Things seen as impure, ugly, and unholy are…wrongly seen out of context."

I wondered, "If everything is a passage to perfection, Swami, then why are there so many rules here? Are onions and garlic really obstacles?

Are they seeing rock music out of context?" The ashram felt like a place of contradiction. A spiritual quest couldn't be packaged into thirty-minute slots each morning and night. I wasn't going to feel bliss while being rushed from activity to activity and told how to dress and when to eat.

Looking back, I now understand how the structure of an ashram can be helpful. The rules create a certainty that allows people to focus on spiritual practice. At that time, though, I wasn't ready to trust the process. There was no way that I was going to learn how to love myself between soggy chapatis and disappointing yoga classes.

I'd paid for four days of the two-week course and it was day five. Though I hadn't thought about leaving early, I saw a guy who'd arrived when I did. He had packed up and was heading for a bus. He told me, "No regrets. Just ready to move on." I was envious until I realized that I could do the same. I was gone within the hour, en route to Varkala.

Descending through verdant mountains toward the coast, the now-familiar salutation to Ganesh played in my head. I was as excited to leave the ashram as I'd been to arrive. I savored seeing plows in the fields, oxcarts, and rickshaws. All were symbols of hard work, but also of something unquestionably *real*, unlike the ashram. As the bus swerved downhill toward the ocean, the occasional whiffs of burning trash smelled like freedom. I felt like a rubber ball, eager to bounce around India, discovering more each time I landed and easily rerouted by the slightest nudge in any direction.

I checked into a hotel with a good rooftop and ordered a seafood pizza at a restaurant above the ocean. The pizza wasn't great, but it allowed me to violate many of the ashram's rules in one bite. Back at the hotel, I rolled up a joint on the rooftop. I hadn't smoked in weeks, but I wanted to now, specifically because it had been forbidden at the ashram. In order to find my own path, I needed all paths to be available. Now high under an orange sky, I set up my mini-speakers and listened to *Help on the Way* by the Grateful Dead. The first words, "Paradise waits, on the crest of a wave," had popped into my head as soon as Ganesh's chant left it.

In 1973, the Grateful Dead lost singer, keyboardist, and founding member Ron "Pigpen" McKernan to alcohol-related disease at the young age of twenty-seven. If not the heart of the band, Pigpen was definitely their soul. On stage in his signature leather vest, he would fire up crowds with improvised lyrics. His tombstone was inscribed with: "Pigpen was and is now forever one of the Grateful Dead."

The band trucked on with a new keyboard player, but Pigpen's death hung an even larger shadow over the band than their massive speaker towers did. Though they were achieving creative heights and commercial success, tours now included a regiment of roadies and a growing gaggle of hangers-on. Chemical consumption by all prompted concern about who might next be enshrined as a forever member of the Grateful Dead. Instead of finding out, they agreed in late 1974 to put down their instruments for an undetermined hiatus.

The break didn't last a year, but when the band returned, their sound system and entourage were vastly reduced. They invited fans to a small venue in San Francisco, auspiciously named the Great American Music Hall. They arrived with new compositions and arranged to broadcast the show on FM radio. That recording was what I listened to on the rooftop in Varkala. The music tasted like a hungry man's first meal in days and I imagined that the 1975 crowd may have felt the same way.

Bill Graham, the Grateful Dead's promoter, loved to introduce the band. On that night, the rhythm section started playing before he had a chance to introduce all seven band members. As Graham said, "On lead guitar and vocals, Mister Jerry Garcia," the first chords of a new song burst forth. When he concluded with, "Would you welcome please, the Grateful Dead!" the band announced their return, on their terms.

> "'Cause I love what I love and I want it that way."
> – *Help on the Way*, Grateful Dead

At sunset in Varkala, I felt the same way—floating in the ocean at sin-cleansing Papanasham Beach.

The next morning, I checked email for the first time in five days. There was no word from Liz, but I emailed to tell her that I'd left the ashram. My best friend, Matt (aka Chez), was logged in to a chat application. For him it was the middle of the night.

Mark: Chez, what are you doing awake?

Matt: Can't sleep.

Mark: Got goddesses on the brain?

Matt: Huh?

Mark: Girls! From your last email, I figured that thinking about women might be keeping you awake. There was the skiing girl, the situation with Martha...

Matt: Ok, you're right. I have goddesses on the brain.

Mark: Do tell...

Matt: Oh, nothing really interesting. I'm just trying to decide what to do about that cute girl who I went skiing with. I was trying to forget about the Martha thing, but thanks for bringing it up.

Mark: I think it sounds interesting, but don't let it keep you up, neither of them are the right goddess for you anyway.

Matt: What's up with the goddesses?

Mark: Oh, I was reading about Tantra where you see the divine in the image of the goddess. We aim toward higher consciousness by sharing intimate experiences with a human goddess.

Matt: Holy shit.

Mark: Exactly. :-)

Mark: It's a divine pursuit, but really only once you've found the right partner for you. Until then, girl chasing results in "untransformed indulgence." It distracts from spiritual growth.

Matt: You may be on to something. Any suggestions on how to sleep?

Mark: Well, you obviously have thoughts to process, so those probably have to run their course.

Matt: I did some sun salutations.

Mark: At night? This I would not recommend. It will wake up your body. It's better to do them in the morning. Try laying on your back, scanning your body, and observing your sensations.

Matt: Thanks guru. Enough about me, tell me about the goddesses in India.

Mark: I think Liz is in Rajasthan, but I haven't heard from her in a bit.

Matt: She sounded pretty special.

Mark: Yes, I think she might be the right goddess for me.

Matt: So, what are you waiting for?

Mark: She's with her friend Fran, and three is a crowd. Also, I'm not convinced that I should dive into goddess worship at this point.

Matt: I think it's a little late for that.

Mark: Thanks Chez.

    I stayed in Varkala for a few days. The manager of my hotel was a friendly fellow around my age named Shaji. He would check on me while I was alone on the rooftop playing tabla. Once when a pair of long-legged women climbed the hotel stairs, he implied with a glance that he could introduce me. I shook my head and said, "It's okay."

"You don't like girls?"

"I'm taking a break from girls,"

Then he asked if I had a "real love," as opposed to the love of an arranged marriage.

"I might, I mean… I think so."

"You do!"

"Well, she's far away right now, and I haven't known her for very long…"

He didn't care about the logistics. He wanted to know "What does *real love* feel like?"

It was a difficult question, but I'd been thinking about it since the night of the singing swami. I told him, "It's when you look at each other and think, 'All that's good in life is right here.'"

"This person is everything?"

"No, the rest of the world is still important, but its natural goodness is all there, in front of you, in the shape of your true love… your *real* love."

Shaji was fascinated. I continued, "I know… it sounds exclusive, but it isn't. It brings acceptance and appreciation of everything else."

"You have felt this before?"

I thought of Ronit and said, "Yes, but it faded… The connection went away."

While I wondered for a moment if the connection would eventually fade with Liz, Shaji said, "You are very lucky man that you have felt this."

It was helpful to be reminded of my good fortune. Late that night, as the shrinking moon shone through thin curtains, I wrote in my journal, "Like a beautiful sunset or an impressive mountain, love of one person is an extreme example of how good life is. Our love for that person can be a catalyst that magnifies our love toward the rest of the world."

I had the theory down, but I still wasn't starting with love for myself. The Sivananda Ashram may not have been the answer, but I wasn't going to learn anything by smoking joints on rooftops either. Still, Varkala was a nice place to divert to before forging ahead on my spiritual journey. Only once I was comfortable would Shiva lop my head off and force me to begin again.

CHAPTER 26

Varkala: Sin City

I was born in Toronto and lived there with my family until I was three years old. I have no memories from inside the house, though. I can't tell you what the kitchen looked like or where my bedroom was. All I can remember is riding outside on my orange tractor. It had big wheels in the back and a steering wheel connected to a smaller front tire with pedals. I would ride around the driveway of our brick house in red overalls and blue and white sneakers.

We lived on a hill, so at first, I'd roll from higher up the sidewalk and into the driveway while my mom stood guard. By the time the leaves turned the bright shades of an Ontario autumn, I was riding past our house to the bottom of the street. My mom would stand at the corner, monitoring my right turn to ensure that I didn't end up in traffic.

It was late 1977 and my third birthday was approaching, as was our move to Edmonton. My dad had been relocated to western Canada for his job. He didn't have to go, but as North America lingered in post-Watergate recession, the young father knew to follow the money. Alberta had oil.

One afternoon, my mom let me out to ride. I pushed my tractor uphill past a few neighbors' houses. I assumed that my mom was proceeding to her usual spot at the street corner, but she must have been delayed because, once I started moving, I saw that no one was there. The vehicle gathered speed and I took my feet off of the spinning pedals. When I passed our house, I heard my mom call "Maaaark!" as she ran across the lawn. I wanted to look back, to respond, but it was too late—the tractor was out of the barn. I had to focus on the upcoming turn.

I dug my rubber soles into the pavement to reduce velocity. I knew just how much I needed to slow down to turn without skidding. I had done it many times—never falling—but always with a spotter. This time, Mom could do nothing but watch. Trusting my instincts, I leaned to the right as I yanked the steering wheel and made the turn.

My mom was upset with me, but not for long when I agreed that it would have been safer to wait for her. She had always been there, so I assumed she would be again. She may have been more upset with herself than with me, but I told her not to worry—I knew what I was doing.

Two dozen years later, I was telling my parents the same thing. First, they worried about me visiting an ashram and being converted to a new religion. Now that I was out of the ashram, they worried about me having no itinerary. I wrote that there was a method to my meandering and that they needn't be concerned. Varkala was a vacation destination and I was doing just that—taking a vacation from whatever it was I was supposed to be doing. There was no rooster, alarm clock, or ashram staffer to wake me up early and I loved it.

One morning, I sat alone at a café sipping chai when a European woman called to me from the next table. She had a deep voice, strong accent, and broad shoulders. I'd guess she was ten or fifteen years older than I was. She wore a sleeveless top, with blond hair tickling her shoulders. Her name was Fabia and she was a massage therapist from Italy. She invited me to her table and as I sat down, she said, "You are prac-ti-cing yo-ga."

I was impressed that she could tell. I told her about Krishna and my short trip to the ashram, and that word lit up her blue eyes. "I spent time at O-sho's ash-ram. Do you know it?"

"I know *of* it." My friend Josh was planning to go and I recalled the abundance of merchandise and lack of enlightenment that Galit, one of the Israeli women at the Yogi Lodge, had left Varanasi with.

"It was Valentine's Day… I was there for a tan-tric medi-ta-tion. Do you know tantra?"

"I've… read about it."

Fabia smiled, remembering aloud how a coed group of participants entered a shared space all wearing saffron robes. They were guided through a meditation and then encouraged to express themselves to each other through touch in the spirit of the romantic holiday. The robes came off and… Fabia left the rest to my imagination. After my recent experience, I was surprised to hear what went on at another ashram. I asked if it was really a spiritual experience or "untransformed indulgence" and Fabia shook her head. "Oh, no… it *was* trans-form-a-tive!"

I smiled. "*And* indulgent."

The tantra talk had charged me up and I needed to cool down. I decided to go for a swim and Fabia said that I could find her at the café anytime. I ran down the cliffside stairs to the beach, kicked off my sandals, dropped my journal in the sand, and sprinted into the sea.

I dove into a wave and realized that the sunglasses that had been on top of my head were now gone. I looked around, but realized that it would be futile to search for them. I'd worn those yellow, cheap, scratched, perseverant shades for most of the last few months, but I told myself not to care that they were gone. The shades were *stuff* and I didn't want to care about *stuff*.

Instead, I floated on my back in the warm sea and thought of Liz. Why hadn't she written me yet? Did she somehow know that I'd betrayed her trust? Was she so good at suppressing her desire that she was forgetting about me?

When I returned to the rooftop for a private afternoon yoga session, it was humid and I felt loose. While holding a pose, I fainted. It wasn't a rush to the head like the previous time in Hampi. It was a sudden blackout.

Curled in a ball on the ground, I was "fresh born," as Krishna would say during savasana. I opened my eyes, but saw only darkness. I felt around with my hands and touched the concrete. After a second, my vision returned and I saw the rooftop, but remained clueless about place, time, and circumstance. I unpeeled my limbs from the floor and looked around. My first thought was, "I remember this place." The spot where I had been practicing yoga seconds earlier had become a memory.

I was observing someone who'd fallen, but I had an odd angle—I was too close. I could only see legs and ground, not the whole person. For a surprisingly long few seconds, my identity remained blank. I slowly discerned that I was in India, in my underwear, on a rooftop. I couldn't remember the name of the town, but I knew that I was alone. Then I thought of Liz. Before my family, my home, or my friends, I remembered Hampi and Kochin and Palolem and the ashram, and then I knew that I was in Varkala.

When I checked email that night, I found this message:

Hi Mark,

I'm glad to hear that you escaped the sweaty yoga place.

I am in Udaipur, enjoying myself beautifully. I washed a bucket of clothes today. I almost scrubbed them on the ghats, but the water was too green and slimy.

Sima, the tailor, had Fran and I over for dinner last night. She is such a precious woman. I had to walk out of her store today because I was overwhelmed with kindness.

I certainly am thinking of you... Sima suspected I had someone on my mind when I walked into her store because I was not interested in looking at her silk scarves. She's fixing my sleep sheet... wonderful.

All these are little details to let you know that you are with me, and I think of you.

Travel in light.
Liz

I replayed her words, "you are with me, and I think of you," in my head. She hadn't written in a while and was all the way up in Rajasthan, but she hadn't forgotten me. Though I wasn't welcome on her trip with Fran, I could still tag along in Liz's mental sidecar.

In Varkala, I was a nowhere man. I had no plans and I wasn't learning anything new on drums or in yoga. I practiced both alone on the rooftop, but *adi guru* (the guru within) was inexperienced. I started feeling a tug to try another ashram. I flipped through *From Here to Nirvana* looking for ideas. Mysore had been the launching pad for Liz's monk hunt and it had some teachers who looked interesting, including a music swami and some yoga gurus.

I joined Fabia for coffee the next morning and told her what had happened on the rooftop. I kept thinking about the feeling of being outside my body and even outside of my mind. Who was that watching? Was it my true self? The Atman? As Liz had earlier, Fabia equated fainting with a suspension of consciousness. "Osho teaches a meditation for 'the no-mind' where you witness yourself from a distance." She thought I had caught a glimpse of that phenomenon. She said that she could suppress her thoughts while giving a massage. Perhaps inspired by the conversation, she promised that if I returned in the afternoon, she would massage me.

To me, Varkala was Sin City, an alluring temptress at the deepest base of India, offering transformative indulgence—the anti-ashram. When I had first arrived there, I slept with Robin before seeing daylight. No amount of cleansing in the sea would make me forget that sin. But now, with no schedule and no one to answer to, Varkala continued to lure me in. *Have a massage, learn about tantric orgies, eat anything you want, smoke some weed, go for a swim…*

When I returned to Fabia, it was just as hot as it had been the previous afternoon when I'd passed out. I told her that she didn't need to massage me—we could just sit and talk. She wanted to keep her promise, though. I entered her room and, as directed, stripped down to my underwear and rested facedown on the bed. Fabia kneaded and stretched me while I recalled observing my body from the outside. I knew that fainting was unsafe and I wasn't going to try to replicate it, but the experience had opened a door that would never close again.

I was a beginner in the meditation game, but I knew that the aim of the practice was to move beyond our thoughts to something more profound.

I also knew that the point of yoga was to bring our mind, body, and spirit into unity, but I didn't understand how they were separate in the first place. It was all just theory to me. In the fleeting moment when I found my body tangled on the rooftop, I had *felt* a separation. With no sense of time or place, *I* was still there. Watching. Aware. From that moment forward, I no longer doubted that "I" was something beyond my body and mind. Call it spirit, the self, the soul, or even God. It didn't matter. I *knew* from my own experience that it was *real* and beautiful. That non-judging observer held the answer to how I could love myself. If yoga could take me deeper toward that "I," then that was what I wanted to do. I recalled the warning sign at the ashram in Hampi: "The search for self is essential. Life without this realization is a waste." It was time for me to stop wasting time.

Fabia wiped her brow in the extreme heat. Her tank top was drenched with sweat, but she didn't seem to mind. When she was done, I rose from the bed, thanked her with a firm hug, and said, "I'm leaving tomorrow."

She was disappointed. "But you're my yoga rebel."

I laughed and thought to myself that I *was* a yogi and perhaps even a rebel, but I certainly was *not* hers. This rubber ball was going to bounce out of Sin City and onto a train north.

Heading toward Karnataka the next day, I thought about Liz and "real love." What if she *was* the one? I'd thought of her when I hardly remembered who *I* was. It was Friday, two weeks since Liz and I had reunited for Shabbat in Kochin. The next full moon was another two weeks away. That seemed like a long time to wait, but instinct was leading me back toward yoga and, besides, I didn't want to commit to anyone. The word itself sounded criminal. Would I be committing the crime of self-delusion in pursuit of pleasure? Would that commitment be rewarded, punished, or both? I wasn't quite ready to find out, but still, I was moving north, in Liz's direction.

CHAPTER 27

Mysore: Gurus

Indian trains carry a collective consciousness across the country. Passengers bring anticipation on board at each station and as the train rolls away, it rocks from side to side like an overloaded shopping cart. When it achieves full speed, people hold on to avoid careening off the walls. When the pace is steady, travelers connect with each other while not being anyplace at all. Then darkness falls and everyone retreats to their bunks for the night.

As cramped, loud, and smelly as those steel rods of human energy were, I loved being on board. I relied on the vendors for food or chai—I was too afraid the train would leave without me if I got off to buy something. I would write in my journal or read, but my favorite part was observing it all. The forward momentum was a steady reminder that change was happening. Whenever I was on an Indian train, I was sure that I was moving in the right direction.

Indian Railways seated foreigners together for long rides. This designation included more than just westerners with backpacks. I also met travelers from nearby countries like Nepal and China. On the early morning that I rolled into Bangalore on my way to Mysore, I sat with a group of Tibetans. All were young men in their early twenties, some in monks' robes, some in regular clothes. They shared the excitement of a road trip and seemed comfortable with each other. One monk slept on a friend's lap. Some looked out the window, others looked at me.

I wondered what it was like to be a young monk with a vow of celibacy and a life devoted to spiritual study. Many Tibetans, including their exiled leader, the Dalai Lama, live in India as refugees. Because Tibetans are known for their nonviolent resistance to Chinese oppression, I was surprised when a monk landed a solid punch on the arm of one of his friends. It was friendly, not vicious, but it surprised me and I gasped. My reaction caused their whole group to turn toward me. Everyone was silent for a second, and then we all laughed together.

Of course, a Tibetan monk isn't nonviolent *all* of the time, but I didn't know that. These young men were just guys being guys. In a life devoted to spiritual practice, a monk didn't have to give up his personality. I took it as a reminder that I didn't have to give up mine either.

Neither the ashram nor Sin City had offered me the right balance, so I hoped to find it in Mysore, a city filled with gurus. Still, I remained skeptical, in part due to an experience I'd had at home, months before coming to India.

I'd heard some of Ronit's friends talk about going to see someone named John. Then one day, my buddy Arlo called and said, "Let's go see John the Prophet! You've heard of John the Prophet… Let's go to his lecture tonight. It'll be cool." Arlo was always up for new experiences and could be very convincing. I didn't know what to expect, but if this guy was considered a prophet by some, I thought it might be interesting. It sure was.

We followed the directions to St. Albert, a tidy suburb that I wouldn't have considered a new age haven. It was winter and the nondescript hall was as white as the snowbanks surrounding it. The scene inside was like a dressed-down version of a church or synagogue with everyone in stackable chairs facing the front. I was glad that I'd declined Arlo's offer to smoke a joint in the parking lot because the energy in there was odd enough without herbal enhancement.

John was seated on a low stage, not saying a word. I put my hand on a seat near the back, but Arlo whispered, "We need to be close. It's all about his *energy*."

Arlo had never seen John before, but he was right. People were clustered at the front, as close to John as possible. The hall contained around a hundred people and all were transfixed. They didn't seem particularly happy, just focused. As we found a pair of seats in the third row, no one looked at us. They were all watching John.

He had blond hair and looked normal—just a guy in a button-down shirt and khakis—but he was not acting normally. He had everyone's attention and by the time we settled into our seats, he *still* wasn't talking. His brow hung like a stone slab over piercing blue eyes. He would stare at one audience member for a long time and then move on to someone else. He slowly crossed the room, shifting from person to person.

I looked around for familiar faces and found none. When I looked back at John, his eyes were making their way in our direction. I got a bit nervous, but then he started talking. His expression was stern and he spoke slowly. He used words like "beingness" and "magicalness."

I couldn't make much sense of it, but I focused on the eyes. His stare-at-one-person-for-a-long-time tactic struck me as a form of manipulation. People wanted him to look at them, and they drank up the attention when he did. A young woman raised her hand. She was sitting on the floor in front and holding a notepad. In an Israeli accent, she asked how one could maintain "beingness." She was probably in her early twenties and fresh out of the army. I was shocked: She'd traveled to Edmonton in the dead of winter to see *this* guy? The young woman was thinking about going home, and her question was about how not to lose the feeling she was having in John's presence.

John looked firmly at her and she held his gaze like it was a staring contest. He said that the "beingness" would fade if she stopped "knowing," implying that to keep "knowing," she should stay for longer. That wasn't the answer that she wanted and I felt bad for her.

Blue granite went back to scanning the room. Ignoring raised hands, he was coming our way. After looking at a few people for a couple of minutes each, he was on me. I stared back and tried not to blink, wondering if I would feel something.

I did. Though I felt squirmy, it was special to be the one engaging with the leader. I'd been there for only half an hour, most of it in silence, but his stare had an odd magnetism. He moved on to Arlo, who started to glow now that it was his turn.

This is a mind fuck, I thought. It didn't matter *what* John said or if he was really a prophet. He could make people feel special because they all felt that *he* was special. He had amassed enough power that he could quote cat posters and his followers would feel uplifted. This was how Jim Jones convinced all of those people to drink the poisoned Kool-Aid, I thought.

Later in the parking lot, I asked Arlo, "Did you feel anything?"

"Yeah…" he said. "When he looked at me, I did…"

"Me too… It was intense. Why do they call him a prophet?"

"They say he's enlightened…"

"It felt pretty dark to me…"

"Definitely, definitely…"

I could see how sitting with someone enlightened might be an efficient way to sense clarity, but I hated the idea of a guru controlling a group of followers. John made early adopters feel special—their questions were answered, they got longer looks. Newcomers wanted that. It was a spiritual pyramid scheme.

I carried that mistrust with me toward Mysore. I wanted to take yoga deeper, but didn't want to be a *follower*. It was a delicate balance. *From Here to Nirvana* described a "healing by music swami." I wasn't looking for healing, but thought the swami sounded cool.

On the way to Mysore, I had to change trains in Bangalore. Standing at the ticket window, I had my backpack and tabla at my feet. Somehow, while I bought a ticket, a thief sliced into my backpack and stole my camera. I turned around to see a diagonal scar across my pack but no sign of the thief. I was astonished at how quickly he had located the camera and vanished, but I was relieved to still have my bank and credit cards and my passport in the money belt around my waist.

It was disappointing to lose the camera, and though the device was more valuable than the sunglasses that I'd lost while jumping into the sea, I had decided not to worry about *stuff*. I saw the incident as a test. I was upset but tried to shake it off. My first stop in Mysore was at a tailor shop where a woman stitched up my backpack. Then I checked into a hotel that featured nightly Indian music concerts in an open-air restaurant. There was no flat rooftop for my practices, so I settled for a quiet corner near the utility closet.

The next morning, I heard that Mysore Palace would be lit up that night—a Sunday tradition. I thought, "If only I had my camera…" I had tried to move on from stuff, but India was a spectacular visual experience that I wanted to remember and share when I returned home. Thank goodness I'd only lost about ten pictures as the rest had been developed already. I recalled a quote from *What Buddhists Believe* by Dhammanada: "The Buddhist should reduce his strong attachment to possessions which, if he is not mindful, can enslave him to greed. What he owns or has should instead be used for the benefit and happiness of others."

So, for the benefit of myself and others, I bought a used camera similar to the stolen one. I captured the Mysore Palace lights and felt the joy of discovery through art.

The music swami turned out to be away on tour, so I checked out a yoga center that was also in the book. There I met an elderly yogi who was a specialist in the hatha yoga that I'd been practicing already. Two students practiced familiar poses in a windowless concrete room in his urban ashram.

The octogenarian yogi expounded on the benefits of spending a month under his instruction. For one hundred dollars, he would teach me daily and I would share in the benefit of his community of pupils. I wondered if there were more than two of them. When I asked if it would be possible to participate for a shorter time, he did not relent.

"It is necessary you stay one month. One hundred dollars."

I was not interested at all. His austere studio seemed stifling and I wanted to be free. I thanked him for his time and the rubber ball bounced back onto the Mysore street.

When I was in Palolem, I'd browsed one of Josh's books by a scholar named Krishnamurti.

Krishnamurti was a twentieth-century scholar from India who had, as a boy, found himself in the unusual position of being groomed to be a guru. By the time he was a teenager, an entire order was established around his teaching. He lectured around the world and gathered thousands of followers. Then, at the age of twenty-seven, he experienced what many considered enlightenment. Krishnamurti refused to say so and insisted that he wasn't special. He dissolved the order, returned all donations, and spent the rest of his life as an unaffiliated spiritual educator.

In Josh's book, I'd read this quote: "If you have money, you can go to India. But I do not know why you go. You will find no enlightenment there. Enlightenment is where you are." I was amused to read that quote in a book that Josh had carried all the way from Canada. Still, it was easy for

Krishnamurti to say that India wasn't important. He was *from* India. The country's spiritual ingredients were already baked into his cake.

I was bouncing around the country hoping to build on the magical moments I'd already experienced, but I was growing frustrated with using a guidebook to do it. I tried to exchange *From Here to Nirvana* at a bookstore, but they wouldn't take it. I browsed for a while and pulled Krishnamurti's *The Awakening of Intelligence* from the shelf. These words caught my eye: "I can't find a strong enough word to deny that whole world of gurus of their authority, because they think they know. A man who says 'I know,' such a man does not know. Or if a man says, 'I have experienced truth,' distrust him completely." Krishnamurti went on to explain that by sacrificing freedom for a specific system, a spiritual seeker ends up with "a mind which is incapable of subtlety, swiftness, and sensitivity."

I valued my teachers, but I was learning that spiritual practice is inherently a do-it-yourself endeavor. Krishna was only able to share the timeless teachings of yoga with me because I was open and ready to receive them. For me, it was never about the guru, it was about seeing what had been going on with me and having the motivation to change it. At that beautiful beach in Goa, I could see that I'd been living in a fog for years. And since those first days at Palolem, I'd been reconnecting with parts of me that had always been there, hiding below the expectations, judgments, and compulsions.

I wanted to keep on digging, but Mysore wasn't feeling like the place to do it. I left the bookstore and returned to my hotel in time to shower before the dinner concert. I dressed casually with a long black lungi around my waist and a black T-shirt. I found a spot near the stage as tabla and sitar music filled the dining room. Relishing the atmosphere, I was taken aback when the waiter called me "Swamji." I shot him a puzzled look. When he did it again, I asked why he would call me that. He eyed my outfit and said, "You are holy man, yes?"

A holy man? Hilarious. Perhaps I'd found my guru after all.

CHAPTER 28

Palolem: Breathe

My guru hunt in Mysore had turned out to be even less successful than Liz's monk hunt nearby. When I emailed to tell her, she responded:

Hello Mark,
 You're in Mysore... Wow... You are far away from me.
 I have been thinking about you and I am becoming somewhat clear on my feelings... As my fingers warm up on the keys, maybe I'll spill a little about what I feel.
 I loved Udaipur, romantic, cold, and beautiful. Now we are in Pushkar feeling the intensity of being in a holy city. We might run off to Delhi or more likely to Rishikesh to do yoga along the Ganges.
 How do I feel? A Spaniard in Udaipur helped me figure it out... passion... I feel passionately for you... una gran atracción (a big attraction). When I left home to travel at age seventeen, my sister Julie gave me a card of the full moon rising over the desert. She wrote, 'Dear Lizzie... Always follow your head, your heart, and the full moon.'
 Well, at the risk of... whatever, I will say that with you, I feel that these three are in sync. Yes, I feel passion in my heart. My head sees that there is a connection with you. You are kind to me and good, and the full moon...
 So... there's passion with potential. That's how I see it. No pressure... no rush... I trust you to know when the time is right for you to find me... I

am willing... Except you know that I am still involved with my adventures with Fran. I want very much for you to have time alone and only you can know how to give that to yourself.

Mixed messages? Too verbose? I have a feeling you understood this all anyways.

Namaste
Liz

I did understand. Two weeks after blowing like a leaf in the wind, Liz felt "passion with potential." The timing was up to me and she was "willing." I didn't know if I should go to her yet, but I knew that Mysore wasn't where I wanted to be. I went right to the train station and said to the fellow at the ticket counter, "I want to go to Goa tonight."

"No train, sir."

"How about a bus?"

"No bus tonight."

"Is there *any way* to get to Goa tonight?" I'd learned not to accept the first answer.

"Yes, local bus possible, have to changing in Coondapura." His waddling head indicated that I'd finally asked the right question.

"Local bus" turned out to be a euphemism for uncomfortable bus. I wanted to bounce around India and that's what I got—on a hard seat for many hours.

While unable to sleep on the bus, I listened to Pink Floyd. Their ethereal instrumentals suited traveling in darkness, and in the early-morning hours, their lyrics seemed particularly profound.

Pink Floyd was already famous in England in 1967 when they asked David Gilmour to fill in on vocals and guitar for their brilliant but erratic front man, Syd Barrett. Gilmour was a childhood friend of Barrett's and he was happy to help.

Gilmour fit in right away. He was a talented musician and he was reliable. Barrett, on the other hand, had been consuming copious amounts of LSD and it may have permanently damaged his brain. He had become so incommunicative that the band didn't have to kick him out. They just stopped picking him up for gigs.

By the time Syd Barrett was twenty-seven, he was living as a recluse, and Pink Floyd was celebrating the release of one of the most successful albums of all time, The Dark Side of the Moon.

When I arrived at the Ocean Breeze the following afternoon, Povi greeted me. "Number Four, you want hut number four? Where is Number Five?" I told him that I wasn't sure where Josh was, but that I was happy to be back. After settling into hut number four, I walked to Patnam Beach and savored the sea air as the words of *Breathe (In the Air)* replayed in my overtired mind.

As I swam in the ocean at Patnam with that album's lyrics still in my head, the first words of the opening track—"Breathe, breathe in the air. Don't be afraid to care"—struck me as a meditation on the prana in breath.

Pink Floyd's follow-up to Dark Side *was an album called* Wish You Were Here. *By 1975, no one had seen Syd Barrett in years, but the album title made it clear that he was still on their minds.* Wish You Were Here *began and ended with a cautionary tribute to their estranged former member, an epic composition titled* Shine On You Crazy Diamond. *They had recorded the instrumental track—including a spectacular guitar solo by Gilmour—and were working on the lyrics in their studio when an overweight, bald stranger appeared. He had shaved eyebrows and said nothing. He seemed odd but also…familiar. The stranger sat in a corner and got up frequently to brush his teeth. The band members assumed that he was a member of the crew. After about forty-five minutes, they realized that it was Syd Barrett.*

The band approached Barrett, but he said very little. He left the studio without incident and returned to obscurity. Shine On You Crazy Diamond *included the lyric "Nobody knows where you are, how near or how far," but somehow, on the very day when those words were being recorded, Barrett emerged to bear witness to his own tribute. It may have been a coincidence, but perhaps, even without his sanity, Syd Barrett had remained within the collective consciousness of Pink Floyd.*

As I floated in the sea at Patnam Beach, I thought of what steers someone back to a particular place where their life has turned. After reading Liz's message, I hadn't spent a moment considering any options other than coming back to Goa. Instinct had turned me toward the site of my *rebirth*. The spectacular setting had cleared up my confusion before and as I floated on my back with saltwater covering my ears, I asked the sea for guidance one more time.

Liz sounded ready for me, but I also wanted to go deeper into my yoga practice. The ashram had been stifling and Mysore wasn't the answer. Palolem would be different with Josh gone, but maybe I needed more time there? As I swam back to the shore, Pink Floyd offered a solution: "Look around, choose your own ground." I accepted that I should take things one day at a time.

I surprised Krishna the next morning when I came to his early advanced yoga class. I was the only student—and proud to show him my developing headstand. He insisted that I also stay for the beginner class. His familiar voice soothed me in savasana and it felt like I was home.

When the beginner class began, I noticed an Israeli woman with curly brown hair in the group. She looked familiar, so I wondered if I'd seen her before or if it was just that I found her attractive. She spoke with Krishna like an old friend, but I couldn't place her.

After the class, I returned to the Ocean Breeze for breakfast and noticed the Israeli woman at another table in the restaurant. We exchanged smiles and when I returned to hut number four, I discovered that she was my next-door neighbor. Number Six, as Povi would surely have dubbed her. On the dirt path leading to the Ocean Breeze's outdoor shower, I introduced myself, mentioning that I had spent three weeks there a few months earlier. Her name was Orly and she had been at Palolem for three days.

Orly had clearly made an impression on Krishna because that afternoon, while I was playing tabla, the yogi paid a visit to the Ocean Breeze. It was the first time I'd seen him there, and though he listened attentively to my drumming, he had clearly come at Orly's invitation. They talked for hours at a plastic table until orange hues painted the sunset sky.

I joined them for dinner and Orly told me that her name means "light" in Hebrew, which I knew already. I still couldn't tell why she seemed familiar. Then she asked, "What sign are you?"

I knew nothing about astrology except for recently reading about my sign in Linda Goodman's *Sun Signs*. "Scorpio. I'm action-oriented and

brutally honest with a weakness to love. It could ruin me. Also, Scorpio is skeptical and doesn't believe in astrology. You?"

"Cancer. I'm emotional and tough to get to know."

Okay, that wasn't it.

The three of us walked to another sandy restaurant/bar in the bay of Colomb Beach. When the conversation turned to meditation, Orly asked Krishna, "How long do you *not* think for?"

He didn't understand the question, but I knew what she was asking. I told her that I wasn't much of a meditator, but that, "When truth pervades consciousness, we're riding the time, not tracking it."

Orly liked my answer and then asked us our ages. I was twenty-seven and Krishna was a year older than I. Upon telling us that she was thirty, Orly said, "Some guys don't like it when they find out that I'm older than they are after I've been with them."

What was that comment about? Krishna was unfazed, but I looked at Orly differently as she visited another table to ask for a cigarette. I hadn't been thinking about her that way and wondered if there was something in her interactions with me or Krishna that I hadn't picked up on?

While Orly engaged in typical post-bumming-a-smoke conversation at the other table, Krishna leaned back in a plastic chair, staring at the stars. There was no moon. Tiny waves lapped just short of his toes. Barely audible, he asked the universe, "Where is Liz?"

The brakes squealed on my train of thought. I'd been wondering if Orly was interested in me, and then, as if he were guiding me in a yoga class, Krishna adjusted my mind.

Liz was on her way to Rishikesh, I told him. He didn't say anything—just kept stargazing. I wondered when the moon would be full, when the time would be right to go and find Liz. I still worried that, by following her, I'd fall into my old patterns of depending on someone else for my happiness. Before leaving the beach, I wanted Palolem to tell me if I had changed.

After a while, Krishna began his walk home. I stopped by the table to tell Orly that I was ready to do the same. She stood and asked if she could walk with me. On the walk she asked, "Do you listen to spiritual music?"

"No, but I've been noticing spiritual meaning in the music I do listen to."

She asked for an example.

"On the bus here, I was listening to Pink Floyd, thinking for the first time that *The Dark Side of the Moon* isn't just about life, it's about a *spiritual* life. In *Breathe (In The Air)*, they sing, 'All you touch and all you see is all your life will ever be.' It sounds like Buddhism to me. There's no God, only our experience on earth. It's up to us to make the most of it."

Now she wanted to hear the album. We found ourselves at bamboo hut number four and Orly was inviting herself in. As I reached for the mini-speakers, she said, "No, it's late and I want to hear it loud. Do you have headphones?"

I offered her a seat on the bed, but she insisted on sitting on the floor of sand. Respecting her boundary, I queued up the music, sat next to her, and handed her an earbud. I held my head close to hers so that the cable would reach. The woman whose name means light brightened up as the heartbeat introduction of *Dark Side* pulsed into her ear.

Breath is vital to yoga and meditation. When the lyrics "Breathe, breathe in the air. Don't be afraid to care" began, Orly nodded in understanding as

I had on the bus the night before. I rested my arm on her shoulder. She put hers around my waist, but somehow, even in that dark and intimate setting, I felt no sexual energy. Side by side in the sand, we were spiritual siblings, sharing the backseat on a road trip to a new phase in our lives.

When the cacophonous clocks of *Time* kicked in, Orly pulled out the earbud and hugged me goodnight. She still felt familiar, but I hadn't figured out why. She'd invited herself in, had a musical bonding experience, and was done within minutes.

In bed a moment later, I picked up the Leonard Cohen novel that I'd been reading. He writes, "Do you know what the ambition of our generation is, Wanda? We all want to be Chinese mystics living in thatched huts, but getting laid frequently."

And there I was, in my thatched hut, feeling mystical, but not thinking about getting laid. I wasn't feeling *desire* for Orly, but still, there was something about her… Was it our shared interest in music and yoga? She had said that people with her astrology sign were tough to get to know, but I hadn't found that at all. The issue wasn't with Cancer, though, it was Scorpio. *Sun Signs* was right: I *am* brutally honest and action-oriented with a weakness to love. The *rebounder* would have given into that weakness and pursued Orly, but this time, brutal honesty about my feelings for Liz protected my heart from the pain of committing another betrayal. The rebounder was gone.

But why did Orly seem so familiar? She didn't look or sound like anyone I knew…

Then I finally figured it out.

It was her *shakti*—her goddess energy. She was confident and curious, spirited but not reckless. A yogic radiance magnified her natural beauty. I enjoyed her company, but it still wasn't like being with Liz. Orly felt like a test to see if I could tell the difference. My connection with Liz was about more than music, yoga, tantra, *or* shakti. We had a *personal* connection—we understood each other deeply after a short time. Our union was too special to ignore despite the obvious risks. Even the goddess of light couldn't blind me from that.

Memories rolled in as I drifted toward sleep. I was in the bed I'd shared with Robin, worrying that Lina might hear us from the next hut. The one where I shed tears listening to *Suzanne* after Hampi. Staring now at stars through bamboo, I remembered my plan to take things one step at a time. I asked the sky what my next step should be, and within seconds, I heard a train whistle in the distance. I took it as a message that I should get on a train as soon as possible and find Liz. Action-oriented with a weakness for love?

Nah, I don't believe in astrology.

CHAPTER 29

2,673 km: General Class

The rooster woke me up in time for Krishna's early advanced yoga class and I stayed for the next one too. Orly didn't make it to either. On a straw mat in paradise, I kept thinking about heading to the Himalayas to find Liz. When Krishna pointed out that I'd be near Mount Kailash, I sensed his story about Shiva and Parvati coming on, and excused myself to send an email to Liz. I wrote only, "You move me (to Rishikesh)" and included a photo of us on the rocks in Hampi surrounded by Indian children.

Orly wasn't at the Ocean Breeze when I returned, so I left her a goodbye note in *From Here to Nirvana* and slid the book under her bamboo door as a gift. No more guidebooks for me—it was time to follow my instincts.

I hadn't smoked pot since Varkala. I often craved it, but also felt a countervailing influence. After the two yoga classes a day at the ashram, I'd noticed how the joints in Varkala made my throat feel awful. As much as I enjoyed the buzz, the smoke felt polluting. I still had a stash, but decided that it was time to travel without my vice. I returned the gift to Krishna on my way out of Palolem.

I headed an hour north to a town called Margao, where a direct overnight train to Mumbai would make for a more efficient exit—or so I thought. The train station was bursting with negativity as hundreds of Indian men jostled for position toward the ticket window. A White man in a khaki hat tried to shout his way to the front with the force of his own stereotype: "I'm American. Don't you know how much foreign aid money we give to this country?"

I lingered in line, trying to feel the irrelevance of time, but that got me nowhere. I actually lost ground as Indian men pushed in front of me. Then I realized that it was a game and I started to shove back. The protocol wasn't about fairness (or entitlement for that matter), it was straight-up Darwinian. If you could push past someone, you stayed there. I used my hips to shimmy forward each time the human multi-beast shifted in any direction.

At one point, I was slightly ahead of the American. He wouldn't stop complaining until, in a surprising moment of collaboration, the Indian men decided that they couldn't endure him for another moment and cleared a path to the counter for him. He shouted "Thank you!" with disdain. I didn't want to be associated with him, so I stayed put. The swarm resealed, but it wasn't long before I reached the front as well.

Indian trains have three main classes: General Class, Second Class Sleeper, and Second Class A/C. There must also be First Class, but even the A/C prices were high for my budget. Second Class Sleeper was what backpackers would take. There were usually six passengers to a cabin,

sharing the benches that double as beds. To get from Margao to Mumbai that night, my only option was to ride General Class. I was anxious to go and after what I'd endured in line, I felt that I should take the lower-priced ticket.

Why was I rushing? Was it that it was a day before Valentine's Day? Spring fever? Time running out on my six-month Indian visa? More than any of that, it was the realization of a shared feeling. We had only spent a total of eight days together and Liz trusted me to find her again when the time was right. I couldn't wait another day.

The situation in General Class came as a shock to this North American boy. The queue-jockeying masses of Margao were now subdued neighbors in tightly packed railcars. Cabins that would have held six in Second Class had thirty or more people in them. I couldn't find a place to sit and hardly anyone had luggage. In the constrained space, my backpack and drums were as conspicuous as a limousine in a slum.

Gone were the tea and snack vendors—the paying customers were clearly elsewhere. Indian men sat shoulder to shoulder on the benches. Instead of upper platforms for sleeping, there were metal luggage racks lined with men resting. I tried to squeeze onto one but couldn't fit, so I sought space near the bathroom. The toilets were holes in the train floor, revealing evidence of a lot of bad aim. Men slept on the floor, uninterrupted by others stepping over them on their way to the facilities. The smell made staying there prohibitive, so I wandered from car to car. Each one was the same.

Eventually I noticed another traveler, an Israeli fellow who stood out as much as I did. He was seated on his backpack against a side wall of the train and nodded at me with tribal instinct as I approached. I kneeled in the aisle to say hello, and he told me his name was Eyal. The windows don't close in General Class, so it was hard to hear each other. I didn't know if my plan was brave, stupid, or just naive, but it was comforting to see that another traveler had made the same choice.

Forced to move each time someone walked past in the aisle, I was about to continue searching for a space when the Indian man next to Eyal shoved over just enough for me to squeeze between the two of them. Eyal had been traveling with his girlfriend of two and a half years. They'd just spent a week apart to give each other space. Eyal said being alone was amazing, but he missed her. He was in General Class for the same reason that I was: love.

As we approached the Mumbai station, Eyal asked if I had any rolling papers. Until that day, I'd *always* had rolling papers, but I had given them to Krishna along with the pot. The ride had been so rough that I would have joined Eyal for a puff, but with no papers, there was no smoking.

Disembarking in the dark Mumbai morning, I immediately asked about a ticket to Rishikesh via New Delhi. I was determined to continue north, but not eager to endure another sleepless night. Again, there were no Second Class Sleepers, but this time I had a choice between General Class and Second Class A/C. I opted for the forty-dollar A/C seat. It cost more than I'd often spend in a week, but I knew that I had a whole night of sleep to catch up on. I also bought a Second Class Sleeper ticket from Delhi to Haridwar, near Rishikesh.

The train classes seemed symbolic of India's caste system. There were four main castes, going back thousands of years. Below the lowest caste were the backward people, or untouchables, the term itself implying that they were too dirty to come in contact with. The fellows in General Class were from the lower castes, but the untouchables had it worse. It bothered me how Indian society viewed them as subhuman. When I read an article in a Mumbai newspaper about a human rights organization called The Society for the Advancement of Backward Peoples, I asked myself, "But which way are they advancing?" Again, my issue was with the wording. You need to be facing forward before advancing or you won't actually get anywhere.

I felt the same way about myself. I was moving quickly, but was I really pointed in the right direction? Sleeplessness invited uncertainty into my mind. Before my next overnight train, I put my bags in a locker and went to an internet café to see if Liz had responded to my email. I wanted an indication that she would welcome me, but found none. I wrote to tell her when I expected to arrive in Rishikesh, and I left to explore Mumbai. I liked the energy of this city that was formerly known as Bombay. People on the street wanted to talk about politics and culture. I shopped for books and saw professional women, students, and cute kids. Streetside salesmen encouraged me to look at their tables of combs, clocks, batteries, and books. I bought a book on tantra.

Popping into a café, I gulped a Duke's lemon soda while hiding under a fan from the oppressive midday heat. Then I walked along Mumbai's shoreline where giant concrete blocks protect the city from storms. It was a rare uncrowded spot with a breeze. I brought my fingers to my lips to puff an imaginary joint. It was where I would have lit up if I still had a stash. I recalled Eyal's request for rolling papers and knew that I would be feeling worse if I had gotten high at that early hour. I was thankful that I hadn't had any. My day was better for it.

I paid a couple of rupees to weigh myself on a big red scale in the train station. The scale produced a small yellow card that said 71 kg. (157 lbs.). My stomach had been bothering me for months and I knew that I had lost weight, but was surprised to find out how much. I had weighed 84 kg. (185 lbs.) when I left Edmonton. The back of the card had a fortune, which read, "You are on the threshold of worldly success. Splendor and achievement will color your life."

I appreciated the optimistic message as I boarded the Panjab Mail train to Delhi early in the evening. I was the only one in the cabin. For the price, I expected a palace on wheels and that was what I got. I was eminently thankful for a padded bed, air conditioning, and twenty-four hours of cleanliness. I reviewed my tickets, did the math, and wrote a note in my journal:

> Goa – Mumbai   797 km
> Mumbai → Delhi   1,539 km
> Delhi → Rishikesh   337 km
> ───────────────────────────
> Total   2,673 km
>
> Hey Liz, guess what? You have the power to lift a 71 kg man 2,673 km in 3 days! (Not even counting the trip from Kerala to Goa).

Train staff brought me bedsheets and a towel. Under the sheets and with the towel over my head, I laid down for a nap. I felt the train begin to move as I dozed off.

CHAPTER 30

2,673 km: Second Class

I awoke to the smell of curry and the sound of children's voices. My top bunk was aligned with a small window on my right. To my left were the aisle and four more perpendicular bunks. The floor of the train car was now filled with enough plastic containers of food to feed the vibrantly dressed Indian family who collectively placed palms together and greeted my opening eyes with a "Namaskar" blessing as I sat up. My high perch felt like an altar.

Then the adults said in unison, "Eat something." Their kindness was overwhelming. I had expected to fill up on samosas and chai from the vendors on the train, but the family insisted that I share in their curries, rice, and home-baked flatbreads. I was hungry and appreciative. The food was a little bit spicy but delicious. The taste reminded me of lunches with Keshav's family after tabla class in Varanasi.

Two beautiful little girls smiled up at me on my bunk/altar. The family kept referring to me as their "guest." I was confused by that reference at first: I had simply bought a ticket in the same railcar. Then I realized that I was a guest in *their country* and understood that they wanted to welcome me with abundance. After my night on the previous train with their less fortunate compatriots, I soaked it up. They were on a family trip to visit relatives. It felt like their celebration had already begun and I was invited to be a part of it. They asked where I was heading and why. When I told them about Liz, the mother and main food distributor asked with patrician inflection, "It is a love marriage?"

"Well, it's not a marriage... We're still getting to know each other."

"Yes, of course. I met my husband before we were married. It's important."

"Right... it's kind of like that."

She smiled and asked, "So, you *will* marry her?" If anyone had been looking down at their food, they weren't any more. All eyes were on me.

I shrugged. "If I'm lucky..."

The group erupted in laughter. Like "real love," "love marriage" in India is when the partners choose each other rather than their parents arranging it. The idea that I had to convince Liz to marry me was hilarious to them because in India it is often the daughter's parents who have to convince the groom and his parents to take their daughter.

I passed around the photo of Liz sitting cross-legged in the Hampi treehouse. The matriarch said with certainty, "She is so *very* beautiful. You will have a happy life together."

Speechless, I waddled my head, and six more waddled back at me.

The fortune from the scale in Mumbai had said, "Splendor and achievement will color your life." What was I achieving? I wanted a happy life whether things worked out with Liz or not. As Buddha had taught, "achievement" isn't about job or status, it's about realizing the truth behind our existence, our pure loving nature. I thought of the Indian man in General Class who had made space for me and my bulky bags. On a difficult night, that act of kindness reminded me of the essential goodness in others. Now showered with the generosity of my new neighbors, that truth was presented to me in colorful splendor.

Then everyone started getting ready for bed. I went to the sparkling bathroom and brushed my teeth. I found it hard to sleep again because of my long nap and also because I felt so appreciative and full. I knew I needed rest, but didn't want to close my eyes. Being awake was too good. I felt like a happy child fighting bedtime.

I eventually drifted off and awoke early, ready to move my body. Morning yoga had become an essential part of my routine and I felt that I needed to stretch. In the aisle, surrounded by my sleeping "host" family,

I stood up and reached to the sky, then down to my toes, straining to balance as the train shifted from side to side.

That morning, I didn't have a chance to check email in New Delhi before switching from the palace on wheels to the Second Class Sleeper bound for Haridwar, a town across the river from Rishikesh. My cabin was empty, and it felt peaceful, almost meditative, to be back in my regular class of railcar, with no one else around except for the occasional chai vendor or floor sweeper. As I gazed through the barred window at the flow of farms and communities, I recalled how the same-sized space had been filled with thirty or more people in General Class. I imagined that the men leaving Goa must have been there for work and were returning to Mumbai with some money in their pockets—a hard commute. I felt fortunate to have the means to explore freely.

It was a long and quiet day. When evening came on—my third in a row on a train—it finally felt like February. The outside air was crisp and less polluted. I put on warm clothes and climbed into my sleeping bag. The

cabin filled with other passengers as I prepared to sleep. I must have knocked out early because I awoke at 4:30 a.m. feeling rested. It felt like Christmas morning but we had hours to go, so I stayed bundled in my bag and listened to music to drown out the snores and misty morning calls for "Cha-i."

After a few more hours and with only one more hour to go, the train car was empty again. I packed up and opened the tantra book I'd bought in Mumbai. Ashley Thirleby writes, "Love, in the *tantric* sense means simply: 'I recognize and accept your essence.'"

I told myself that when I found Liz, I should be accepting of her essence, beyond her appearance or reaction to seeing me. Then I lost interest when the author began describing how to squeeze your penis muscles. I put the book away and admired the landscape.

A white-haired Indian couple sat down in my cabin and asked my "good name," where I was going, and why. I kicked off my shoes, crossed my legs, and leaned back on the window.

They asked if I was planning to practice yoga in Rishikesh and I said that I surely would since I was already practicing every day "except today, because I'm on a train." They were also yogis. I wasn't surprised to hear it because they shared a familiar glow. Observing my reclined posture, the husband said to me, "You're not in any hurry…"

I laughed because it was *and* wasn't true. I had certainly rushed the 2,673 kilometers from Goa and I was anxious to find Liz, but in the moment, I was savoring the morning air. Having traveled so far in such a short time, the transformation was palpable. Just as Goa had been a striking opposite to Varanasi, and as Kerala had felt culturally distinct, the state of Uttarakhand seemed like a secluded, sacred, and serene part of India.

During a pause in conversation, I imagined living with a yogi wife into our sixties. The two of them seemed so content and comfortable together. I couldn't hope for anything more. Could Liz and I have that? There was only one way to find out.

The senior yogis got off the train before I did, leaving me to end the journey alone. Their farewell blessing was "May all of your dreams come true."

I said thank you, feeling that perhaps they already had.

Beams of sunlight jumped onto the street outside the train station. Approaching the rickshaw drivers for a ride to Rishikesh, I was struck by a visceral and familiar image: an enormous bust of Shiva, over ten feet tall and adorned with offerings of flowers. Remembering that I was now close to the source of the Ganges, I realized that Rishikesh must also be "Shiva's city," another place where the destroyer reminds us not to get too attached, because everything changes.

I squinted at the statue though the morning light and thought, "Oh yeah, *you*. Don't worry, I remember."

CHAPTER 31

Rishikesh: Light Workers

Riding on a rickety rickshaw to Rishikesh, I asked to be taken to the nearest internet café. When I arrived, I learned that the electricity had gone out. I'd last written to Liz from Mumbai two mornings earlier, telling her that I would reach Rishikesh on February 16th at around 9:30 a.m. I was on time, but hadn't been to a computer since then, so I still didn't know how she felt about me coming or where to find her. As I waited for the power to come back on, doubt began to creep in. Had I read too much into her messages to me? Could she already be gone?

After playing whack-a-mole with pessimistic thoughts for more than half an hour, lights came on, machines whirred, and I was able to read two messages from Liz. The first one was from the previous night—she was surprised but pleased that I was coming. The next was from that morning, guiding me to meet her at the fittingly named Shiva Café.

I knew of Rishikesh because the Beatles had visited in the late 1960s to study meditation, but it has been a spiritual hub for centuries. Surrounding mountains contain caves where holy men sit for extended periods, often without food or water, aiming for spiritual perfection.

I crossed a narrow footbridge and watched the Ganga flowing green over boulders around a bend. In Varanasi, the river appeared too thick and toxic to touch, but in the mountains, it seemed inviting, particularly as I hadn't showered in days.

The Shiva Café was on a narrow road lined with yoga schools and restaurants. I didn't see any familiar faces when I entered, but I discovered a stairway to an unfinished rooftop where construction cables jutted out of concrete blocks. A group of travelers sat around coffee and pastries at plastic picnic tables perched above a rocky riverbank.

And there she was. I'd been looking at the same picture of Liz for weeks, but now I could see her for real. Sun shone on her orange salwar kameez, curly hair rested on her shoulders. At the sight of her smile, I immediately felt that the journey had been worth it.

A young man at the table was speaking, and Fran's back was turned to me. She must have noticed Liz's expression because she turned around, jumped out of her chair, and hit me with a bear hug just as I laid my tabla bag on the ground. I peered over her shoulder and met Liz's smile with one of my own. The fellow kept on speaking, though he seemed perturbed by the distraction.

Liz looked shy, perhaps embarrassed that she'd lured me across the country in such a short time. I walked over to where she still sat in her chair and squatted down to meet her face. She said, "Hi, Mark," laying her words down like a dam, designed to hold back all emotion.

"Hi, Lizzie! Want to give me a hug?"

She got up from her chair. As I wrapped my arms around her, she greeted me with hesitation. "It's...nice...to *see* you."

I kissed her on the cheek, held both of her hands, and looked in her eyes. She dropped my hands because it was India and said, "I didn't check email for a few days."

"And you were surprised?"

"Yes...but I'm glad you're here." She tilted her head. "Did I ask you to come?"

"Not exactly... You said it was up to me...and that you were willing."

"You were so far away..."

I giggled that I had closed our geographical gap so quickly. I still intended to give Liz and Fran space to travel together, but in that moment, I wanted her all to myself. I wanted to hear about the palaces of Rajasthan and everything on her mind, but I had interrupted the momentum of a conversation and Liz didn't want to be rude. She introduced me to everyone and invited me to sit down. After three days on trains, I didn't want to.

The guy speaking was Liam. He was from England and sported Indian robes and clunky studded Elton John sunglasses. Fran seemed fascinated with his discourse, but Liz kept peeking over at me with looks that seemed to ask, "Are you *really* here?"

Liam was explaining that, like humans, the planet Earth has chakras, or energy centers. Rishikesh is one of the chakras, and Liam was from another one of them, the Isle of Wight. He said that these areas are connected with each other and charged with a certain power.

"Well," I said, "Rishikesh's power was out this morning, so that's why I was late. Sorry."

Liam ignored my joke and told us of certain people known as *Pleiadians*, or "light workers," who are more sensitive to spiritual power than others. Liam explained that Pleiadians are spiritually evolved humans who live among us, but also act as messengers from the outer galaxy. They are on a mission to shed light upon the ultimate reality for others, hence their title of light worker. Liam was a Pleiadian, and believed that the rest of us on that half-built balcony in Rishikesh were as well, by virtue of our interest in yoga and meditation.

Liam also explained that the universe has nine dimensions. I asked him what dimensions four through nine were and he answered with a suggestion: "Check out the Galactic Council. I'm on their email list. They're talking a lot about 2012."

"What's happening in 2012?"

"You haven't heard about 2012? A *lot* of shit's going to go down. It's the end of the Mayan calendar. They predicted an apocalypse, but the council believes it will be a time of spiritual transformation for the world." Liam assured the group that we Pleiadians would fare well through the end times. Yoga and meditation would carry us through.

Was Liam a false prophet spouting nonsense? Probably, but I tried to not judge him. The sunglasses made it hard, though. At a pause in the conversation, I stood up to go and Liz did too. On the street, Liz said, "You're crusty." She was talking about my hair, but I didn't care.

We walked to her guesthouse, where the owner, a thin Indian man in a button-down shirt, said, "I will show you a rooftop room, you might love it. The guests there are all yoga and meditation people." From the open-air rooftop, we saw the Ganga winding around temples and forested hills. Not only was the view impressive, I wouldn't have to create my own yoga spot. With straw mats covering a spacious floor facing the river, it already *was* a yoga spot.

Three rooms faced the open space and the mountains beyond. A young couple sat on their bed with the door open, looking at the view. A long-haired young man sat shirtless on a lawn chair reading *The Yoga Sutras of Patanjali*, a historic text that contains the philosophical foundation of yoga. Then I realized that I was *also* a long-haired "yoga and meditation" person, and that the owner was probably right that I'd love it there.

He led us to the third room on the rooftop and turned on the light to reveal a bold-colored, handpainted mural of Shiva above the bed. I laughed and said, "This must be the place."

I was about to have my first shower since Goa when Liz asked me not to because she had a surprise for me. Then she guided me upriver and away from the buildings of Rishikesh to a forested area where the stone road became a dirt walking path. Sadhus nodded at us as we walked past. After a while on the trail, I heard rushing water and then saw a waterfall, about fifteen feet high, with an icy pool at the bottom. Liz threw her clothes off and I followed her lead. I washed off the showerless days and then we kissed and floated in the cool pool, keeping warm by holding each other—free and alive.

We had no towels, so we dried off naked in the open air. Then, as soon as we finished getting dressed, a group of a half dozen Japanese tourists appeared, led by their Indian guide. We laughed at our good timing, and made our way back to town.

Our rooftop neighbors turned out to be two couples who had also met in India. They radiated with the joy of travel, yoga, and new love. Sam from Italy was the shirtless one, still reading in the sunshine when we returned. His accent made the ancient philosopher "Pa-tan-jaaali" sound like a culinary delicacy. Sam was traveling with a smiling blonde German woman named Jaana. They seemed thrilled to be in Rishikesh and together.

The other couple included Laura from England, who had long brown hair and freckles, and her new partner, Nibodhi. He was the toughest to figure out as he wore the orange robes of a holy man along with brown dreadlocks and prayer beads. He walked pole straight, as though someone was pulling on a string attached to the top of his head. Though he looked as though he had just emerged from one of the meditation caves around Rishikesh, his American accent revealed that his history was more similar to Liz's and mine than his swami image implied.

Nibodhi spoke of sweat lodges, reiki, yoga, community living, and an organic greenhouse with vegetables planted in the shape of a goddess. Though he had to be around our age, he seemed comfortable in the role of a teacher, sharing his gathered knowledge with the rest of us. Unlike Liam the Pleiadian, Nibodhi managed to preach without pretention, using aphorisms such as, "You're a stick of bamboo, channeling energy from the earth and sharing it as you choose."

On the guesthouse rooftop that evening, I pulled out my tabla for some long overdue practice. Nibodhi asked if I had another drum so that he could join me. I gave him the small drum I'd bought from the seller on the corracle in Hampi. Unlike on that tiny boat, I had the force of the tabla pacing the rhythm this time. I rolled through beats and Nibodhi filled the space between them with quick taps on the smaller drum. I roared faster and he kept up with me. Jaana began to sing wordless melodies above the rhythm. My hands vibrated as prana surged up my forearms and through my spine. I sat up straight to allow the energy to flow through my bamboo body. I couldn't stop smiling.

Most drum jams go on and on until someone breaks the collective vibration by stopping or losing the beat. As I'd learned from Keshav, tabla rhythms have a planned ending called chakradhar. It takes elements of the main theme and doubles them up, leading to a dramatic end point. In a classical Indian music concert, you might hear the tabla player call out "chakradhar" to indicate the impending finale. When I tried that with Nibodhi, he understood. I played the final section the customary three times, and he stopped right when I did, with an emphatic, "Pop, Boom!" The group laughed in unison.

It was a marvelous end to a spectacular day. I was expressing myself through music on a cool night along the Ganga, among friends and a special young woman. I was glad I'd left the *just right* days at Palolem behind.

In a quiet moment, Liz said to me that the rooftop was like "three mirrors facing." I didn't know what she meant at first, but then looked at our neighbors and understood. If we wanted to know what *we* looked like, we only needed to look around.

I appreciated being with people who understood what we were going through. When Nibodhi asked if Liz and I were traveling together, I said, "I put a spell on her earlier today." As the group laughed, I thought to myself that the opposite was probably more accurate.

I returned to my room to put away the drums and Liz arrived with a gift for me. It was a postcard-sized print of Gustav Klimt's famous painting, *The Kiss*. The painting depicts a woman lying with a man who presses his lips to her cheek. The previous night, Liz had sat under the evening sky on the yoga rooftop and written on the back of the print:

R   A moment by a candle with a sliver of a moon
I   Sheer cold, pure as ice, radiates off the Ganges
S   Rapidly flowing from the source to the source.
H   Smoke from the lantern in the cloudy star sky
I   Rises like smoke from the engine of your Bombay train.
K   Beauty, you come to greet me,
E   The flame of the glass lantern warms my cheek.
S
H

Mark, I have a print of Gustav Klimt's The Kiss that I cut from a box of chocolate. Delicious love, richness be mine, WOW... Am I feeling this way, or just writing to warm these Ganges dancin' fingertips...
LOVE on a winter's eve, in the Himalayas.

Sliver of a moon, I thought he would come when you grew full.
The mere hint of your light brings him to me.

CHAPTER 32

Rishikesh: The Deeper You Go, The Higher You Fly

When I first rolled into Rishikesh, the rickshaw driver had asked if I knew who the Maharishi Mahesh Yogi was.

"Sure," I said. "He was the Beatles' guru."

The driver then pointed to a collection of structures that had been overtaken by the forest and said, "That was his ashram." Talk about impermanence—thirty-four years on, the site looked more like an ancient ruin than the abundant retreat center I'd seen in photos from 1968.

Back then, George Harrison was noticing that, despite all of his worldly success, he still wasn't happy. Marijuana and LSD weren't the answer, but they had revealed a glimpse of the type of joy that he couldn't achieve by material or carnal means. Happiness lay somewhere deeper and Harrison wanted to go there. He brought the other Beatles to meet the Maharishi at a talk in England. The diminutive swami had long white hair and a high-pitched voice. He taught a type of meditation where each student receives a mantra that connects with their personal rhythm. The method resonated with the musicians. As Paul McCartney said, "He was out to save the world, and we were ripe for saving."

Soon afterwards, the band agreed to study with the Maharishi in India. The Beatles found it liberating to have a break not only from media attention and business dealings, but also from their own thoughts. Once, when the Maharishi was boarding a helicopter, John Lennon asked if he could come along, saying later, "I thought he might slip me the answer."

The Beatles wrote many songs while they were in Rishikesh, including Dear Prudence, about a fellow meditator who was so engrossed in the practice that she wouldn't leave her room. The Maharishi's modern spin on Hindu philosophy inspired Beatles lyrics such as "The deeper you go, the higher you fly. The higher you fly, the deeper you go."

I was also flying high in Rishikesh and had at last found a supportive setting to go deeper into yoga. But when I woke under the mural of Shiva the morning after our drum jam, I should have known better than to get attached to a situation that seemed so perfect.

After waking up next to me, Liz joined me on the rooftop's straw mats for yoga. Everyone else was still sleeping. Yellow and orange sunrise light reflected on the Ganga. I was stiff from traveling, but my body awoke more with each stretch. We practiced for over an hour in the morning air before chanting "Om" cross-legged with the sunlight on our backs.

Liz went downstairs to change. I followed a few minutes later, and found Liz in an awkward conversation with Fran. I was surprised to see Fran awake so early in the day, but she wasn't talking. Liz was trying to get her to express herself, but she wasn't getting through. I returned to the rooftop to wait for Liz.

When Liz came to fetch me for breakfast, I was the one getting the silent treatment. She talked only enough to determine where we would eat. Then finally, after crossing the footbridge, settling into seats, and ordering food, she said, "We're leaving tonight for Shimla."

"We? You and Fran? May I … join you?" I was happy in Rishikesh, but clearly Fran was ready to move on. They both knew that it would be a controversial choice with me.

Liz, her lips devoid of expression, said, "You should do what's best for you."

Hoping to break the tension, I said, "What's best for *me* is to be with *you*."

"I can't *stop* you from coming,"

That stung, but I understood. Liz was *trying* to appear indifferent to my decision, but she wasn't a very good actor. I said, "Look, I know that you and Fran are on your own trip, but I didn't take three overnight trains so that I could spend a day and a half with you. I'm coming."

I knew that I had put Liz in an awkward position, but I wanted us to overcome it together. I dropped my shoulders, held out open palms, and Liz smiled. She reached across the table, put her hands in mine, and exhaled deeply. She seemed relieved that she had done her part as a friend. She wouldn't admit it, but I don't think she was ready to say goodbye to me either.

My heart hurt as we walked out of the restaurant and back across the river. I appreciated that Liz was willing to have me join them in Shimla, a city on a mountain in the next province, but I was also disappointed that she hadn't advocated more strongly for it. I told myself to give the two friends some space before our overnight bus ride.

The previous night had been amazing, but now I wondered if Fran had felt like a seventh wheel up on the rooftop. I would have loved to stay longer in Rishikesh. There were ashrams and yoga teachers everywhere, and I'm sure I would have found Indian music, too. But Rishikesh wasn't going anywhere, Liz was. She was why I had come, and she was why I would leave.

I was packing up under the Shiva mural when Liz came into the room with an invitation. "Want to go swimming in the Ganga with Sam and Jaana?"

"Swim... in the *Ganga*?" It did *look* inviting, but I hadn't actually considered going in.

"People say that it raises your spiritual vibration."

"I'm more worried about what it will lower."

The Ganges was so polluted in Varanasi that, for me, the thought of swimming in it was akin to diving into an outhouse. But we were thousands of miles upstream from Varanasai. In Rishikesh, the water looked clear and I hadn't seen any dead cows floating in it. Perhaps it would even be refreshing.

Even more refreshing was Liz's transformation back to the woman I'd come to know, leading with her beautiful smile and adventurous spirit. I put on my bathing suit.

As we walked downriver and past the town, Sam asked in his Italian accent, "Do you have any ma-ri-juaaana?"

"No, man, I stopped carrying it a little while ago."

"That is very smart." When I asked him why, he said, "A policeman searched me on a train. I didn't have any drugs, but he forced me into a corner and searched my bag. He pulled out some hashish, but it wasn't mine."

"He planted it?"

"Yes, for *baksheesh*. You know baksheesh?"

I did. It loosely translates to "tip," but also includes bribes as well as charity. Porters at hotels and beggars on the street ask for baksheesh, but as I understand it, the real money makes it into the pockets of public officials like the police. If they have you cornered, as Sam had been on the train, they urge you to "donate" to avoid the consequences of India's complex bureaucracy and legal system. My friend Ramesh in Nepal had warned me about corrupt Indian police, but I was still shocked as Sam continued his story. "He wanted one hundred American dollars. I said no at first, but he planned to take me off of the train at the next stop and arrest me."

"So you paid him?"

"I had to. I gave him all of my rupees and he let me go."

"That's awful, Sam..."

"Don't travel with drugs. If they catch you and they are *your* drugs, it could be worse."

I thought of all of the train rides I'd taken with a film canister of pot stuffed deep in my backpack. I hadn't realized how dumb that was and I wasn't aware of how bold and corrupt the police could be. Sam's story gave me second thoughts about leaving our rooftop sanctuary, but I looked at Liz walking in her orange salwar kameez, chatting with Jaana, and knew there was only one right choice.

Though we had nothing to smoke, Sam's reaction upon jumping into the Ganga indicated that the river carried a buzz of its own. He howled with glee and tossed around in the cold water. Jaana and Liz waded in next and I didn't wait much longer. If I was going in the Ganges, I wanted to fully immerse myself—to go deep as the Maharishi had taught. I took a running start and cannonballed into the river.

We laughed and splashed and I eventually climbed onto a sandy riverbank, dripping and freezing. It may have been the cold, but I felt tingly for the rest of the day. Even with clothes on, I felt as though I was wearing the sacred Ganga, somehow shielded by Shiva's grace. The *destroyer* was back at work. Liz's declaration that she was leaving wasn't meant to separate us. It simply signified the end of the yoga rooftop that I'd quickly become attached to. She and I weren't done learning and growing together, but I needed to remember that it wasn't going to be *that* easy.

A few weeks into the Beatles' time in Rishikesh, things turned sour when members of their group suspected that the celibate Maharishi was being inappropriate with some of his female students. This revelation, combined with the Maharishi's desire for media attention, caused some of the Beatles to lose confidence in his teaching. One by one, they all decided to leave. On the way out, John Lennon wrote a song about how the world was waiting for a lover but that Maharishi made a fool of everyone by breaking the rules. George Harrison begged his friend to change the title and subject of the song, so it is called Sexy Sadie *instead of* Maharishi.

My reaction to ashram life had been similar. Like the Beatles, I fled at the first hint of hypocrisy. As I walked through Rishikesh for the final time that evening, I looked at the ashrams, certain that some contained authentic teachers like Keshav and Krishna. I hung back as I followed

Liz and Fran to the bus station. I wanted them to feel that things hadn't changed much. Though we'd now met up three times, this bus ride was our first time traveling together. They were nimble in their tiny backpacks while I labored along with my tabla in my arms. Fran still wasn't talking. She seemed bothered that I was tagging along, but I believed that she would come around. I knew that I was imposing, but I had a good reason.

It wasn't just attraction. My connection with Liz felt stronger than any I had felt before. Sure, two and a half months since breaking up with Ronit felt too soon to have a new girlfriend, but Liz felt like much more than a *girlfriend*. We understood and accepted each other. I had never felt anything like it. I couldn't let her travel on, leaving a trail of email breadcrumbs while I wondered what might have been.

After we boarded the bus, Liz sat with me, held my hand, and apologized for hurting my feelings during breakfast. I said that I respected her loyalty to Fran and that I would give them space to explore together. I was happy doing my own thing. When she asked about my travel plans, instead of admitting that I had none, I told her that while many places in India seemed fascinating, she was more important to me than any of them. I shared what I'd realized at the ashram in Kerala: "I'm working on loving myself as much as I love you."

The dark bus full of Indian people wasn't the most romantic place to say "I love you" for the first time, but it was a way to explain my actions. My feelings for Liz weren't a distraction from my spiritual journey, they were an essential part of it. Still, I told Liz that I would leave if she wanted me to. Until then, I would follow my heart. She put her head on my shoulder as the bus headed north.

I usually attracted a lot of stares from Indian men curious about the long-haired foreigner, but while transferring at the bus station in Dehra Dun, I was completely ignored—as an accessory to the two pretty White girls in Indian clothes. While they stretched their legs on dusty streets, I chose to sit alone in a restaurant away from the traffic. I was happy for a moment of solitude, but the exhaust-filled air hung low. Pollution scratched my throat and my eyes were stinging. To make breathing tolerable, I tied a red bandanna over my nose and mouth and moved to a back corner of the restaurant, a lone cowboy writing in my journal.

I decided that I needed to talk with Fran. This sojourn wasn't going to last long unless I could get her on my side. It wasn't as though we weren't familiar with each other. We had spoken a lot already, I considered her a friend, and she was the one who had suggested that I might want to move to California. The two things that *had* changed were that we were actually traveling together now, and our time together didn't have a defined endpoint. I was sure that those two factors bothered her, and I wanted to diffuse the tension.

When we boarded the bus again, I told Liz that I wanted to sit with Fran for a bit. I sat down and smiled at Fran. She hadn't talked to me all day, but still smiled back. I began by saying, "I'm sorry." We Canadians say it *all the time*. It wasn't hard.

She laughed and said, "It's okay."

"I know… I wasn't supposed to come yet. It's just that…"

"She's made a profound impression on you?" she said, repeating my line from Hampi.

"Yes… And it's more than that…"

As I glanced over my shoulder at Liz, further back on the bus, gazing out the dark window, Fran said, "I know… You guys are beautiful together. I'm happy for you."

"Thanks for saying that, but also, I didn't want to wait. This feels like an opportunity."

"Listen. If I felt that way about someone, I wouldn't want to wait either. I already told you, I think you are good for her."

Her tone now sounded as positive as it did when she would talk about their co-op house in Berkeley. That place was all about inclusion and Fran wanted to include me. Still, every supportive sentence carried an unspoken thought in a backpack: "Sucks for me, though…"

I returned to the back row of the bus and saw Liz trying to sleep against the window. I traded spots with her so that she could lay her head on my lap and sleep. I put my headphones on and listened to the Beatles.

A few years after their trip to India, emotions had cooled and all of the Beatles spoke positively of their time in Rishikesh and even of the Maharishi. The impropriety accusations were never corroborated and all of the band members later said that meditation had been helpful in their lives. For each in his own way, Rishikesh had been a necessary step on the journey.

The Beatles didn't break up in India like Ronit and I had, but it was the last time that all four of them traveled together. After being at the Ganga, the band was never the same. Each of the musicians returned to England with a unique creative and personal vision. Once Shiva had his way with them, each one had to forge his own path, not as a Beatle but as his own man.

As our bus rolled through mountains in darkness, I felt the same way—that my short time near the source of the Ganga had given me a peek into my future. It might not manifest for a while, but it was coming into view. I knew that with authentic teachers and a supportive community of like-minded yogis, I could go deeper and fly higher. But first, I wanted to know who I would be on the journey with.

CHAPTER 33

Shimla Happens (Part One)

*"I have nothing new to teach the world.
Truth and non-violence are as old as the hills."*
– Mahatma Gandhi

Shimla is the hill station capital of Himachal Pradesh. It was established as a political center in the early nineteenth century by British colonialists. Liz and Fran wanted to go there to meet a professor, Dr. Bhatia, with whom biology classmates of Liz's had studied in Shimla. He had extended an invitation for any of their friends to visit him there.

The small city is perched high in the mountains and the streets were sprinkled with snow when we arrived. We found a hotel with a view of hills beyond and a valley below. Out of a third-floor window, we noticed schoolboys in uniform, throwing snowballs at each other. The Californians were a bit out of their element in the cold, and I was surprised by how different it was from India's steamy south.

I chose a room and Fran chose another. Liz did her best to ignore the process, which became harder to do as Fran haggled over the price with the manager. It wasn't expensive, but Fran seemed perturbed with the idea of paying for a room all by herself and having to sleep alone in it. Liz offered to split the cost with Fran, but the haggling continued. I settled into my new room, hoping that things would sort themselves out.

In the end, Liz put her bag in my room but paid for half of Fran's, and we went out for breakfast together. The Park Café's owner was a friendly local named Deepak. He had a stack of CDs and let me choose a jazz album to play on his stereo. After the commotion at the hotel, it felt normal to be a group of three and I was relieved for it.

After breakfast, we went out to explore the town. On the wide, open street, we walked past a golden statue of Mahatma Gandhi, known as the father of India. He led the movement for Indian independence from Britain in the mid-twentieth century, and was known worldwide for his successful application of ahimsa, or nonviolence, in political protest. Trained as a lawyer, he was a religious Hindu who dressed in the robes of a holy man while remaining at the forefront of the most pressing political issues of his time.

"Did you know," Liz asked, "that when he died, all of Gandhi's possessions fit into a shoebox?" I didn't and it made me wonder for a moment if I could downsize from my backpack, drums, and the orange day pack that I'd been carrying.

Shimla looked more to me like Switzerland than India. Gingerbread houses lined a large open town square fronting a broad blue sky. Sunshine warmed the mountain air and Fran bought an ice cream cone. Liz skipped through the square. The town felt freer and more open than other Indian cities I'd been in, until a mustachioed Indian man in matching khaki pants and button-down shirt approached me and said, "Let me see your passport."

Stunned by his demand, I asked, "Who are you?"

"I am police."

"Can I see your identification?" I'd been warned of sketchy characters posing as police officers. I had also been warned about sketchy characters who *were* police officers.

He pulled an ID out of the back of his wallet, covering most of it with his thumb. It had lamination peeling off of a card with a typed name and crookedly cut photo. It looked more fake than any fake ID I'd ever seen. Unconvinced, I said, "How do I know that you're really police?"

As I waited for his answer, Liz quietly said to me, "This is how I got robbed in Bolivia."

My passport was in the hotel room, but even if I did have it, it wouldn't have felt right to hand it to this random person. I recalled the advice that Ramesh in Nepal had given me: "If you get into trouble in India, never go to the police. Go to anyone you know, but never to the police."

The man then insisted, "Come with me to police station."

I thought of how Sam had been cornered on the train. Hoping to avoid such a situation, I said, "My passport is at my hotel. I'll go get it and bring it to your office." I thought that tactic would give me some time to consider how to proceed. He wasn't on board with my plan, though.

"No. Come now."

I was enjoying the morning and had done nothing wrong. Why was this man suddenly focusing on me? At a time when I felt so independent, someone telling me that I had to go to the police station was particularly bothersome. He gave no reason, only saying, "You must."

In hindsight, this is probably the moment that it would have been best to submit. He *may* have had corrupt intentions, but I suspect that ego was more at play than anything else. If all three of us had gone to the police station, we may have experienced a simple and safe exchange. Unfortunately, that wasn't what happened. I continued to insist on returning to our hotel. If my passport was what he wanted to see, he could see it there, with the hotel manager nearby. I also hoped that the walk would tire or bore the mustachioed man, but instead, he repeated with a parrot's persistence, "Come now. You must. Come now. You must."

As we walked toward the hotel, more khaki-clothed cops surrounded me, blocking Liz and Fran to the outside. I now believed that they were all police, but also thought, "This is shady…"

I turned down a cobblestone street, aiming to shake them off. Liz and Fran followed and so did the khakis, talking to each other in their native tongue and laughing out loud. They insisted that I (and *only* I) go into their station, which also felt suspicious. Why would the girls have to stay outside? I saw no good reason to follow their orders, and clutching my day pack in wary recollection of Sam's train incident, I continued to scurry away.

Local Indians stared at the scene, but no one volunteered to help. Again, I heard Ramesh in my mind: "Go to anyone you know, but never to the police."

I looked over the cops' heads and shouted to Liz, "Deepak!"

I turned toward the Park Café so that I could ask for Deepak's advice, but at that moment, five cops grabbed my arms. As I yelled for help, the crowd of spectators grew. Liz and Fran shoved their way through the cops to me and caused a diversion by taking my backpack off of me and away from the circle of police. The cops wouldn't touch the women, but with all of their eyes on the two girls, I wiggled myself free of their clutches and ran down the stairway to Deepak's café. They didn't follow me in.

Deepak's chairs were up on the tables—the café was closed for cleaning. Noticing my frightened expression, and apparently wanting nothing to do with the situation, Deepak said, "They're cops. Give them what they want and they should leave you alone."

"That's not what I hear about cops in India," I said, summarizing Sam's story while the khaki cops shouted from outside the closed glass door.

"In this town, it should be okay."

"*Should* be?" I remained unconvinced, and I was peeved that Deepak wouldn't advocate for me. I looked back at the booth where we'd sat for breakfast. It had a missing person poster that I'd read while eating. It was unclear what had happened to the young, long-haired Israeli man and I was beginning to wonder if it had been foul play.

I looked at the angry pack of moustaches shouting at me through the windows of the empty café. Liz and Fran were nowhere to be seen. I entertained the thought of a James Bond-like escape through a back door, but without Deepak's support, that wasn't going to happen.

"Okay, I'll go," I agreed. "But remember that you saw me."

I opened the café door a crack and found the eyes of the cop who had started all of this. I repeated what I had already said to him many times: "I will go with you to my hotel. There, I will get my passport. Then we can go to the police station."

"Okay, Okay," the cops said, waddling their heads collectively. They leaned into the door and shoved it open enough to pull me out. The break had calmed them slightly. As we continued our slow walk toward my hotel, I noticed the gold statue of Gandhi again. I looked over the heads of the Indian cops for Liz and Fran, but couldn't see them. Still, I had regained a bit of control over the situation. To try to keep it, I picked up the pace, keeping the cops behind me. Indian people on the street started following my long, curly hair and bright orange shirt and the wake of khaki trailing me. I stood out like a schleppy movie star leading an entourage.

Then we passed another police station and in response to a couple of shouts, six more cops came out. They suddenly grabbed each of my limbs, pulled in all directions, and tugged my hair with their fists while punching me in the head. They lifted me off of the ground and carried me into the streetside station. As they forced me inside, I noticed flashbulbs popping and a gasping crowd. I shouted for help, but though their faces seemed horrified, no one responded.

The police sat me in a chair in a small office, still in view of the horde of locals clustered at the door to get a closer look. Bruised but not bleeding, I had stopped resisting and most of the cops had let go of me, but one hothead continued to hit me in the face while I sat. It took all of my will to not retaliate.

I tried to speak, but the punches made it impossible. I looked angrily at the assailant and then closed my eyes to convince myself not to hit him back. In darkness, I saw the golden image of Gandhi in my mind's eye. Instinctively, my palms came together in prayer position in front of my chest and I quietly repeated, "Namaste, namaste…"

The hothead pulled his punches and the room quieted. He seemed embarrassed, as though a priest or a parent had caught him being bad. My humble salutation had reminded him of his faith and surely that faith preached nonviolence.

Ramesh had told me that India is a "high-strung country." I observed that the strings would tighten as soon as I did. Looking back, I know that resisting was my mistake. A balance of wariness and compliance would likely have been more effective than my insistence to do things my way.

"If a person foolishly does me wrong, I will return to him the protection of my boundless love. The more evil that comes from him, the more good will go from me. I will always give off the fragrance of goodness."
– Buddha

Buddha was in India when he said that.

CHAPTER 34

Shimla Happens (Part Two)

I wasn't in the police station for long. After the last cop stopped punching, they led me—sore but able to walk—into the back of a marked station wagon and locked the hatch. I panicked as the crowd, still minus Liz and Fran, gathered around the rear window. I shouted for help, but they only gawked.

The subsequent drive was a very long minute to the police station in the town square where moustache number one had originally wanted me to go. A fat cop behind a desk told me to sit, that I was "under arrest," and that I was *not* entitled to a phone call, adding, "We get your TV shows, you damn fool."

I hadn't asked for a phone call, or anything for that matter. He was mocking cop shows and aspiring toward them simultaneously. The other cops were gone and the door of the station was open to the courtyard. I contemplated running, but I stayed and listened to a lecture about obeying the police. "This is not your country. You need to listen to the authorities..."

The rambling scolding was far easier to endure than the attack had been. He was condescending but not intimidating. As I wondered what would happen next, Liz and Fran walked in. I realized that I was still worked up when Liz reminded me to breathe. Her presence was comforting as Fran demanded the officer's attention. She was there to negotiate and forced the cop to get to the point: What did he need from us?

He wanted me to apologize.

"Give me some paper," Fran commanded. "Pens."

I was impressed with how she took control. We each wrote individual letters of apology to the Shimla police as dictated by the cop, with literary flourish added on the fly by Fran. Our acknowledged sin was non-cooperation, but it was becoming clear that the entire incident was no more than a power struggle. In the former summer capital of British India, the present-day authorities felt compelled to flex some muscle on a noncompliant English speaker. I might be overanalyzing, but it felt like I was being punished for something that I had nothing to do with.

Then, without ceremony, I was *un*-arrested. Liz, Fran, and I walked out of the station, unaccompanied, to get our passports from our hotel, just as I had originally suggested. The cop said, "Come back in twenty minutes," but then he looked at Fran and added with a head waddle, "Or thirty. No problem."

No problem? The irony burned, but I walked out without looking back. We took a route that did not pass the streetside police station.

When we returned thirty minutes later, the cop was still at his desk. I showed him my passport and was ready to leave, but Fran wanted justice. After hearing my story on our walk, she expressed her displeasure at the behavior of the other officers. She was an angry American and she wasn't taking any shit—she was giving it. I felt so done with the situation that I interrupted her to say, "Please, Fran, let's move on."

She had more to say, though, and as I got up to leave, the cop said, "Sit down, you are under arrest." I had been *un*-arrested for a half hour and I liked it better that way. I needed this ordeal to be over. Fran insisted on obtaining the officer's name and ID number. When she eventually did, I seized on the moment of transition and stood. He repeated, "Sit down, you are under arrest."

Annoyed, I sat back down and tried to be patient. I surveyed the officer's desk and noticed a quote on his desk calendar: "The only way to end a situation is to go through it."

Heeding the advice, but staying seated in deference to his authority, I looked the cop in the eye and said, "I've done everything you have asked. I *need* to go now."

He paused and, with a drop of mercy, said, "You are no longer under arrest."

I stood and looked to Liz and Fran as if to say, "Can we go?"

"I'm not done here," Fran insisted, with swinging American balls.

Without a word, Liz conveyed with her eyes that I should get the hell out of there and that there was *no way* she was leaving Fran alone.

I returned to the hotel on my own and locked the door. I thought about barring it with furniture, but I didn't go that far. It took hours for Liz and Fran to return. As I stewed while waiting for them, I stabbed pen into paper and wrote:

> *Whose karma was spared? I'm boiling with hate for them, especially the one who saw that I was defenseless and repeatedly punched me in the head anyway. Bullying just for the sake of it and hiding in their numbers. My guard was up and I was overpowered. What's the opposite of empowering? Getting trampled for who you are. In the back of that car, I wondered if mine would be the next image of a missing backpacker on Deepak's wall…*

I couldn't find a silver lining for the incident, but I appreciated that I had channeled Gandhi's message of nonviolence when I needed it most. I was still angry though, and wondered if the anger needed an outlet. A parting shot would have felt really good.

Still alone in the hotel room, I realized that it was all about the feelings. I wanted to cry, I wanted a hug. I wanted my parents to know that I was okay. I held it all in while waiting for Liz to return. When she finally did, we held each other for a long time and she told me not to worry—it was over. She started to recount Fran's debate with the cop, but I didn't need the details—I wanted to move on. Day became night and we stayed in the room, turning our focus away from the mad world.

The next day, Fran slept in as usual. Liz didn't want to wait all morning before going out, so she invited me to meet Dr. Bhatia. I would have preferred to leave Shimla immediately, but Liz was determined to visit the professor, so I agreed to go with her. While we waited for a bus, a young man put his hand on my arm and I flinched. He wasn't a cop, though. He had a newspaper stand and pointed at it as he said "Sir, you..." My bright orange shirt was on the front page of a local paper. My face was distressed, and my hair flapping as angry cops pulled me unwillingly through a doorway. The people taking pictures of the incident were news photographers. My photo was in three papers and all included descriptions of what had happened. I bought one of each to take with us on the bus.

The university campus was peaceful and Dr. Bhatia was a gentle man. He and Liz talked biology and he gave us both books as gifts. When I told him what had happened with the police, he wasn't surprised; he didn't trust them either. He translated the newspaper articles regarding the "tourist incident." The three columns apparently ran the spectrum from sympathetic (incidents like this will harm tourism and damage the economy), to neutral (they didn't know what was going on—who did, really?) and finally, supportive of the police for their handling of the uncooperative tourist.

The varied perspectives helped me to step back from the situation. Who was the long-haired guy in the orange shirt? An artist? A troublemaker? He could be whatever you wanted him to be... even if you were him. On the day of the incident, I had gone from carefree to stubborn and then pious within moments. I didn't want to get bilked for being gullible, but a little more faith and trust might have helped.

We returned to the hotel in the late afternoon. The only trace of Fran was a note. "Gone to Manali" was all it read. Liz was upset at her travel partner's departure and regretted leaving without her in the morning. She wanted to follow Fran, but it was too late in the day to begin the journey to Manali.

We walked to the Park Café and found an apologetic Deepak. He had heard about the beating and felt horrible about sending me out to face the wrath of the cops. He offered us a free meal and CDs to borrow.

Then Liz and I walked past the golden Gandhi statue to a balcony outside our hotel lobby that overlooked a mountain sunset. I sat in a chair and Liz stood behind me. She wrapped her arms around my shoulders and we admired purple clouds over the forested valley. From that silence, Liz expressed carefully and for the first time, "I am loving you."

Instead of saying "I love you," she'd used one of India's active "ing" verbs. She wasn't describing something static, but rather a dynamic feeling existing in that moment. She was *loving* me that day. And maybe tomorrow, who could say?

We listened to music and ate chocolate in our hotel room. The growing moon shone through a hilltop window. We stayed up for most of the night, catching only a few hours of sleep. When morning light burst through the room's many windows, *Here Comes the Sun* by the Beatles announced the new day. I still felt defeated from the police incident, but the music assured me that things would be alright and I believed it. Liz's support dissolved my anger. Her kindness reopened my heart.

CHAPTER 35

Himalayan Honeymoon

When the sunrise colors faded to a clear blue, Liz had only one thought in mind: going to Manali to find Fran. Our bus rolled into a rainstorm as it climbed higher through the Himalayas. We ducked into an internet café on Manali's main street and Liz checked for an email from Fran. Our next clue was another three-word message: "Off to Solang."

I interpreted Fran's brevity as practical. She wanted us to know where she was for safety reasons. Liz read it as Fran feeling hurt. I suggested that we stay dry somewhere, but Liz wanted to go to Solang, wherever that was. We learned that Solang is one of India's rare ski hills, fifteen kilometers northwest of Manali. Fran was a downhill skier and must have been curious to experience the sport in India. I was pretty sure that she wasn't sipping hot chocolate in a cabin while waiting for us. She and Liz were both enrolled in a Buddhist meditation course in Dharamsala in less than a week. We were sure that Fran would arrive on time for the course, but Liz didn't want to wait that long to make things right with her friend. I didn't even want to find Fran, but I wouldn't admit it.

We asked an auto-rickshaw driver to take us up to Solang. The three-wheeled doorless vehicle had just enough room for us to load in with backpacks at our feet and my tabla on my lap. I asked the driver if he could make it uphill in the rain, and he waddled his head, confident that it would be "no problem."

Most vehicles were coming down the mountain, not deeper into the storm as we were. Our legs got soaked through the open sides of the rickshaw until, at higher altitude, all became silent. Liz asked if the rain had stopped and I declared with Canadian confidence, "Snow."

It was hard to see because the flakes were melting as soon as they hit the road. A bit higher up, though, they painted our path in white. Daylight was fading and we slalomed uphill on the now-icy road. The rickshaw's motor strained as the driver repeated that it was "no problem." We gripped the sides of the car while the L.A. girl marveled at the falling flakes.

Not wanting to say it out loud, I thought, "We are sleeping back in Manali tonight." After a few more unsafe minutes, our driver acknowledged that it was time for him and his vehicle to descend, but the two of us didn't have to. Solang was only a short walk away. I was skeptical since all I could see were heavy piles of snow, and I wasn't eager to be dropped in the middle of nowhere. Liz made it clear that it was my call.

"Solang is there." With an elbow up high, the driver waved his forearm toward a snow-covered forest. I asked him how far. Still waving into whiteness, he said, "Buildings are there."

I knew that Liz would be disappointed if we didn't make it to Solang and I wanted the Fran hunt to end. I also trusted that the vehicles still descending to Manali could be our backup plan. I nodded at Liz and then at the driver. He turned and zipped back down the mountain.

We trudged through the wet snow. It was perfect for snowballs and I tossed one at a tree. Liz tried to hit me with one, but it fell apart in the air. The snow was four feet deep, and our shoes filled instantly with it. Liz was surprised that the path was penetrable at all, but I plowed a trench for her to follow me through.

It was getting dark and we were wet and cold. After a few minutes of uncertainty, we spotted two cabins, neither of which had a sign. We entered the lobby of the one that looked like a hotel, but no one was there. In the other cabin, we found a young Indian man surrounded by a collection of skis and snowboards. It was a rental shop with a restaurant upstairs. He'd seen Fran, but she had left today for… he didn't know where. There was no internet in Solang and just the one hotel. We returned to the hotel to ask about Fran. This time, a receptionist emerged and confirmed that

Fran had stayed there the night before, but hadn't indicated her next destination. The case of the frustrated friend had gone as cold as our icy toes.

Liz's face relaxed as it had days earlier in Rishikesh when she told me she was leaving for Shimla. Again, she had done her best and was ready to let it go. She would see Fran in Dharamsala.

The hotel manager led us to a spacious room with log cabin walls, a bed piled with blankets, and a bundle of wood next to a furnace. We would be the only guests, just as Fran had been the previous night. We were relieved for the opportunity to get warm and dry.

I started a fire in the furnace and we laid our socks next to it. We were still cold, so Liz suggested that we dance to warm up. I plugged in my speakers and put on James Brown's *Funk Power*, a CD that emanated heat even before I put it in the disc player. The red and black cover features the Godfather of Soul singing with his eyes closed and sweat dripping down his cheek. At the first burst of horns and rolling bass line, our hips spun the room into a dance party. Liz twirled toward me and away again. I followed her lead.

By fleeing, Fran had given us a gift. We now had a week with no plans, no commitments, and no connections other than to each other. The first time I met Liz and Fran in my chicken room in Hampi, Fran had suggested a dance party. Five weeks later, Liz and I were finally having one, thanks to Fran shaking us off of her trail.

As flames warmed the room, Liz peeled off layers of wet clothing and placed them by the furnace to dry. Her spirit seemed different than before. I'd always found her beautiful and interesting, but until then, she had been serious and constrained. Snowed in at that cozy cabin, Liz loosened up. She helped me out of my clothes, teased me with her eyes, and danced away. The cold rain and snow had brought on yet another transition. Still recovering from the ordeal in Shimla, we had each other, the James Brown band, fire, and a bed for the night. In that warm cocoon of a room, the two of us were all that mattered.

The snow stopped falling by morning, and with excited thoughts of fresh snow on the mountain, we put on layers of clothes and trod through deep powder to the rental shop. I rented a snowboard and the owner threw in an inner tube for Liz for free. Inner tube? That made me wonder

how big this mountain actually was. In Canada, we didn't use inner tubes on our ski hills. You would gain too much speed and lose control.

The owner directed us to the hill, which was only a short walk away. When we arrived, I had to laugh. The "mountain" was what Canadians would call a toboggan hill—we had one two blocks from my childhood home in Edmonton and we'd spend winter days climbing it and sliding down.

And that's what Liz and I did. There was a ski lift, but as was common in India, it was broken. I hiked up with my snowboard and enjoyed a few turns on the ride down. Then I retired the board and rode the inner tube with Liz. She was nervous at first, but I steered it with my feet and we shared a lot of laughs.

A rental shop at the bottom of the hill provided rubber boots and fur coats to visitors. An Indian man sporting rented gear asked me how I could walk so well on the snow. It was the first time that he and his companion had ever experienced the stuff. I told him that I was from Canada and I showed them how to dig in their heels for traction. Then, on a hunch, Liz asked the woman, "Are you on your honeymoon?"

She smiled and said, "Yes, we were recently married. Are you married?"

Liz scrunched her nose and said, "No, I'm not ready."

It was cute to see Liz have to answer that question. I would be lucky to marry Liz, but I wasn't ready either. Then the Indian bride said, "We met three times before our wedding. That was enough time to get to know each other."

Just for fun, I waved my index finger back and forth between me and Liz and said to the couple, "We've met three times also."

"There you have it!" said the woman, beaming at Liz.

As we turned uphill for another round of tubing, I realized that everyone else on the hill was wearing the same rented fur coats and rubber boots. They were *all* couples, most likely all newly married and touching snow for the first time. Solang wasn't so much a ski hill as a novelty destination for a honeymoon.

Then we met a Hawaiian surfer couple who asked if we knew about the nearby hot springs. We thought going there sounded like a perfect après-ski activity. We followed their directions to a nearby town called Vashist, where the sky cleared to reveal snow-covered mountains all around. Boys played cricket between snowbanks on the road to the hot springs.

The springs were in a Hindu temple, with separate changing rooms and pools for men and women. On my side, Indian men in underwear soaked in a large square pool. Stone deities were built into the walls of the open-air space. Steaming water poured continually from a carved spout. Men and boys scrubbed each other's backs with cloths soaked in the mineral water.

I floated with my ears submerged and felt my body calming. I hoped I hadn't created a conflict between Fran and Liz, but I was so thankful for the time alone with Liz. We were unable to communicate from the separate pools, so I had to guess when she would be done. I walked out clean and dry and she arrived a moment later. Inside, a young Tibetan nun had scrubbed Liz's back and invited us to visit her temple on a hillside in town.

The sun was setting and we needed to find a hotel. First, we stocked up on comfort food: graham crackers, carrots, peanut butter, and chocolate. The hotel room we rented was drafty, but there weren't any better choices in tiny Vashist, so I taught Liz ways to keep warm, like tucking your long underwear shirt into your pants. We used a space heater and piled on so many blankets that they were heavy to lie under. Exhausted from hiking up the ski hill, we fell asleep quickly under our mountain of blankets.

In the morning, Vashist felt blissfully remote. We practiced yoga facing a mountain view and then walked through town. Liz wanted to accept the nun's invitation, so we stopped by and caught a glimpse of her life. The temple was ornate and impressively built into the side of a mountain. The nun invited us both to her room. She had a bed, a desk, a chair, and a few books, but that was all. Her days were dedicated to study and meditation. She would walk and visit the hot springs, but nothing else. Liz's new friend had chosen a life of austerity. It was so simple.

After we left, Liz said, "A part of me would like to live like that…"

"But then we couldn't be together."

"I know… that's the other part."

"Are you looking forward to being silent for ten days?"

She was, but said that she expected to think of me every day. I knew that I would think of her, too. We stayed in Vashist for another two nights, went to the hot springs each day, and didn't check our email. We saw the Hawaiian surfers, Steve and Allie, again, but we also spent a lot of time resting and enjoying each other's company—our own Himalayan honeymoon.

At night, we repurposed the space heater as a makeshift toaster and warmed our graham crackers, peanut butter, and chocolate into delicious combinations. We fed the treats to each other as we took turns playing DJ on the CD player. Liz said that she was learning about winter, but more than that, we were both learning what it was like to be together. She was sweet and curious, playful, and kind. I loved spending all day and night with Lizzie.

We left the blinds open at night, letting moonlight shine onto our pile of blankets. In that sanctum, we were free of distractions. No family, friends, responsibilities, or schedules. We were present with one other and tasting love, like drops of melted chocolate on our tongues.

CHAPTER 36

Dharamsala and Delhi: Karma Yoga

When we were done hiding from the rest of the world, Liz and I boarded an overnight bus for Dharamsala, an Indian city best known as the home of His Holiness, the Fourteenth Dalai Lama. The Dalai Lama is the political and religious leader of the Tibetan people and has lived in the small Indian city as a refugee since 1959. His community of Tibetan refugees have fled their homeland due to Chinese oppression. After we arrived in Dharamsala, we learned that the great monk was meditating for three months, so we wouldn't be seeing him in person.

Our bus arrived at four in the morning. As we disembarked, I reached for my money belt, but it wasn't there. I normally wore the belt around my waist, but while curling up to sleep, I had moved it from around my waist to the cargo pocket of my pants. I'd buttoned the pocket closed, but now it was open. I began checking if I'd stuffed the money belt somewhere else in the night. Liz and I searched for it back on the bus, but the driver had to leave for Kashmir and we got off.

We found a hotel that answered their bell at that early hour. Under bright lights, Liz helped me search through my bags and clothes. How had I been so stupid? Money belts are designed to be hard to steal. In my pocket, it was no better than a wallet. I could have dropped it, but that seemed unlikely. It must have been stolen while I was sleeping. I was angry at the thief, but even more so at myself.

I no longer had my passport, credit card, bank card, rupees, or dollars—everything that you aren't supposed to lose. I called the bus company and they promised to check the bus again in Kashmir. When I called later, of course it wasn't there.

A passport is a traveler's most important piece of identification. Guesthouses ask to see it and, as I had recently learned the hard way, police expect you to keep it on you at all times. Most importantly, I would need it to travel out of India. I also didn't have any money on me. I had some in the bank, but I couldn't access it without a bank card. I didn't have a separate stash or a card kept outside of the money belt.

Liz was starting her meditation course the next day and I would be on my own. The Canadian embassy was in New Delhi, an overnight bus ride from Dharamsala. That was fortunate, considering how huge India is, but to get there, I would need money.

Liz bought me a ginger tea at a rooftop café with a view of the mountains. She sipped and said, "I have cash. How much do you need?" What would I have done if she weren't there? Just getting to Delhi would have been complicated with no money at all. Back in our room, Liz dug deep into her bag and pulled out two U.S. one-hundred dollar bills. "Take them. My mom stuffed them in my pocket as I was leaving. She gives me too many of these…"

I remembered first seeing Liz's small dirty backpack outside the Ravi Chandra guesthouse in Hampi, before I had even met Liz. The bag sat unattended for hours, and I chuckled to think that these two hundred-dollar bills were sitting in the bottom of it that whole time.

Good karma had spared Liz from being robbed, but for me, it was the second time in India. When my camera was stolen, I felt violated, but I got over it quickly. This time, it was harder to forgive myself. I was ashamed to be so desperate, but Liz's compassion made things easier. I'd been so busy living in the moment that I had no plans for what to do during her meditation course. Now I knew what to do: I needed to get a bank card and a passport.

We left the hotel and walked uphill on a steep single-lane road. There we saw a blonde smile shining above tanned Tibetan faces. It was Fran, looking as happy as I'd ever seen her. She hugged us both and immediately started telling stories. After Solang, Fran had explored the valley south of Manali, an area even more remote than Vashist. The valley was renowned as a hub for the growth and production of marijuana, and Fran had met some interesting characters there. She seemed invigorated and happy to see us. She was on an errand, but she and Liz agreed to catch up that evening. They would have to get all of their talking in before their course began the next morning, when they wouldn't be allowed to speak to anyone for ten days.

The following morning, Liz and Fran stood at the gate of the monastery, about to ascend a long, forested stairway for their course. Holding Liz, I said, "If you start to doubt my feelings for you while we're apart, tell your mind to *shut up!*"

"That may be the sweetest thing you've ever said to me." Then she added, "I'm going to think about how we can grow together and separately."

I kissed her on the forehead and they were off. Liz's words made me realize how much we had grown together already. When we first met, we were finishing each other's sentences. By the time of our "Himalayan honeymoon," we shared thoughts with as little as a look. But all honeymoons come to an end, even fake ones. It's what you do next that determines if a relationship can last.

I'd mostly ignored the question of how to grow separately since deciding to go to Rishikesh. After their course, Liz and Fran had a bit more time in India and were then flying to Nepal and then Thailand. Now that they were reunited, I intended to let them complete their travels together. To be alone with Liz again, I would have to meet her in Thailand. That journey would begin at the Canadian embassy in New Delhi.

After I bought my ticket, I went into a restaurant to wait for the bus. As I sat in a booth facing a forested valley, a Tibetan monk sat down across from me. His name was Kunchok, he was in his midtwenties, and his bald head shone like a light bulb above his saffron robes. His chatty friendliness implied that he wanted something. I'd been asked for money hundreds of times in India, but it never took this long. I heard about his escape from Tibet and his current religious studies. It was interesting, but I kept waiting for the pitch. "I have this friend," he said, and I braced myself to say no. "He needs to learn English in order to find work. I don't speak it well enough to teach him. Will you spend some time with him?"

That was it? My relief must have revealed an openness to the idea, because Kunchok waved another Tibetan man over from the other side of the restaurant. Tsultrim was twenty-four and his rough complexion and leather jacket might have been intimidating were it not for his smile and gentle brown eyes. As he sat down in the booth next to Kunchok, I said that I'd be happy to spend time with him but that I was leaving town that day. I didn't know how long it would take to get a new passport, but I'd look for him when I returned.

The Canadian embassy in New Delhi was a tidy white building with a wall of booths outside. A long but orderly line of well-dressed Indian people waited their turn. It was as though the Indians who wanted to go to Canada knew that pushing to the front wasn't going to be acceptable there. I went to the back of the line and anticipated being there for a few hours. Then a security guard asked, "Are you Canadian, sir?" I nodded and he said, "This line is not for you."

I felt guilty as I bypassed the line and entered a spacious room with a sign that said "Citizens' Entrance." It had a high ceiling, stone walls, plants, and a spotless floor. There were Canadian flags and another row of glass booths. My sense of privilege deteriorated as I waited a long time to be seen. When I was finally called up to speak with an agent, it was by phone through double-paned glass like in prison movies. That made me feel even less important.

I was given a list of documents that I would need for obtaining my new passport and then set out to start gathering them. I got my photo taken and then went to a lawyer who would prepare an affidavit on how my passport was stolen. She was a young Indian woman in a grey pantsuit who transcribed the tale of my missing money belt in handwriting on wide sheets separated by carbon paper. When she was done, I asked about the incident with the police in Shimla. She was empathetic but not surprised at all. "If you take action, they will arrest you."

I shook my head at the lack of justice. She shrugged and said, "India is not like Canada. You cannot trust the police here." I tried to combine the lessons of Shimla and Dharamsala: I should keep my passport with me, but not get it stolen. I was starting to miss home.

While I was in New Delhi, I stayed in a tourist hub called Paharganj, where everything was "cheap and best" and they had it all: food, lodging, trinkets, and drugs. One vendor said, "You can get *anything* in Paharganj." As I walked around, I was constantly surrounded by men with ideas of how to separate me from my money. My white skin seemed to indicate that I was a human ATM, but the irony was that I couldn't even use a real ATM.

I practiced yoga in my hotel room because the outside air was too polluted to even consider the rooftop. I played tabla in the room at midday when everyone else was out. It felt like I was on an odd and inefficient business trip. My new bank card showed up first, arriving in an envelope with the familiar handwriting of the office manager at my workplace in Canada. It was nice to know that people back home were supportive of my damn fool idealistic crusade. When my passport documents arrived, I hurried back to the embassy to submit my application. I was told to return in a week.

Liz would be out of her course in three days, so I returned to Dharamsala. I wanted a break from New Delhi's minefield of feces and pushy people. On the ride back, Indians were throwing bags of trash out of the bus window and down the mountainside. I wanted to stop them, but I knew that I couldn't change India.

As my disillusionment with the country grew, I remembered the promise I'd made to help Tsultrim, the Tibetan refugee. I found him at Kunchok's upper-floor apartment. Tsultrim received a small stipend from the Tibetan government-in-exile, but it wasn't enough to pay for housing, so he was staying with the monk. Tsultrim cooked lunch for the three of us, and then he and I went on a hike. I learned that he was the first one in his family to leave Tibet. He wanted to work in the tourism industry and support his family from afar. As we walked and talked, the grumpiness I'd accumulated in New Delhi rolled down the Himalayan mountainside like garbage dumped from a moving bus.

A yoga teacher once told me a story about her guru. In his ashram, students were required to practice karma yoga each day. Whenever the students would report to the guru that they were making great spiritual progress, he would say, "Good! Now go clean the toilets."

It wasn't a punishment. Progress in meditation can be quickly reversed by the belief that it is making you better than other people. Karma yoga dissolves the ego, the enemy of spiritual growth. After becoming fed up with humanity in New Delhi, I might have hibernated in the hills if I hadn't been asked to help Tsultrim. Thank goodness Kunchok hadn't asked me to scrape the moss off of a terracotta pot.

CHAPTER 37

Dharamsala: Sivaratri

Afternoon hikes around Dharamsala with Tsultrim became a part of my daily routine. We'd walk to remote villages and chat. He became a good friend. I could tell him anything.

After a few days, Liz's course was about to end, so I wrote "now it's your turn to find me" on a note for her at Fran's guesthouse. When I returned to my own guesthouse, I was surprised to see Nibodhi and Laura, the American swami and Englishwoman from the rooftop in Rishikesh. They were my new next-door neighbors. We hung out that night, jamming on drums and sharing stories. Their friendship distracted me from the uncertainty of Liz's return. Still, I could tell that I was nervous when I awoke in the morning with stomach pain. I stayed in bed until mid-afternoon, when I became tired of waiting.

I ventured into town and saw Liz on the road, wearing a shy half-smile. She looked calm and beautiful. I hugged her and leaned forward to kiss her cheek, but she backed away. Ouch. She opened her mouth to explain, but only silence emerged. After ten days of not talking, she hadn't found her voice yet.

"Hi, Lizzie, how are you? How was it?"

"Mark… It's nice…to see you, but I need to spend some time alone now."

I wasn't prepared for such a quick sidestep. As her body turned away, she said, "I don't want to become too attached." Then she walked down a street that I didn't recognize. Where was she going? How could I find her? Had she experienced greater joy in silence than she had felt with me? I stood alone on the street with only questions.

I imagined what I'd do if the leaf in the wind blew away. I wanted to believe that I would be fine—I'd learned so much from being alone. Still, that didn't make it hurt any less.

I didn't have the motivation to find Tsultrim and my stomach was still bothering me, so I ate toast, drank tea, and retired early. I tried to imagine where Liz was. Not knowing was hard. Light poured through my window, and I walked over to look. The moon was full. It was the time when I'd planned to come and find her, back on the rooftop in Kochin, thousands of miles and so many feelings in the past. It felt like I had found *and* lost her since then.

I invited Kunchok and Tsultrim to join me for breakfast the next morning. There was something about discussing girl problems with a celibate monk that made them feel less severe. Kunchok wasn't worried about it and Tsultrim advised me to be patient: "She doesn't know, you don't know." He was right, but the uncertainty was hard for me.

Back at my guesthouse, I found a note from Liz that told me her location. As I stood in the lobby with her hand-written note in my hand, heavy rain rolled in. I wondered if the storm was signaling another transition—the end of my time with Liz? Had she meditated away her feelings for me? I grabbed my raincoat and marched uphill into the downpour to find out.

When I arrived, my head was drenched and socks sopping. A brown-haired woman smiled as she opened the door of a large suite. "You must be Mark," she said. "Liz is here." There were a few people inside—friends from the meditation course. I took off my coat and Fran gave me a hug.

Liz rested like a reclining Buddha on a bed in an alcove with windows overlooking a forest. Her smile carried both joy and regret. When I squatted on the floor next to her, she said, "Mark, I'm sorry." I sat on the edge of her bed and stared into her eyes for a sign. I suspected that I was about to be dumped. After a moment of silence, she said, "I came to find you. I just need some time." She still seemed distant, but I trusted her words. Then she said, "I missed you."

Her feelings *hadn't* faded. I took her hand in mine as her friends tried to look busy. I told her that I missed her, too, and asked about the meditation course. She said that she loved being in silence. She wanted to bring the peace of mind she'd felt on the mountain into her daily life. Then she asked, "Did you see the moon?"

"Yeah, it's full. Should I have waited?"

She shook her head. "I'm glad you didn't."

After a while, I mentioned that Nibodhi and Laura were my neighbors at the guesthouse. I promised to coordinate a meetup with them and then I made my way toward the door. I wanted to give Liz the time and space that she'd asked for. I already had what I needed: hope.

The next morning, we all met up at a Tibetan restaurant: Nibodhi, Laura, Liz, Fran, and I. When Nibodhi saw me, he said, "Your aura, it's not as bright as usual…"

"My aura? What's that? There's light… around me?"

"No, not *around* you. It *is* you. Your aura seems dimmed, particularly your heart chakra."

While I wondered if anyone else could tell that I was emotionally damaged, Nibodhi began doing *anuloma viloma* pranayama breathing exercises at the table. I knew the practice from my yoga classes. It involves holding your hand to your face and covering one nostril while breathing out the other, then alternating. As we watched, Nibodhi said, "I have to balance my *nadis*."

Fran asked, "Aren't you supposed to do that without your hands eventually?"

"I don't believe in suppositions." That package of swami knowledge blew my mind. My whole life was about suppositions. Even after being away from work and home for more than six months, I still constantly made plans for how things were *supposed* to go. The idea of dismissing that notion altogether was revolutionary. I loved it.

While I wondered how broadly I could apply Nibodhi's declaration, Liz pointed out that the restaurant's sign included the words Gyudmed Monastery. That was the name of the monastery in Karnataka where she and Fran had gone on their monk hunt after Hampi. The object of their hunt was Lobsang Tsering, who had worked on a Tibetan charity initiative with one of Liz's friends. When they arrived at Gyudmed in Karnataka, another monk named Sherap Lama had told them that Lobsang was in northeastern India. Liz and Fran had stayed at the monastery anyway, and Sherap Lama had shown Liz a photo of Lobsang.

Liz asked the cashier if the restaurant was affiliated with Gyudmed Monastery in Karnataka. The cashier spoke little English, so she pointed Liz toward a tall monk who was standing nearby. As Liz approached him, the monk turned around. He had a thin layer of black hair atop his tanned head.

"Are you Lobsang? Lobsang Tsering?"

With a huge smile, he replied in perfect English, "Yes, I am."

Her monk hunt was finally over.

Lobsang was a special kind of monk. He led tours of North American cities with a group of Tibetan artists who created colorful sand *mandalas* to raise money and awareness for their community. He invited us to an art school for Tibetan refugees later that day.

The school's forest setting was beautiful and the art was lovely. It was great to spend time with friends and especially Liz. At the end of the day, we returned to our separate guesthouses. Though I wanted Liz as close to me as possible, I knew that it wasn't going to happen until Thailand—if I could get there before she left.

The next day, Nibodhi mentioned that it was *Sivaratri*—a Hindu holiday in honor of Shiva. He had coordinated to host an all-night puja ritual at a firepit near the white-tiled altar outside of our guesthouse. He asked Liz, Fran, and Laura to gather patties of cow dung to help start a fire and sent me looking for dry wood in the hills. He asked me to get a lot—the fire would be going all night.

I arrived after sunset with my tabla and all of the wood that I could gather. Nibodhi had incense, *ghee*, oil lamps, and prayer beads. His forehead was adorned with the horizontal white-powder stripes of a *Shivaite* and he chanted Shiva's names while preparing for the ritual. He tossed the dung patties into the firepit and led our group of eight friends in call and response chants. Nibodhi poured ghee into the fire, and when the blaze was at a sufficient height, he pulled out his chillum, the conical hashish pipe that is popular among Shivaites. He guided us to honor the god by raising a fist while inhaling from the chillum and saying, "Bom Shiva" while exhaling. Liz hadn't smoked pot in years, but took a puff from the pipe since it was a sacrament.

I thought about all of the times Shiva had graced my path since I'd first learned of him. He had laid waste to my already broken relationship in Varanasi. I hated him for it then, but thanked him later. He watched over every one of Krishna's yoga classes in Goa, and I'd chanted his name at an ashram in Kerala. He'd welcomed me back to the Ganga in Rishikesh and now India's change agent was having a birthday. Nibodhi handed me the chillum and said "Bom Shiva," amidst a billow of smoke. I did the same and then added a salute to Nibodhi: "No suppositions."

Hashish and incense mingled with wood and dung smoke from the pit, enveloping the outdoor temple and rising toward the stars. The full moon rose over the mountains as Nibodhi chanted and I accompanied him on the tabla. The buzz from the chillum livened up our group as the others began to dance by the now-massive fire. As the hours rolled toward morning, the air cooled and our group thinned, but the fire blazed on. So did Nibodhi. He planned to chant until sunrise and I had no doubt that he would make it. Laura remained bundled by his side in a blanket.

When the first light of dawn overcame the smoky haze, Liz and I shared a look that said we were both done. Without my saying a word, she followed me upstairs to my room. I had expected her to join me there days earlier, but she'd dismissed that supposition.

She was seeing the room for the first time even though I'd been there for a week.

I drew the curtains and we pulled the blanket over our heads. We held each other for the first time in over two weeks and raced to close our eyes before daylight. Our embrace felt familiar but somehow also new. I'd stopped expecting her to come back to me, so I appreciated her touch as much as I had the first time, or perhaps more. As she fell asleep in my arms, I thought, "Happy birthday, Shiva. Thanks for all the changes."

CHAPTER 38

Dharamsala to Delhi: Compassion

The morning after Sivaratri, Liz and I were climbing the stairway of my mountainside guesthouse when I saw Tsultrim on his way down. He was looking for me. He and Liz still hadn't met, but before I had a chance to introduce them, he asked, "Do you want to see the Dalai Lama?"

We were interested but also surprised. "Isn't he...meditating?" I asked.

"Not today. Tibetan Uprising Day."

We hurried up the stairs and followed Tsultrim to the temple. Tibet had been annexed by China in 1951. Tibetan Uprising Day commemorates an unsuccessful rebellion against China in 1959. I'd often noticed travelers wearing T-shirts that said "Tibet will be Free." I'd mutter to myself, "That's a nice thought...for a T-shirt." Though Tibetan freedom had gained popular attention, practical support from the U.S. and other powerful nations was scant.

In just the months since I'd left on my trip, China was admitted to the World Trade Organization and Beijing was awarded the 2008 Summer Olympics. When I was in Dharamsala, George W. Bush, the president of the United States, was visiting China. Developed countries showed more interest in the massive nation's growing economy than in its atrocious human rights record. The Tibetan people had been torn apart, either living as refugees in exile or as oppressed minorities in their homeland.

Many families, such as Tsultrim's, had people on both sides of the border. I didn't expect Tibet to be free anytime soon.

Tsultrim led us through the incense-scented halls of a Tibetan temple, past sculptures of deities carved in butter. We joined leather-faced seniors motoring along with canes, smiling children in colorful wool hats, adolescents, monks, and nuns. We settled into a tight spot in a courtyard. Anticipation and chatter filled the open space. Almost the entire audience was Tibetan, most of them holding paper flags. Someone handed me one, along with an English transcript of the Dalai Lama's prepared speech. The Tibetan flag depicts a yellow sun radiating beams of light over a mountain where two snow lions fight over a burning jewel. The flag has been banned by China since 1959. I held mine high in solidarity.

The Dalai Lamas are a succession of monks who have led their people for over three centuries. They aren't royalty and they aren't elected—Dalai Lamas are found. Tibetan Buddhists believe in reincarnation, so locating their next leader involves detective work, analysis, and a little bit of magic.

After the death of the thirteenth Dalai Lama in 1933, the council of monks waited for signs of where his spirit had gone. Then a senior monk had a vision of a lake in the remote east of the country. A monk from the Sera Lama sect led a group of fellow monks disguised as pilgrims to the home of a two-year-old boy named Lhamo Thondrup. The head monk held a rosary that had belonged to the previous Dalai Lama, and the boy immediately asked for it. The disguised monk said, "If you know who I am, you can have it."

Though the toddler lived far from Lhasa, the capital of Tibet, and his family spoke a different tribal language, he said, "Sera Lama, Sera Lama" in the Tibetan accent of the people of Lhasa. When the group returned later, they revealed their intentions to the child's parents and subjected Lhamo to a series of tests, including one where they would put two items on a table and ask the boy which were his. Spectacles, a pencil, and a bowl were some of the examples. Young Lhamo was remarkably accurate in saying "It's mine!" about items that had belonged to the thirteenth Dalai Lama. Before long, the search party felt certain that they had found their new leader.

The boy went to Lhasa to train, and lived there through a tumultuous time in Tibetan/Chinese relations. He assumed power at age fifteen in 1950, the same year that China invaded Tibet. *The young leader, who had mainly studied religion, was thrust into an untenable political situation. He attempted to negotiate with China, but found himself caught between the loosely structured rebellions of his people, his own belief in nonviolence, and a communist government in China that abhorred religion and believed that Tibet's land was theirs. It was in the wake of the Tibetan Uprising of March 1959 that the Dalai Lama fled through the Himalayas on a perilous nineteen-day journey to India.*

Forty-three years later, the Dalai Lama appeared joyful as he walked briskly through the crowd, smiling and waving at his fellow Tibetans while a small entourage of Indian security guards followed him to a lectern. The audience bowed in reverence. Seemingly embarrassed by the gesture, the Dalai Lama encouraged everyone to rise.

I read along in the transcript while he spoke in Tibetan. He addressed contemporary political issues, such as 9/11 and the American response to it. Though we were commemorating an uprising, the Dalai Lama emphasized nonviolence and compassion, consistent with his Buddhist faith: "The most devastating cause of human suffering has been the culture of violence in resolving differences and conflicts. The challenge before us, therefore, is to make this new twenty-first century a century of dialogue when conflicts are resolved nonviolently." In addition, "We are all interdependent and have to coexist with one another on this small planet."

The Dalai Lama was optimistic about meeting the challenge. "The global trend today is toward more openness, freedom, democracy, and respect for human rights," adding that China would have to follow the trend. I was skeptical and surprised to read his pragmatic approach to the plight of his people: "My position on the issue of Tibet is straightforward. I am not seeking independence. As I have said many times before, what I am seeking is for the Tibetan people to be given the opportunity to have genuine self-rule in order to preserve their civilization and for the unique Tibetan culture, religion, language, and way of life to grow and thrive. For this, it is essential that the Tibetans be able to handle all their domestic affairs and to freely determine their social, economic, and cultural development."

He thanked the international community and particularly the people and government of India for their "unsurpassed generosity and support." He concluded by acknowledging the Tibetans who had sacrificed their lives for freedom. As he followed the speech with some unscripted words in Tibetan, it began to rain. His Holiness left the stage while a choir of children serenaded him and got soaking wet.

As we walked out, I asked Tsultrim what the Dalai Lama had said after his prepared speech. "He said, 'Everybody go down.'" I didn't understand what that meant at first, but then I noticed people gathering on a road downhill. A mass of monks and students were charging down the muddy hill for a ten-kilometer protest walk. Tibetan elders chastised anyone who turned toward home, grabbing young Tibetans by the arm and even striking them with their canes. We followed along to shouts at a decibel level that I could only compare to a playoff hockey game. The chants included

"Long Live Dalai Lama!" and

"What we want?... Freedom!" and

"We want... Justice!"

The drenched crowd eventually gathered in a town square, still shouting in the pouring rain. Tibetans waved flags, held signs, and chanted. Monks waved fists in the air and children stomped their feet. I was disappointed to see no cameras other than mine. There may have been more

news coverage of my "tourist incident" in Shimla than of this protest. In the midst of that desperate mass of inspired youth, I had to wonder if anyone else was listening.

As Liz and I hitched a ride back to my guesthouse, I considered if the rain signified a transition for the Tibetans. It didn't appear to. They were mired in a generation-spanning standoff. It was a transitional rain for me, though. The embassy had called. My passport was ready.

Liz and Fran were leaving the next day for Varanasi. If I could get my passport quickly enough in New Delhi, I could meet them in Varanasi before they left for Nepal. I said goodbye to Tsultrim and the other friends I'd made in Dharamsala, packed my bags, and caught the overnight bus.

Winding down the road, I used the day's last light to read a card that Tsultrim had handed to me. The front had a photo of a young boy wearing traditional Tibetan robes and hugging a holy book while standing on a grassy hill with yaks in the background. On the inside, Tsultrim wrote:

Dear brother Mark,

Thank you very much for the time you spent with me. Our friendship has developed very quickly over the last few days. During that time, I have come to know that you are a wonderful man, and human being. I feel honored to know you—you are very special. I feel deep, abiding love for you that will never change in any number of lifetimes.

I have a very hard life this moment, so I really need some help and support, please if you can little bit support me and even you ask some of your friends, that will be very great to help my life. If you can't, I don't mind.

That's all for today. I wish you happiness and peace surrounding your life.

Much love, your brother, Tsultrim

Twisting past forests and villages, I felt more in touch with my new friend than at our goodbye an hour earlier. His openness in writing reminded me that his struggle was far more pervasive than anything I had encountered on my trip. I wanted to help him more, but for the moment, I was satisfied that we'd already helped each other. I opened a book I'd bought the last time I was in Delhi and read these words of wisdom:

> "If you maintain a feeling of compassion and loving kindness,
> then something automatically opens your inner door.
> Through that, you can communicate much
> more easily with other people."
> – *The Art of Happiness*, The 14th Dalai Lama

My time with Tsultrim *had* opened something in me. I was more accepting of an uncertain future than I had been before. Recovering from the theft of the money belt helped me to see how fortunate I am and what I have to give. I didn't *need* to be with Liz, but I wanted to be. I wanted to keep improving myself, and as Tsultrim helped me to see, one of the best ways to do that is to support others.

I went to the Canadian embassy to get my brand-new passport. There I learned that you need to clear immigration not only to enter India, but also to *leave* the country. I was surprised as I had never encountered immigration agents while leaving Canada or any other country. The embassy directed me to an immigration office in Delhi.

First, I ventured into the market madness of Paharganj for lunch. Walking down the road, I saw Fran wearing her salwar kameez and a sly smile. I hadn't known that she and Liz would be stopping in Delhi on their way to Varanasi. As I got closer, she asked, "Are you following us?"

"I was going to ask you the same thing."

Then her eyes pointed to a bookstore nearby. "She's in there."

I found Liz in the bookstore, looking at books by the Dalai Lama. She said that she was happy to have more "bonus time" with me, but I could tell that something was on her mind. We walked out onto the road, but couldn't have a conversation because vendors interrupted us with pitches at every step. To hide from the horde, I led Liz into a hotel lobby and toward a staircase. Sitting on the stairs while I stood at her eye level, Liz told me that she'd been reading a book by a famous Vietnamese Buddhist monk. "Thich Nhat Hanh says that people are not supposed to engage in sexual activity without a long-term commitment."

"I don't believe in suppositions," I said, proud of my callback to Nibodhi.

She didn't smile. "He says that being attached to someone is like an illness. That's why it's called being 'lovesick.'"

"Well, I'm not interested in getting relationship advice from a monk."

She finally laughed and touched my hand. We spent the rest of our "bonus time" browsing bookstores until Liz and Fran had to catch their train to Shiva's city. I kissed Liz on the cheek and suggested that she and Fran check out the Yogi Lodge as a place to stay.

Of course, the immigration office in Delhi couldn't stamp my passport. I could feel my frustration building as the officer tried to explain why. It was turning into a pretty disappointing day, but I tried to remember the Dalai Lama's advice. Compassion could help me to understand others and make it easier to communicate with them. I had to trust that the immigration officer was doing his best, and so was Liz. I needed to listen and try to relate to their perspectives.

Liz had caught a glimpse of monastic life in her meditation course and she wanted to maintain the purity that came with it. I couldn't think of anything purer than our few days alone together. I hoped that she would eventually agree with me, but if she didn't, I'd have to be compassionate about that, too.

Then the immigration officer told me that the most efficient way to get an exit stamp was to return to my original point of entry. Fortunately, that was Varanasi, which was exactly where I wanted to be.

CHAPTER 39

Varanasi: Bhakti

"Varanasi is older than history, older than tradition, older even than legend, and looks twice as old as all of them put together."
– Mark Twain, in 1897

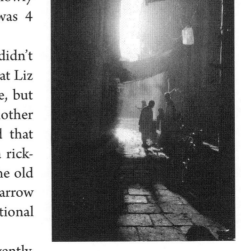

The smoking stench of burning trash crawled through the barred windows of the train car as it rattled slowly through predawn darkness. It was 4 a.m. and I was back in Varanasi.

Groggy from a poor sleep, I didn't know where to go. I suspected that Liz and Fran were at the Yogi Lodge, but its doors would be locked for another couple of hours. I remembered that Keshav awoke early, so I hired a rickshaw to take me to the edge of the old city. Then I walked through the narrow winding streets to the International Music Centre (Ashram).

I knocked on the door gently, thinking that if Keshav and his family were asleep, they wouldn't hear my quiet tap. I heard a shout from upstairs and a moment later, Keshav opened the door, his potbelly protruding from an undershirt and his cheeks filled with paan. When he realized it was me, he grinned with a huge, red-stained smile. Shifting the paan to one side of his mouth and talking out of the other, he said, "Oh, hello! You have just arrived?"

I had been a little embarrassed to come knocking so early, but the feeling dissolved when Keshav invited me inside. He asked about the past three months and how long I would be staying. I told him I'd be there about a week. I hadn't thought of returning to Varanasi as a homecoming, but my tabla teacher made it feel that way. He served me chai in a single-use clay cup and we scheduled a lesson for 10 a.m. that day.

Before the lesson, I went to the Yogi Lodge to get myself a room. I had the crooked cobblestone walk to the lodge memorized, including which blind corners to peek around to check for unyielding cows. When I approached the building with the monkey-cage rooftop where Ronit and I had broken up, I felt a wave of emotion. I didn't regret what had happened there, but tears welled in my eyes nonetheless. I was feeling bad for my past self, for how I had waited and hoped for something better until my patience and faith had dried up, making change inevitable.

Because I was carrying my drum, I couldn't wipe my wet eyes. When I reached Dasaswamedh Ghat, I instinctively joined the beggars and pilgrims approaching the river. Before facing more history at the Yogi Lodge, I would visit India's ghost-eradicator, the sacred Ganges.

I stopped at a ghat where men bathed. As they splashed soap and holy water on their bodies, I recalled my conversation with Liz on the staircase in Delhi. I was frustrated with her, but also wondered if she might be right. Had my blind attachment to having a relationship really died at the Ganga months before, or was it simply the end of a cycle, only to begin again? I wanted to believe that I had changed, but I knew that only time would tell. I wanted the Ganga to help me see the truth before I left Varanasi again.

In contrast to my warm welcome at the International Music Centre, my check-in at the Yogi Lodge felt anonymous. I was one of many shaggy travelers who had stayed there and the owner revealed no recollection of my recent history at the place. I'm sure he didn't remember when I had used the telephone in his office to call my parents and tell them that Ronit and I had broken up, or that I'd received a call shortly afterwards from my sister, to see if I was okay. Nor would he have known how humiliated I felt when my ex-girlfriend sent her Israeli cuddle buddy to my room to get ointment to rub into her back. No, he simply confirmed from his register that Liz and Fran from USA were staying in his dorm and then he checked me into a private room on that same floor.

I went upstairs to the dorm where a hashish and opium joint had once filled the air with potent smoke. Now the space was clean and the beds empty except for one with Fran sleeping in it and another with Liz's backpack next to it.

I put my bags down and walked up a level to see my old room. It was locked, so I went up to the rooftop. The haze was familiar, but the air carried the newness of spring, sunlight pushing through smog. I looked forward to practicing tabla in that spot again.

On my way back downstairs, I saw Liz in a towel, returning from the shower. Her mouth dropped open in surprise from seeing me there so soon. We hugged quietly since Fran was still asleep. Liz remained speechless through her gaping smile. I offered my room for her to get dressed in and invited her to breakfast at one of my favorite local restaurants.

After eating, we walked along the Ganga and Liz said, "This place feels like…"

"A different world, a different century?"

"Yeah, it's like we've traveled through time."

Though she'd been in India for almost six months, Varanasi still felt different to her. I'd always found the river's death and defecation unnerving, but on that walk, the Ganga's eclectic cavalcade felt normal because it was *familiar*. I knew where the funeral pyres were and how to avoid the open toilets. It was like I was touring her around an odd hometown.

I took Liz to a temple along the river where devotees chanted among candles and burning incense. Those clean and peaceful ghats are where locals and pilgrims practice *bhakti*, the yoga of devotion, the most popular path of yoga in India from what I could tell. Though Hindus believe in one God just like my ancestors did, they give their Lord many names and faces. It is through those images that Hindus connect with the divine.

There is something in a god or goddess—their legend or their energy—that opens the heart of a devotee. I saw it at the temples. Indians would bow their heads all the way down to the ground in humility before their Lord. It was always surprising to me because, from an early age, I had been told to *never* worship idols. Besides, I was more of a stand-up type anyway. You wouldn't catch me bowing to anyone, and certainly not to a statue.

As Liz and I walked further along the riverbank, our feelings traveled back in time also as the Ganges washed away the tension between us. We still cared about each other up in Tibetan town, but the connection of our "Himalayan honeymoon" had been swiped along with my passport. In Varanasi, Liz seemed to reopen in the warm air. She asked if I would be meeting her in Thailand. After some time in Nepal with Fran and then a visit with her mom in Thailand, Liz would have three weeks available and wanted to spend them with me.

It sounded great, but I was hesitant. Save for those blissful days in the Himalayas, she always seemed to be pulling away. My trip had begun with a painful breakup; I didn't want it to end the same way. Still, I knew that I'd never find out unless we tried. I told her that I *would* meet her in Thailand, knowing that it wasn't a real commitment until I bought a plane ticket. Only then would I decide when to leave the place that was older than history and jump into an uncertain future.

The time for my tabla lesson approached, so I guided Liz back to the lodge and left to meet Keshav. I arrived at the Music Centre as an Indian student bowed and touched Keshav's feet before departing. Bhakti is also visible in the guru-disciple relationship. The guru is a representation of God and teaching is considered a divine act, so students would touch the bare toes of their guru at the start and end of a lesson. I didn't do that and Keshav didn't expect me to.

As we began my lesson, Keshav invited me to sit and asked, "You have been practicing?"

"Yes, every day," I said with pride, and he asked me to show him.

I had been playing for less than a minute when he stopped me and said, "This is what you've lost."

I nodded as he corrected the placement of my hands. It felt wonderful to be under his guidance again. He was a kind man and a master of his craft. At the end of the lesson, Keshav extended an invitation: "We are having concerts this week for Shiva. It was Sivaratri recently and we are having many musicians at the ashram to perform for Shiva."

I respected Shiva's continual reminders to not get too comfortable, but I didn't feel any bhakti for the destroyer. I was wary of things that I couldn't control, not affectionate toward them, which was why I wouldn't bow to a god or a guru. Still, I was happy that I would have more chances to hear beautiful music at the ashram. When I told Keshav that I had friends to bring with me, he was glad to hear it. Then I said, "I should tell you, Guruji, you were right that I am no longer thinking about my old girlfriend. You were also right that I have found another woman who is very special to me."

"Good, bring her to my concert tonight!"

My news wasn't a profound revelation for him. He knew it would happen because he had seen it so many times before. Though his marriage was arranged long ago, he understood that we westerners would cycle through many relationships before settling on a partner.

Later that day, I was back among the collection of kites surrounding my old practice spot atop the Yogi Lodge while the huge orange sun hid in the haze of the horizon. With my hands on the tabla, I recalled Keshav's words: "This is what you've lost." As kite battles raged on neighboring rooftops, I thought that technique wasn't all that I'd lost. Since my last visit to Varanasi, I'd left behind a partner and our plans for a life together. I asked myself again if I'd also lost my attachment to being in a relationship.

Back on the rooftop, the question didn't seem important anymore. I *knew* that my life was richer with Liz in it, and if she stopped feeling that way about me, I would be okay. Was I loving myself yet? I did love how much I'd changed since the last time I was in Varanasi. I'd gained enough confidence to persevere through the challenges I would inevitably face going forward.

Moments later, the sun was officially down. I knew because Muslim chants echoed from the minarets. I saw the ghosts of my past only if I looked for them, including myself, circa 2001. Liz found me on the rooftop, and as if she knew what I'd been thinking about, asked if she'd recognize me from back then. I replied, "You would, but you might notice that I was sad."

That night, I was excited to bring Liz and Fran to the Music Centre for the concert. Keshav's teenage son, Sandip, greeted us at the door, his smile expanding his cheeks just like his dad's. I paid for our tickets and Sandip invited us to sit wherever we liked. We were early and the open room's floor space was empty. Instruments sat on the stage and thick, sweet dhoop smoke twirled in the air. Fran admired the room and chose a spot against the wall to sit.

I planted myself right in front of the stage and Liz joined me. "I feel a special energy in this room," she said, looking around as if to find the source of it.

"I believe it. A lot of incredible music happens here."

The room filled with visitors and the performers sat cross-legged with their sitars and tabla. Early on, Keshav chewed paan and spat in a cup occasionally as he and his partner began the slow, first part of the raga. As their pace increased, he stopped chewing and stuffed the paan into one cheek.

While the masters performed, my mind wandered to recent memories, possible futures, and back to the present moment. Liz's presence was comforting during the musical journey. I was *so* pleased to be back in that room and sharing the experience with her. I didn't know what would come next for us, but the music helped me to accept the uncertainty.

The audience followed every note, holding their collective breath in vivid passages and exhaling in relief as the cycles of sound transformed. My eyes and ears became fully engaged in the musicians' interplay toward the finale when they ended their performance with a climactic chakradhar and laughed to each other with the bliss of a peak experience.

I put my palms together in namaste, leaned forward, and bowed low to the ground. Before my ego could step in and hold me back, I was at my teacher's feet, prostrating.

The music was divine; I respected *and* loved it. The musicians were the messengers of God and I was a devotee, a bhakti yogi. But I wasn't thinking about any of that. The bow didn't come from thought. It was the humility of my heart pulling my head down to where it belonged—at the feet of my guru, on the concrete floor of an ancient building in Shiva's city.

CHAPTER 40

Varanasi: Permission to Exit

I awoke Monday morning focused on obtaining a "permission to exit" stamp on my passport. The agent in New Delhi had told me to go to the Superintendent of Police in Varanasi. After Shimla, I was hesitant to visit a police station, but Liz, who would leave the next day with Fran, assured me that it would be fine.

Liz walked with me to the station, where we found six men in uniform drinking chai in a shaded courtyard. Another policeman was inside, talking on the phone. The six officers indicated with matching arm waves that the man on the telephone was the only one who could assist us. I was hesitant to enter, but that faded when the officer poured tea for me and Liz with one hand while holding the phone with the other. We sat across from his desk on wooden chairs as his conversation rolled on and on. When the call finally ended, the officer said that I needed to visit the Foreigner Registration Office (FRO) and he wrote down the address for me. As I thanked him, he said, "It is my duty, for you are my guest." I took it as a reminder not to generalize about people, not even Indian cops.

The FRO was a small, dusty office at street level on a dirt road. Boxes of files piled to the ceiling made it feel as though the walls were closing in. Inside, the situation was similar to the police station because, through some combination of seniority and language, only one of the many employees on hand could help us. That person was, according to the nameplate on his desk, Mr. Yadav. His suit, tie, and trimmed moustache contrasted with his cluttered office. I tried to speak with him, but he ignored me as he shuffled papers between the towers of files.

Liz and I waited among the stacks of boxes. We were blocking Mr. Yadav's path to his colleagues' offices, but there was nowhere else to stand. Each time he got up from his desk, we retreated to the entryway to allow him to pass. I would try to make eye contact with him each time, but that tactic didn't work.

After about twenty minutes, he asked what I needed, but then he walked into the next office before I could finish speaking. Eventually, through sentence fragments separated by paper shuffling, he made the exit-stamp process sound complicated. I asked where I could begin and he handed me a form requesting my personal information. I completed it and handed it back. Then Mr. Yadav promised that the issue would be settled in two days. I should return on Wednesday.

As we hailed a rickshaw toward the old city, I told Liz that it was important to have a clear agreement with the driver before boarding. "He needs to agree to the price first, or else he will insist on a higher rate when we arrive. I make sure he at least nods before I get on. It helps."

When she asked what would happen otherwise, I told her, "When I first arrived here, I asked an Indian man boarding a rickshaw what the price should be to get to Dasaswamedh Ghat. He said twenty-five or thirty rupees, so I would pay thirty, but the drivers would *always* ask for more. I'd hold out the money and they would shout and make a big scene. We'd get into a long debate and it always upset me. Then one time, I stood at an intersection and watched how locals dealt with the rickshaw *wallahs* upon arrival. The wallahs shouted at Indian men in suits for more money, too, but the passengers would ignore them and hold out the fare until the wallah accepted it. That made me realize that I shouldn't take it personally. It's just how things are done here."

On our ride back, we entered a traffic circle where rows of rickshaws, cars, and oxcarts circled and exited with confusing inefficiency. There were no lanes or traffic signals. Two police officers stood in the midst of the chaos, maintaining order with long sticks with whips on the end. They whipped the oxen to prod them onward, but they also whipped the rickshaw drivers. I was shocked. I hadn't seen anything like that before. I was relieved when our driver steered behind the cop's back and then accelerated to avoid the whip.

At the end of the ride, I didn't debate the fare. Instead, I gave the driver more than the agreed-upon amount. After seeing that whip, it felt like the right thing to do.

As Liz prepared to leave for Nepal, she asked again if I was coming to Thailand. When I said, "Once they let me leave, I'm there," I believed it this time. I felt that if I didn't meet up with her, our connection would fade into memory when we both returned home.

The next morning, I walked Liz and Fran through crooked streets to a taxi for the airport. I returned to the FRO on Wednesday, only to be completely ignored by Mr. Yadav again. He dug into stacks for files and would paper-clip pages between carbon paper and write on them. I addressed him every few minutes, but he acted as if I wasn't there, so I found a chair among the files and sat. I kept trying to get his attention when he looked up or walked past me, but he treated me as invisible and inaudible. I thought, "In this situation, is he the passenger and I am the rickshaw driver asking him for more money?" I wasn't going to start shouting like a rickshaw wallah, but I *was* getting frustrated. After a while, Mr. Yadav must have wanted the chair back, because he gave me a form for a visa extension and told me to go down the road and get it photocopied. "But I don't want a visa extension..." My words trailed him out the door.

A few minutes later, Mr. Yadav asked a subordinate to put down the cricket scores he was reading, go down the road, and photocopy the form. The young man returned with the original and a copy. Mr. Yadav handed one of the pages to me and instructed me to complete it. It was similar to the form I had completed two days earlier, asking for my personal information, passport number, and so on. I filled it in and handed it back. "And again," he said. For the third time, I provided my details on an identical form. As I began to wonder if he could actually help me, something magical happened.

Mr. Yadav took a fresh sheet of carbon paper, stuck it between two additional forms, secured the three with a push pin, and started writing on the top page. It was all in Hindi except for my name. I was thrilled with the forward momentum, but also in full realization that *nothing at all* had been done on my behalf until that moment.

Then he said, "Now give me your passport."

I handed it to him, expecting him to copy down some details and return it to me. Instead, he attached it with a paper clip to the package of carbon paper that he had just filled out. He said that he needed to keep my passport for a few days. I really didn't want to leave my new passport among the paper pinnacles of that messy office, but Mr. Yadav promised that he'd return it to me on Friday along with my coveted "permission to exit" stamp. He shooed me off with an arm wave and I left, *sans* passport, again.

Thankfully, the Music Centre's nightly Sivaratri concerts were a perfect antidote to Mr. Yadav's dusty office. I was having daily tabla lessons again and practiced on the Yogi Lodge rooftop in the afternoons. A new batch of travelers in the dorm would join me on the rooftop and jam on their instruments. Those sessions were scented with "manali" that my new friends had bought down by the river. I declined the chillums as a practical matter—unlike my preferred grass, the thicker hashish smoke hurt my lungs and made my head heavy.

I returned to the FRO two days later full of anticipation. Mr. Yadav didn't make me wait this time. My passport had been stamped, *but* it still needed a signature. It turned out that his boss was the only one with the authority to sign, but he was not working that day. Mr. Yadav told me to return the following day. I felt burned by his broken promise and couldn't believe I had to come back a fourth time, but I tried to dissolve my frustration by accepting the fact that he worked in Indian bureaucracy where everyone spent a lot of time drinking chai, procrastinating, and missing deadlines. He wanted me out of there as much as I did and this latest delay was *not* his fault.

When I returned on Saturday morning, Mr. Yadav rushed the passport into my hands like a hot chapati out of the oven, surely hoping that I would vacate his office just as rapidly. I wondered where the pile of paper from my simple request would end up within the FRO's Himalayan filing system. My monthlong business trip was over and I figured I'd better leave India before Shiva made things even more interesting. I went straight to a travel agent in the old city, tapping my money belt frequently on the way to be sure that my passport was still there. I bought a train ticket to Calcutta (now called Kolkata) and a plane ticket onward to Bangkok, Thailand.

I went to evening aarti at dusk. Young priests moved their candelabras in synchronized circles above billowing incense smoke, accompanied by bells and chanting. While I watched them, I thought about a quote that I'd copied into my journal:

> "There is a very close connection between humility and patience. Humility involves having the capacity to retaliate if you wish, yet deliberately deciding not to do so. That is what I would call genuine humility. I think that true tolerance or patience has a component or element of self-discipline or restraint—the realization that you could have acted otherwise, you could have adopted a more aggressive approach, but decided not to do so."
> – *The Art of Happiness*, The 14th Dalai Lama

India was incredibly frustrating at times but also humbling. I was learning how to diffuse my anger when challenged by cops and robbers, beggars and bureaucrats. Mr. Yadav had tested my patience for an entire week, but with my passport stamped, I felt that I was making progress.

My habits were changing, too. By not getting high every day, I had stopped hiding from the opportunities and beauty of life. Drugs don't have

that effect on everyone—many people can enjoy substances in healthy moderation, but I'd learned that I wasn't one of those people. Since I'd stopped carrying a stash of grass and all anyone else had was the stronger, more potent hashish, I'd found that I was better off sober anyway. I was learning how to create sustained happiness through yoga and music. It was more work, but my new practices were helping me to open my heart, rather than hiding it in a cloud of smoke.

As the priests at aarti rotated urns of sacred incense, I reflected on the four and a half months since I'd first visited the Ganga. I'd left home looking for something better in Nepal, but things had gotten worse for me there. It was in Varanasi that I took my first steps toward rediscovering myself. Even if Keshav was right and the changes were Shiva's doing, at least I had known enough to follow the signs forward. It was hard to accept that my long, strange trip in India was ending, but I didn't have to go home *yet*. First, I wanted to have some fun with Liz on a beautiful beach.

I had my final lesson with Keshav the following day. I thanked him for his teaching and his guidance. Booked on an overnight train to Calcutta, I practiced tabla one last time on the Yogi Lodge rooftop before packing up. I had a whole pineapple next to me, and I would carve off and savor slices between rhythms. At one point, I tilted my head upward and saw a sideways crescent moon—a tiny white smile on a wide, light blue canvas. Then, too quickly for me to react, a monkey swooped in and snatched the pineapple. I got up to chase him, but he was on another rooftop before I even got to my feet. I sat back down behind the tabla feeling frustrated—I'd been warned about the monkeys. Realizing that there was nothing I could do about it, I calmed myself with rhythm.

On the train from Varanasi to Calcutta, I had one neighbor in my car, a Buddhist monk from Thailand named Ajay. He was draped in robes like Kunchok and Lobsang, but theirs were maroon. Ajay's robes were orange, in the Thai Buddhist tradition. Before we tucked in for the night, I told him that I was on my way to his homeland.

I next saw Ajay when I awoke at 3:30 a.m. He said that someone had been touching my backpack and Ajay had scared him off. I was surprised that a thief would be so bold since all of my belongings were on the top bunk with me. I was curled into my sleeping bag with my tabla behind my head. My backpack was under my legs and my shoes were tied to it by the laces. I was on the off-ramp from India and didn't want any more mishaps. I thanked Ajay for the warning and tucked my pack in a little closer before going back to sleep.

When we awoke and prepared to disembark, my things were intact but Ajay's shoes were gone. I felt angry about it. Who steals a monk's shoes? Ajay revealed no reaction and simply said, "He must have needed them more than me."

If I'd seen the thief, I might have jumped from the bunk fists first, but Ajay didn't even consider it. While I felt agitated on the young monk's behalf, he had put himself in the shoes of the one who stole his.

Whether it was Ajay's personality, his training in Buddhism, or likely a combination of both, he led with empathy and I admired that. He didn't require generosity to open his heart, it was already open.

As Ajay left to walk the streets of Calcutta barefoot, I recalled another Buddhist lesson: the shoes were impermanent. Ajay knew that before he even reached to put them on and found that they were gone.

CHAPTER 41

Koh Lanta: Libro Abierto

By the time I arrived in Calcutta, Liz was on an island in Thailand called Koh Lanta with her mom. She emailed to invite me to join them, adding, "You would love it here." I was surprised. Meeting Liz's mom seemed like a big step in our relationship, but if she felt ready, that was good enough for me. I decided to go. At the Calcutta airport the next day, I felt satisfaction in flashing the hard-won exit stamp on my passport.

While I waited for my flight, I needed to use the bathroom. The toilet stalls had these labels on them:

INDIAN   WESTERN

I was stunned by this segregation until I opened one of the doors and realized that the labels referred to the type of toilet. INDIAN was a pit toilet for squatting and WESTERN was a North American-style flushing toilet. Though it was the first western toilet I had seen in a long time, I chose the Indian one because I wouldn't have to touch anything. I found it hilarious that I'd chosen the Indian option because it was more sanitary.

At the Bangkok airport, I was among a group of boisterous young Americans with lobster-red skin under bleached-white tank tops, their flip-flops slapping the tile floor. I wondered how I must have looked to that group, bedraggled from eight months on the Indian subcontinent. I was thin and my curly hair came down to my shoulders. My clothes were faded from the sun and infused with the pollution dust that laundry soap can't get out. As always, I wore hiking shoes. When there's poop on the streets, flip-flops won't protect you.

In the airport, I was impressed with the motion sensors in the bathroom and the speed of the luggage carousel. Waiting to go through Immigration, I laughed to see two Indians, finally outnumbered, trying to push to the front of the line. When I told the agent that I needed a tourist visa, he looked at my Canadian passport and replied with a smile, "No, you don't." Things were getting easier.

Normally, when meeting a girlfriend's parents, I'd get a debriefing on the way. My partner would warn me about patterns and pitfalls, but this time, I traveled to southern Thailand without any preparation. After a bus and a ferry, I was stunned by Koh Lanta's beauty. Tall palms and powder-white sand led to deep blue water of a shade that I'd never seen before. When I found Liz's room at a seaside hotel, her mother answered the door. She had short brown hair and the same almond-shaped brown eyes as her daughter. Wearing a T-shirt over a bathing suit, she greeted me with a hug. "I'm Susan, like your mom!"

My mom is friendly, but Cuban Susan was over-the-top gregarious. Before I'd even put down my backpack, she was offering me fruit and making plans for our lunch. I learned that Liz was away for the day, working on her scuba-diving certification—something I'd done years earlier. I looked forward to talking with Liz about it, but first I had to find a place to stay. I told Susan that I would look for a guesthouse and return later, but she quickly dismissed that plan.

Susan was determined to get food into me and said kindly that she didn't want me staying at a different hotel or guesthouse. The Lanta Villa Resort was a lot fancier than the two-dollar-a-night places that I was used to. It had a pool and you could see the ocean from the cabins. Susan said, "I'm going to get you a room here." I tried to refuse, but she said, "I know you're on a budget. I'm happy to pay. It's only six dollars a night. I want you and Lizzie nearby."

Before I could offer any further resistance, Susan returned from the front desk with a key to my new cabin. She told me to drop my bags in the room and join her in the resort restaurant for lunch. After eight months on the road, I was suddenly being told what to do by a mother whom I had never met, but somehow it felt natural.

The restaurant was on an open wooden platform under a palm-frond roof with a view of calm sea. A bowl of fruit arrived at the table soon after I did. Susan asked me a lot of questions, but it didn't feel like an interrogation because she was so friendly. I ordered eggs, sat back, and described my life back home. I told her about splitting with Ronit and about discovering yoga and tabla. I explained my decision to travel so far on multiple occasions to find Liz. I admitted that I was hesitant to date again so soon, but that her daughter was too special to let float away.

Susan said that once she and Liz had arrived at Koh Lanta, she didn't want to leave. She knew that Liz would want to explore, and inviting me was a way to get her to stay put. Susan probably also wanted to size me up, but she did a good job of concealing that intention. After lunch, I settled back into my beach routine with some yoga and tabla.

Liz returned from her scuba course still in her bathing suit and got me wet with her dripping hair. She was vibrant. With the protective shield of the salwar kameez peeled away, she seemed much more relaxed. She thanked me for coming and we went for a barefoot walk on the beach to catch up.

Liz had mentioned before that her family was struggling. She has two older brothers and two older sisters. I learned at dinner that night that, as Liz was about to leave for India, there had been a shouting match between Liz's brothers and their dad. Before the wounds could heal, Liz was on an airplane. Months later, they still hadn't. Her parents and brothers were no longer speaking with each other. Hours of meditation and self-reflection in India had helped Liz to see that her torn-apart family was also tearing her up inside. In search of unity, she proposed solutions, but Susan told her, "You can't fix it, Lizzie. This isn't *about* you."

I kept quiet at dinner, but on a moonlit beach walk later, I held Liz's hand and told her that I thought she was brave. Susan was telling her to leave things alone, but that wasn't in Liz's nature. She had grown up with two sisters *and* two brothers. She wanted it to stay that way.

The following day, I continued my yoga and tabla beach routine while Liz was at her scuba course. I was happy that I'd come to Koh Lanta. I was recovering from intestinal troubles and the strains of Indian travel. Thailand was spectacularly beautiful, and it was special to be there with Liz. That evening, we swam in the emerald blue water. As an orange sunset decorated the sky, we hugged and kissed in the water. I asked Liz, "How can you be so cute, beautiful, and sexy at the same time?"

Her response: "Your perception, your perception, your perception."

The next morning, Susan and I joined Liz on the dive boat. There was a celebratory vibe as Liz's group completed their certification. Susan went snorkeling and I dove with the group. I swam through a cave full of fish and saw a shark that was longer than me. Underwater, I focused on the rhythm of my breathing. I could see why so many people are drawn to the sport of scuba diving. Not only can you witness spectacular sea life, but the deep inhales and long exhales of a dive are meditative. It's rare to find that kind of silence.

In the afternoon, Liz and I went to an internet café to check email. Her mom didn't have web-based email yet, so she was using Liz's account while on Koh Lanta. When Liz saw a response from her aunt—Susan's sister—Liz read Susan's original message. It was in Spanish, so Liz translated it for me. Susan had started out by expressing her relief that I didn't seem like an "old man" despite being twenty-seven to Liz's twenty-two.

Instead, she said, "*El es como* Lizzie" (He is like Lizzie), adding, "*piensa en los pobres*" (he thinks about poor people). She described my tabla playing as akin to a rumbling earthquake and then, in reference to our mealtime conversations, wrote, "*El niño es un libro abierto*" (The boy is an open book). Liz and I were pleased to see that she approved of me.

That evening was our last on Koh Lanta. We would escort Susan to Bangkok the next morning to start her journey home. Fran was in Thailand too, in the north. Liz wanted to find Fran before she went home and then travel just with me, as she'd proposed months earlier.

We three walked barefoot along a row of beachfront restaurants, checking menus before stopping for dinner. As soon as we sat down, Susan started ordering appetizers in an attempt to fatten me up some more. Like Liz, I would be returning home in a few weeks for a sister's wedding. Hers was in May and mine was in June. Susan said that she wanted to help *my* mom.

Before we left in the morning, I picked up a Thai-designed greeting card, wrote in it, and gave it to Susan. I told her that it was delightful to meet her, thanked her for her generosity, and concluded with, "Don't worry. I'll keep an eye on Lizzie while we're traveling. Actually, I can't take my eyes off of her."

CHAPTER 42

Bangkok to Chiang Mai: Baggage

On the bus to Bangkok, Liz and her mom continued their long conversation about life. Susan told Liz not to worry about things beyond her control, such as other people's behavior. I sat alone with my journal and reflected on the things that I *could* control: my demons. If any actions or tendencies weren't doing me any good, I wanted to leave them behind in Asia.

The first demon was addiction. I had fought with myself about smoking marijuana for a long time. I hadn't expected to tackle that tendency in the land of charras and chillums, but another of India's sacred practices had proven to be the antidote. Morning yoga kept my lungs and mind clear, unlike pot which did the opposite.

At home, getting high was an escape from the mundane—an easy way to return to the present moment. But there was nothing mundane about my amazing journey, especially as I found creative expression through drumming and writing. Enriching days helped me realize that smoking marijuana was an unhealthy compulsion for me. Indian sunsets shone a light on that tendency, and yoga pushed it out the door.

With my trip ending soon, I wanted to avoid the tedium that made me want to get high in the first place. I would have to find work that was meaningful to me. In Edmonton, I had been auditing companies in the oilfield industry, which didn't feel like I was helping the world. My clients would admit that their primary motivations at work were a fresh pot of coffee and a paycheck. My motivations hadn't been much different, except that my preferred substance had to wait until I got home.

Back when I was in kindergarten, I worked on a self-profiling scrapbook. On the "What do you want to be when you grow up?" page, I had put "ventriloquist." I thought that throwing your voice was an amazing skill. When my dad saw the book, he said, "You can be a ventriloquist, but you should go to school first so that you have a career to fall back on."

I might have been a bit young for that dream-dampening message, but I eventually accepted that my dad was right. Now that I had my Chartered Accountant designation, I had more options, but I was qualified for many jobs that I had no interest in. To break my pot-fueled cycle, I would have to work *for* something. I'd noticed that my nonprofit clients had an organizational culture that was completely different. The staff worked hard because they believed that they could make things better. I wanted to be one of *those* people. If I could spend my days working toward something positive, I wouldn't feel as compelled to light up when I got home.

My second demon was longing—in wanting a relationship. For as far back as I could remember, I'd pursued a female companion. In that same kindergarten scrapbook, my "best friend" was a brown-eyed girl named Pippa. In grade one, it was auburn-haired Alana, and on it went. Sure, I went for stretches where I didn't have a goddess to worship, but I was always looking. Their beauty was divine, their kindness a blessing. Each time I found one, I did all that I could to make her happy with me.

With Ronit, things went on too long and got too weird because I thought that my search was already over. It was only when Shiva splashed cold Ganga water on my face that I realized that relationships aren't about finding and keeping. They have to be voluntary and enriching for both sides. It seemed so obvious in hindsight: the idea that I *needed* someone else for my own happiness didn't make any sense.

That said, I was aware of the risk of relapse. As I looked out the bus window at rice paddies, I knew that I was worshipping again, but Susan was right that Liz and I were similar. Our paths had merged and we were growing *together*. Liz accepted who I was and encouraged who I wanted to become. I felt sparks when we were together. I didn't know how long the sparks would last, but I wanted to find out. As our bus rolled past palm trees toward the city, I trusted that what we had was good for me. While I vowed to leave my demons behind, I didn't *need* to do it alone.

After Susan departed, I sat next to Liz on a wood-framed bed in an aquamarine-painted room at the Shanti Lodge in Bangkok. As I took inventory of my belongings, Liz told me, "Bring only what you need. We can travel 'Liz and Fran style.'"

I always filled my pack until nothing else could fit, but Liz and Fran kept their bags light by purging unnecessary items. That lightness allowed them to explore with their packs on and hold off until the last minute to decide where to sleep. After Liz had removed the warm layers of clothing that she no longer needed, her bag looked as empty as it had when I first saw it unattended in Hampi. Then she turned to my clothes, instruments, and gear and said, "You have *way* too much stuff."

Her first target was the twenty-pound tabla. Liz knew that I loved to play it every day, but suggested that I leave it behind to enable a nimble traveling experience. It was hard to eliminate such a big part of my new routine, but Liz assured me that I'd have lots of time to practice after she left Thailand for home. I placed the instrument in a corner of the Shanti Lodge's storage closet, and Liz started to sort through the contents of my backpack.

I wasn't attached to any of the clothing and watched as Liz narrowed me down to two pairs of pants and socks, two shirts, and three pairs of underwear. She said that we could wash a pair of underwear by hand each day. Then she surveyed the small pile and advised, "You should be able to fit everything in your day pack." That was a radical suggestion, but I kept an open mind as Liz eliminated items one by one. The sleeping bag had been perfect for Indian trains, but we were using only a bedsheet for the warm Thai nights, so it joined a growing collection of excess items in the backpack that would stay behind.

I put away my old journals, and we each chose one book to read. I kept the Dalai Lama's *Pursuit of Happiness* and Liz selected Kahlil Gibran's *The Prophet*. Our only sticking point was music. Liz thought that I could get by without my CD player for five weeks, but knowing that we had long bus rides ahead of us, I doubled down and suggested that we buy Liz a pair of earbuds so that we could both listen. I agreed to pare down to only ten CDs, but I would still bring the player and speakers. "The speakers?" she asked, eyes wide. "We're trying to travel light." She shook her head at my attachment to amplified sound.

I stuffed the speakers into the orange day pack and bragged that I still had room to spare. Liz may have lost the battle of the speakers, but she won the war. We would travel Liz and Fran style.

Liz's only itinerary requests were to begin in Chiang Mai, where Fran was, and to otherwise stay off of the "tourist trail." I went through the guidebook and drafted a plan. Chiang Mai was in the midst of a water-throwing New Year's festival called *Songkran*. After Chiang Mai, we'd visit Laos, traveling from north to south. Then we would go to see the giant temples of Angkor Wat in the Cambodian jungle and wrap up Lizzie's time in Asia on a Thai island called Koh Chang. She agreed to the itinerary and we set off the next morning.

It felt ironic that on our first full day alone together in Thailand, Liz and I were on our way to find Fran. I didn't mind, though. Fran was leaving in a couple of days, and I'd heard that Thailand's second city was lovely, friendly, and less polluted than Bangkok. We cuddled on the daylong bus ride and listened to a Led Zeppelin compilation and a Neil Young bootleg. I found us a place to stay in Chiang Mai that was centrally located and recommended by the guidebook. It looked like a motel in any town, with a table and chairs across from matching beds with sheets tucked in and a private bathroom in the back. Liz thought it was a bit extravagant at three dollars, but feeling sweaty and tired, I argued that we take it.

Late-day sun shone through the lighter layer of curtains and made the walls look yellow. I sat at the head of the bed closest to the window, writing in my journal, when Liz walked up to me and said, "I think we might be moving too fast." Our debate over lodging had made her think that we might not be compatible. I was surprised: Just as her idea to travel together was manifesting, Liz was tapping the brakes. She added, "It's called falling in love because you lose control."

"Is that more monk relationship advice?"

She nodded and explained that she *wanted* to be with me, but worried that desire could pull her into a bad situation. I told her, "It's okay to *want* to be with someone. Don't take this the wrong way… I love you, but I don't *need* you. I've learned how to be alone, but I prefer to be with you if I can. Either way, I'm still in control. So are you."

She looked puzzled but didn't say anything. Instead, she got up and went to take a shower. I stayed on the bed and got back to writing. When Liz came back out, she said, "No matter what happens in my life, I'll always know that you were good to me."

As I looked at her, standing across the room in her towel, my mind jumped to an image of her in Solang's snow, a memory of her beauty in nature's beauty. I couldn't help but cry. The tears were as unexpected as when I'd listened to the song *Suzanne* in Palolem after leaving Liz the first time. As in my hut, it was the idea of Liz as a memory that set me off. Regardless of the resolutions I'd made in my mind, my heart didn't want to see her that way.

I wiped my eyes and Liz, still standing in her towel, tried to be realistic. "You know, it's quite possible that you won't be the last man I'm with in my life."

Another tear jumped onto my cheek as I stood up and walked toward Liz. I looked her in her eye, shook my head, and said, "I don't love based on probability."

Without the fear of being alone, I had nothing to lose from telling Liz the truth. Still, that didn't mean that I wasn't vulnerable. I *was* attached to her and I wanted to see what we could discover together. Sure, she shook me off from time to time, but every time we reunited, I felt as though I were on a mountaintop, basking in a light I had never seen before.

CHAPTER 43

Around Chiang Mai: Arjuna

Three thousand years ago, on the wide and dusty plains of Kurukshetra, India, a brave young warrior named Arjuna leads the massive Pandava army from a gold-plated chariot. The Pandavas face their equally powerful enemy, the Kauravas, waiting in rows, armed for battle. Arjuna, as the Pandava general, orders his charioteer to take him to the exposed center of the battlefield. There they stand alone in no-man's land, poised to command the attack.

But Arjuna hesitates.

The Pandavas are his brothers and cousins, but as a result of the complicated leadership struggle of the time, so are the Kauravas. From this closer vantage point, he can see familiar faces on the enemy side, clutching their weapons and waiting for war. As the Pandavas look to their leader for a sign, Arjuna steps off of the chariot and sits in the dirt, despondent. His charioteer asks him what's wrong. After a silence, Arjuna says that he would rather wander the earth as a beggar than fight. The charioteer knows him well; he is Arjuna's closest friend and advisor. He's also overqualified for his current position since he is the god, Krishna. He tells his friend to get on with it.

"Get up, Arjuna. It's embarrassing."

This tale is the *Bhagavad Gita*, the most revered section of the epic *Mahabarata*, from the Indian *Vedas*, which form the basis of yogic philosophy.

Krishna questions Arjuna on the cause of his hesitation. It is out of love, the warrior insists. How can it be right to slaughter one's own family for territory? As rational as that sounds, Krishna manages to tear down Arjuna's every defense, rendering him even more vulnerable and confused.

But then Krishna builds the beleaguered soldier back up with compassion and empathy. He convinces Arjuna that not only is he prepared for battle, it is his sacred duty.

Far from a literal call to arms, the Gita teaches that one must fulfill one's destiny. You may face uncertainty and even terrible luck, but you can't let that stop you. You could die from disease or a madman's delusion, but those are things that you can't control. What you *can* do is charge ahead with your heart open and your mind focused. Then you are bound to be successful.

Still, the Gita has not been translated into hundreds of languages simply because of its motivational message. It is revered for the metaphor that unfolds in Krishna's words, verse by glorious verse. The Pandavas are the positive actions that we take to improve the world for ourselves and others. The Kauravas are our demons. Both are a part of each of us and we love them both. We live with the enemy Kauravas every day. These brothers and cousins represent our *desire* or, in my case, the *craving* for a perfectly rolled spliff or the *perceived* need to be with a brown-haired girl.

All too often, we find ourselves like Arjuna, in a fetal position in the middle of a battlefield between the two, not knowing how to proceed. That's our conscious mind. While changing allegiance from one side to the other, and back again, we often freeze in the middle.

Krishna is the god within us, the Atman, the observer. He reminds us that, as long as we are taking in breath, it is our duty to fight for good. That's why yogis do "warrior" poses—to strengthen the body and clarify the mind in preparation for the battle within. In the best moments, being a yogi means being a humble warrior in service to your highest self. You must attack your beloved enemies, the ones you grew up with and trusted until you understood that you would be better off without them. Send them packing because it is your duty. Be a man.

"You gotta pay your taxes, so you might as well be a man."
– James Brown

On our first morning in Chiang Mai, I was slumping through my own battlefield. When Liz and I emerged from our motel, youngsters squirted us with water guns in celebration of Songkran, the water festival. Though it was hot outside, I tried to avoid the assaults. I wasn't in a playful mood after our conversation the night before. Though I'd said that I didn't want to know the odds that Liz and I would stay together, she had made me consider them.

I kept quiet through breakfast, but perked up after drinking some Thai iced tea. It comes with condensed milk and and a large amount of sugar. Though it's best to drink it sparingly, Liz asked for hers with no straw. She didn't want to add plastic to the earth.

We had planned to meet Fran at our motel, but before the appointed time, we saw her on the street, also buying a Thai iced tea. Liz ran to her and they embraced for a long time. They looked so different in tank tops and shorts instead of salwar kameez. I was already familiar with Fran's bear hugs, but it felt different this time. Without the question of how long I'd be hanging around, she seemed genuinely joyful for the "bonus time" with Liz and me.

The street party was in full swing. Kids sprayed us with water as we passed ecotourism offices and Thai massage schools on a walkable main road.

I realized that since leaving home, I had celebrated many New Year's: Rosh Hashanah (Jewish) in Pokhara, Divali (Indian) in Varanasi, and good old December 31st at Om Beach. It seemed fitting since everything felt new to me that year. I missed Losar (Tibetan) while in New Delhi, but I liked the spirit of Songkran.

The three of us rented bikes to ride on the hills around Chiang Mai. Kids on the side of the road soaked us with water guns and hoses. The splashing ambushes were refreshing as we pedaled uphill in the heat. Then Fran suggested that we join the battle. She stopped her bike at a roadside shop and bought a water gun. Liz and I followed suit and we became a mounted posse of happy warriors, firing back in the spirit of celebration.

The next morning, we packed up for an excursion to a famous cave that housed thousands of birds and bats. It wasn't my first choice, but I surrendered to the flow. When we met up with Fran, she was surprised to see my small bag and exclaimed, "We've converted you!" Well, not quite.

After our trek through the cave, we hiked a couple of miles to a riverside at the foot of a guesthouse that looked like the Ewok village in *Return of the Jedi*. The rooms were treehouses connected by wooden bridges. It looked awesome to me, but Liz and Fran wanted to sleep on the riverbank. They thought it seemed inviting, but it was getting dark and I didn't like the idea because I didn't know the local wildlife—animal or human. Besides, the Ewok guesthouse probably cost only two or three dollars, and it was so close that we could hear voices coming from its bar.

Feeling like Liz and Fran were being irresponsible, I declared that I would get a room at the lodge and they could come if they wanted. Liz called my bluff and said that she was going to stay on the riverbank. I was disappointed but kept quiet since it was Fran's last night with us.

I took a few steps uphill, but I began to worry that something might happen to them. I felt compelled to protect them from their own naïveté, so I stopped and turned back. I had nothing to sleep on and neither did they. They wanted to simply lie in the dirt with their heads on their backpacks as they had in Goa months earlier. I sat against a tree, an indecisive Arjuna, grumpy about my predicament and unable to act.

Then the gods intervened on my behalf—it started to rain. Not the heavy, transitional kind, just a light-enough sprinkle to make it unpleasant to sleep outside. I stood up and repeated my earlier declaration: "Okay, I'm going to the guesthouse."

Fran nodded at Liz, acknowledging that with Mother Nature now on my side, the balance of power had shifted. I turned uphill and heard their footsteps on the leaves behind me. I suggested that they wait in the bar while I inquired about rooms. To avoid any further debate, I booked and paid for a room with two beds, a double and a single.

The next morning, the three of us walked a few miles with our packs on to a bamboo café on stilts above a river. As we sat on a platform waiting for our food, I told Liz and Fran that I wanted to cut my hair. It had been growing for eight months, and it was getting unwieldy and hot. In support, they volunteered to cut it.

I put Jimi Hendrix's *Axis: Bold as Love* on my speakers, handed Liz my Swiss army knife, and she began trimming with the tiny scissors. There was a lot of hair and not a lot of blade, so after a while, her hands started

to hurt. Fran finished things off and by the end, I had short hair with a bundle of curls on the top.

Afterwards, I stripped down to my underwear and jumped in the river to rinse off. With my mane gone, I felt lighter and ready for a new adventure. The water was far too cold for either of the Californians to consider joining me, so Liz wrote in her journal and Fran filmed both of us with her video camera, commemorating our last day together.

Dripping dry in the morning sun, I sat on the riverbank next to Fran, who asked, "Will I be seeing you in California?"

"I'd like to, but sometimes I wonder…"—I looked over at Liz—"if we'll make it that far."

"What makes you say that?"

"She pushes me away."

"She's checking to see if you'll leave."

"She doesn't want me to?"

"I don't know much about relationships, but I *do* know that Liz thinks about you all the time when she's not with you. *And*, in all the time that I've known her, she's never let anyone get this close."

I appreciated Fran's kindness, friendship, and clarity. Then, as though looking down at me from a golden chariot, she said, "She wants to be with you. If you want that too, make it happen."

I got up off of the ground to put on my baggy uniform and prepare for battle. "Alright Fran. See you in California."

CHAPTER 44

Mae Hong Son: The Buddhist Spirit

Back in Chiang Mai, Fran headed for home in clothes wet from water guns, and Liz and I checked email. One of my friends had written, "Check out Pai. It is a cool town close to you." She added, "You must be enjoying the Thai people. They truly embody the Buddhist spirit."

She was right. If India was a "high-strung country," as Ramesh had described it, Thailand was "no strings attached." But what did Buddhism have to do with it? The Buddha told his students that he couldn't improve their lives. Their enlightenment could only be attained through good karma, perhaps over the course of multiple lifetimes.

In his first lecture, Buddha laid out Four Noble Truths. The first is commonly translated as life is suffering, *but because of how uninspiring that sounds, I prefer a different translation:* life is imperfect. *You can have a perfect day, but the next one probably won't be. Acceptance of this truth seemed to liberate the Thai people from expectation.*

I was feeling it, too. I was excited to be alone with Liz, but I knew that it wasn't going to be perfect. She and I boarded a bus near the Myanmar border to meet the Karen people, a refugee community that had fled from the country formerly known as Burma. The tribe was regularly featured in *National Geographic* for the brass rings that the women wear from collar to chin, earning them the nickname "longnecks." We wanted to hear the stories behind the photos. On the way to the camp, the bus stopped along the way and the passengers were offered Songkran blessings with water poured over their heads. Liz told me, "You have to do it. You're the waterlover."

"Waterlover?"

"I called you that in my journal when you were in the river after your haircut. You're so free in the water. Songkran is the perfect holiday for you."

It's true, because I tend to overheat physically and in temperament. In the humidity of Chiang Mai, I had showered multiple times a day to cool down. I accepted the blessing. Once we were back on the bus, a powerful rainstorm came on. I told Liz that, consistent with her theory, I liked the rain and especially a big downpour. I shared my description of a transitional rain: a suspended space signifying a new beginning. She asked what was changing this time. I smiled and reminded her, "We're finally alone."

Buddha's second noble truth teaches that suffering is caused by desire. Remaining detached from specific outcomes makes it easier to be content.

I observed this truth in the refugee camp, where we met a teenage trinket seller named Ma-where. Her neck was adorned in copper rings that stretched it upward and prevented her from moving her head to either side. Her family had fled to Thailand ten years earlier due to oppression in their homeland. The outside world beckoned in the accents she heard every day, but the tribal elders wouldn't permit her to travel farther than Mae Hong Son. The Karen women were a tourist attraction. Their appearance earned the tribe its living. Ma-where said she was happy though, and enjoyed her daily visitors. I was uplifted by her attitude, but still felt bad for her and the women in her tribe.

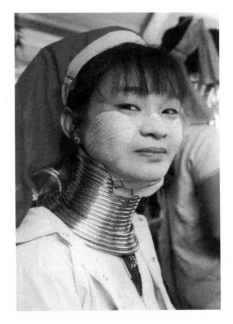

After the bus dropped us off in Mae Hong Son, we'd hitched a ride to the refugee camp with a friendly Thai couple. We saw them again on the way out and they offered us a ride back to town. Tao and his girlfriend, Yui spoke a little bit of English and I guessed that they were in their early twenties. They wore casual clothes and had matching white smiles.

Instead of dropping us at the bus station as I'd expected, Tao took us to a bustling market that reeked of fish. There he insisted on buying us lunch because we were their guests. After the meal, he bought a clear plastic bag of five large, live catfish. I couldn't imagine how long it would take Tao and Yui to eat them all. But then Tao drove to a field of rice paddies and parked. He carried the bag of fish to a stream that wound through the paddies. We all followed, but I remained confused until he knelt for a blessing on the riverbank. He opened the bag and put it in the water, letting the fish swim downstream. When I asked why he had let the fish go, he said, "For freedom. I believe in the next life."

The third noble truth is that suffering can be eliminated. *Before getting to how that's done, a Buddhist must believe that our imperfections and cravings can be transcended.*

I saw it in Tao's eyes when he released the fish. He believed that he was helping them move on toward their next lives and that, through selfless acts, he could too.

Tao and Yui invited us to their home, where we saw further evidence of their respect for all living things. Though the house was impeccably clean, ants crawled on the floor and spiderwebs decorated the bathroom. Because of karma, Tao and Yui wouldn't displace the insects. As Yui cooked dinner with Tao's help, it began to rain and they insisted that we spend the night. While the storm's sounds filled the house, we shared a vegetarian meal. I told Tao that it made me sad to meet the refugees and I asked what he thought about them. He replied, "This life is hard for them, but they can have a better next life."

The fourth noble truth, the path to eliminate suffering, *is where the Buddha's inaugural lecture turns practical—with an Eightfold Path to enlightenment. Similar to yoga's yamas and niyamas, the Eightfold Path guides people toward higher states of consciousness through self-purification. Steps on the path include speaking kindly, acting nobly, and performing good deeds. Once those steps are mastered, one may focus on controlling the mind and concentrating on the key to eliminating suffering. That key, as the Dalai Lama teaches, is having the wisdom to understand that nothing exists independently. We are all interconnected: people of different cultures, even animals and insects. The same life force flows through us all. We work toward nirvana when we support each other.*

After cleaning up from dinner, Tao knelt in front of his altar. He lit sandalwood incense at the feet of a Buddha statue and chanted prayers. Rushes of rain pounded the street and it felt like the house might float away, but Tao's ritual was calming. I listened from a cushion on the floor while Liz fell asleep with her head on my lap, and I ran my fingers through her hair. Tao and Yui had offered us their room, while they slept on couches. When we went to sleep in our hosts' bed, I could truly *feel* the Buddhist spirit.

We left Mae Hong Son in the post-rainstorm petrichor. We thanked our hosts and boarded a bus headed toward Pai, the town my friend had recommended. En route, Liz said that she wanted to keep going to Chiang Mai. She thought that Pai was going to have too many "White people." She wanted to get to Laos sooner because it was more remote.

I thought that Pai sounded lovely. As we each lobbied for our positions, Liz suggested that we might want to spend a few days apart and meet up in Laos. I couldn't believe it. We were finally alone together and she wanted to split up just because she wanted to get away from other travelers like us? I told her that I was hurt that she'd suggest it, but she remained resistant. Finally, I said, "I don't care about Pai. I care about us." Capitulating to her wishes, I paid the bus driver for an extension to Chiang Mai.

I had resisted the urge to fight and instead focused on what I could control, where I would go, and *how* I would react. I breathed deeply, put on headphones, and stared out the window. I didn't regret staying on the bus, but I felt like I was on one side of a fence that Liz was perched on top of, looking alternately from one side to the other.

Back in Chiang Mai, Liz ordered Thai iced tea with no straw from the same stand as before. I didn't say much at dinner because I was still upset, but Liz could tell and she thanked me for agreeing to move on. Afterward, we checked into the same motel we'd stayed in a few days earlier. She got into the shower and I sat on the bed, writing. Wondering how to move on from my frustration with Liz, I recalled how Tao's nighttime prayer had brought calm to his home under a pounding rainstorm. To bring a similar comfort to our space, I sought refuge where I always had—in music. I closed the blinds, turned off the lights, and set up my speakers.

In 1969, the Grateful Dead aimed to capture the spontaneity of their live shows on record. Their sound engineers commandeered one of the first 16-track tape recorders and then, in front of a hometown audience, the seven-piece band performed their most intricate but improvised songs. The result was one of the most revered live albums of all time—a timeless capsule of a sparkling musical moment. Naturally, they called it Live/Dead.

I queued up the CD and joined Liz in the shower. When I stepped in, she said, "Oh hi, Waterlover…" Her smile was calming and so was the water. I told her that I wanted to play some music for her after the shower and she agreed to listen.

Though it was night, the room was still hot. Liz suggested that we skip towels and let the warm air dry the water from our sun-toasted skin. She pulled back the top sheet and laid on the bed farthest from the window. I started the album on the CD player.

The opening sounds of Live/Dead *make it seem as though you've stepped into a performance already in progress. That's because you have—Jerry Garcia's guitar traces notes out of the last song and into the next. The bass, played by Phil Lesh, leads the group into* Dark Star. *The other instruments meander into the mix like familiar friends arriving at a party. Eventually, they synchronize and the sound is enveloping. The track is a jazz song by a rock band, but music writers called it psychedelic because it defies description.* Dark Star *is revered by fans of the Dead not because of how it sounds, but because of what it does. It's more of a transformational vehicle than a song. The band's former keyboardist, Tom Constanten, described it best: "*Dark Star *is going on all the time. It's going on right now. You don't begin it so much as enter it. You don't end it so much as leave it."*

Garcia's long introductory solo enveloped our hotel room and banished the vicissitudes of the day. I looked into Liz's eyes and knew that I'd made the right choice by staying on the bus. The song's lyrics punctuated the impermanence of the moment:

> "Shall we go, you and I while we can,
> through the transitive nightfall of diamonds?"
> - *Dark Star,* The Grateful Dead

Moonlight snuck through the blinds, brightening the droplets of water on our skin. Wrapped in sensation, the musical suite carried us away, together. We listened to the album multiple times, and somewhere between late night and early morning, Liz wrote a poem in her journal and read it to me.

Waterlover and Lunatic

Waterlover, envelop me.
   Tempt me,
      quench me,
drench me.
Waterlover,
   Trace the meandering stream of my bouldering body
   with your fingertips.
You are tide and I am Moon.
   Drawing to the source,
Weight of the sea lifts
   to bring you to my lunar breast.
   Dropping away,
Water of the sea flows
   away from my timid chest.
Tender Waterlover,
   So goes the cycle of moon and ocean.
      Gravity.

CHAPTER 45

Laos: Life Happens Now

Liz and I entered Laos by ferry across the Mekong River. Just after disembarking, I suddenly felt exhausted. It was only midday, but I asked Liz if I could rest in a hotel room. We could have made it to our next stop before nightfall, but I was unable to stay on my feet. After waking up from my nap, I was surprised to feel worse. My head was stinging in an unfamiliar way that was exacerbated by movement and my stomach was tight. Before going back to sleep, I ate a little and drank some water, but still felt terrible. I didn't know what was going on.

The next morning, we decided to push onward. We rode on benches facing each other in the back of a truck. That ride was perhaps the worst one of my life. My head felt like a lemon being squeezed, the pressure increasing with each bump in the road. My intestines were doing backflips. I drank water but couldn't eat. Liz held my hand and kept telling me that we would be there soon. When we finally arrived at our destination, Luang Nam Tha, I was a wreck. Liz escorted me to a tiny guesthouse room and I went straight to the toilet, where it felt like my guts were flushing out of me. From previous experience, I thought that I had severe traveler's diarrhea, but it had never caused such a pain in my head before. Sleep was my only respite from the agony.

Luang Nam Tha was a remote hub for nearby farms, with a main street and a few guesthouses and restaurants. The nearest hospital was far away and I couldn't bear the thought of moving. We had power only from 4:00 p.m. until the early morning. Liz brought me water, rehydration salts, and baguettes—a legacy of France controlling Laos in the first half of the twentieth century. Liz told me to eat one baguette per hour, along with water and rehydration salts, hoping that they would give me strength and digestive regularity. I didn't want to because going to the bathroom felt so awful, but Liz insisted and I obeyed.

For three days, I journeyed into a personal heart of darkness. I could hardly peel myself off the sweat-soaked bedsheets for each painful trip to the toilet. I felt too terrible to read, walk, or talk. At times, I was afraid I was going to die. At other times, I wished for it.

Liz was my solitary beacon of light. If we had been apart when my illness came on, I don't know how I would have made it through. She was caring and diligent, restocking supplies twice a day. She kept me company and calmed me to sleep.

By the fourth day, my sweats had subsided but I was still stuck in bed and my guts were a mess. Though Liz claimed to have no interest in becoming a doctor, the biology graduate had read the health chapter of my India guidebook before I'd passed it on. From memory, she thought that I might have had viral meningitis. It was a serious infection and could even be fatal, but I was already improving and we were doing the right things to treat it. She also found us a nicer guesthouse with a hammock on a porch facing a grassy courtyard—an upgrade from the concrete box we'd been in while I was sick. As we settled into our new place, I said to Liz, "I thought I was gonna die there..."

She told me, "The Tibetan Buddhists say that you should meditate on your own death seven times a day. It reduces fear and helps you to appreciate this human lifetime." She went back into the room, and I laid in the hammock and thought about death and John Lennon.

John Lennon was twenty-seven years old when the Beatles traveled to India. His marriage was on the rocks and his band had been shaken by the sudden death of their longtime manager. LSD had broadened Lennon's perspective and he wanted to sustain that newfound clarity through meditation. His song Across the Universe *includes the Hindu mantra "Jai guru deva om," meaning "glory to the divine guru." Perhaps he simply liked the sound of it,* but I think that perhaps Lennon believed he could find happiness in spiritual practice, if he had the right teacher.

Lennon's marriage didn't survive the Ganga and the Maharishi wasn't the right guru for him, so he drifted away from meditation and into drug addiction. Soon he married Yoko Ono, but fans and associates blamed his new wife for the Beatles' dissolution. Lennon retreated from public view and shared his perspective in a cynical manifesto called God, which begins with a provocation: "God is a concept by which we measure our pain." In God, Lennon denounces the sacred and the profane in such close proximity to one another as to offend almost everyone. Lennon doesn't believe in the Bible, Jesus, mantra, Gita, or yoga. He rejects his hero, Elvis Presley, and even the Beatles, believing only in himself and Ono, and concluding that "The dream is over." With so many fingers pointing at them, I can see how he could feel that way. John Lennon was rock music's libro abierto. The openness of his music reflected the range of feelings that we all have, as painful or shameful as they might be.

Approaching age thirty myself and feeling the magic of India fading, I also worried that the dream was over. My road to happiness had become unclear because I felt so terrible in Laos.

Then Liz came outside and said, "My head feels tight, like something is squeezing it."

"Oh, shit..." I said, knowing that she was about to embark on the same horror ride as I had. The diarrhea and sweating came on so quickly that Liz didn't even have a chance to show me where she had been buying the baguettes. Instead, she got into our new bed and drew me a map. Though I was still recovering, our roles flipped. I ordered her to eat one baguette per hour and take the rehydration salts. She resisted as I had, citing the pain as they passed through her body. I reminded her, "A wise young doctor told me that this will heal you." Those long, fresh rolls were our lifeline.

Luang Nam Tha was an unpleasant place to be stuck. Opium dealers with bloodshot eyes approached me every time I went out for baguettes or to check email. Other travelers were either just passing through or high on opium themselves. Liz and I were there for ten days before she felt well enough to leave the room. As we prepared to move on, we learned that locals were celebrating the coming of spring with a festival, so we rode bicycles to an open field to join in.

In the 1960s and 1970s, Laos was embroiled in the Vietnamese/American war. As soldiers and weapons traveled through the Laotian jungle, the country was decimated by millions of bombs and devastated by the casualties and resulting loss of farmland. Thirty years later, unexploded bombs still littered the landscape. For that reason, I was surprised to see that the spring festival was all about exploding rockets in the sky. We saw a toddler carrying a rocket and another boy riding on a giant one as men carried it to a launching pad. Smaller rockets launched frequently, exploding in bursts of smoke in the sky. I joined a circle of drunken drummers playing, and a group of Laotian women in colorful skirts called Liz over to dance.

It was more fun than we'd had in a week and a half, but the fiery scene was unnerving and we were the only tourists there. As the locals prepared the largest rocket for the grand finale, I asked Liz, "See any White people?" and she gave me a playful frown. It was an authentic experience, but maybe a bit *too* authentic for us. I tried not to worry about safety and just enjoy the atmosphere. The large rocket launched and exploded thirty feet

into the sky. Thankfully, none of the exploded parts landed on anyone. After more dancing and drumming, we rode our bikes back to town.

We left Luang Nam Tha the next morning and, after a few days of traveling and exploring, we floated in inner tubes down a river in Vang Vieng. It would be our last stop in Laos, having squandered most of our time being sick. Drifting in the cool water at sunset, we talked about how and when we might meet up again. Liz had about a week left on her trip and, after our shared illness, she felt essential to me. She wanted me to come to California and I was determined to try. No one could hear our conversation, but as we climbed out of the tubes at the end of the ride, another traveler looked at us and said, "You two met on this trip." Eric was American and his wife, Jill, happened to be from my hometown, Edmonton. We didn't know anyone in common, but it was special to hear her familiar accent. They were on an extended honeymoon, biking through multiple continents. Once it was over, Jill would move to Ohio so that they could live together. We told them that we'd been trying to figure out our next steps and Eric said, "You guys will be fine. You free-spirited Canadians don't have a problem moving away from home."

Later that night, we had big news in our email. Steve and Allie, the smiley surfers we had met on the Indian ski hill, were now engaged. We also heard from Nibodhi, our American swami buddy, who wrote that he and Laura were expecting a child. That announcement was surprising since they hadn't been together any longer than Liz and I had. We walked out of the internet café feeling like the earth had shifted a little. I said to Liz, "We were floating along on that river, planning our future, and these guys were making theirs. It's like John Lennon said, 'Life is what happens to you when you're busy making other plans.'"

On John Lennon's thirty-fifth birthday in 1975, he and Yoko Ono welcomed a baby boy they named Sean. Lennon sobered up, retreated from public life, and stayed at home. He wasn't writing or performing music—he cooked food and spent time with his son. The line I thought of that evening in Laos was written for Sean and appeared five years later on the Double Fantasy *album. Lennon's tone had changed. He was a believer again.*

> "Before you go to sleep, say a little prayer
> Every day, in every way, it's getting better and better"
> – *Beautiful Boy (Darling Boy),* John Lennon

It sounded like he was meditating, but I don't think that was it. Lennon's path wasn't the disciplined practice of ashtanga yoga—he had become a bhakti yogi. Turning inward couldn't have been easy for such a famous person, but he saw the divine in his son's innocence. That purity made him want to improve himself; stop with affairs, drinking, and drugs. His son allowed him to separate from the ambition and judgments of the world, the Maya. Lennon's break from fame allowed him to appreciate life, perhaps more than ever before.

Before Liz and I went to bed on our last night in Laos, she suggested that we meditate on the new being that Nibodhi and Laura were bringing into the world, the flip side of meditating on death. After a five-minute silent meditation, Liz asked, "What did you think about?"

"Life happens now."

John Lennon was shot and killed by a deranged stalker just two weeks after Double Fantasy was released. Many people died a bit that day—there were vigils around the world. Fans lost their working-class hero, the Beatles could never reunite, Yoko lost the love of her life, and Sean lost his dad. Though I became a fan after he was gone, it's hard for me to process the tragedy. My only solace comes in knowing that John Lennon died when his mind was right. He didn't crash a sports car or overdose in a bathtub. He was arriving home after a day with his family and an evening playing music. He'd been doing what he loved *with* the people he loved.

Meditating on death isn't pleasant, but I agree with the Tibetan Buddhists that it can be helpful, even when the reflection is on someone else's life and its end. When I think of John Lennon, I am reminded that, no matter how grumpy I might be on a particular day, I have to start with humility, sprinkle in some faith, and work hard at being a kind and compassionate person. The dream is *never* over and God is not just a concept by which to measure our pain.

The next morning, Liz and I rode bikes to a river that flowed into caves. We put on our bathing suits and explored the crystal blue water.

The sand-colored cave walls curved to form rooms with beams of sunlight shooting through cracks in the ceiling. We swam into a cave, floated, and held each other until the air chilled and we knew that it was time to go. Our time in Laos was ending a lot better than it had begun.

We biked to a restaurant and, after being dry for only a few minutes, a gushing rainstorm hit. Without telling me why, Liz walked across the road to a little store. She emerged with single-use packs of shampoo and conditioner and washed her hair on the street, in the rain. It was coming down so hard that she was able to rinse her long hair in it—twice. I was happy to stay dry in the restaurant, but I admired her spirit.

Life happens now.

CHAPTER 46

Koh Chang: A Gift

In the 1980s, my sister and I watched all of the family sitcoms on TV. We'd watch the old syndicated ones when we got home from school, take a break for homework and dinner, and then watch the new shows at night. One of the afternoon shows was about a dad with three boys and a mom with three girls. They got married and made one big happy family, *The Brady Bunch*. The matriarch declared that they were all brothers and sisters now—equals.

When Liz's mom remarried in 1977, she and her husband, Cyril, merged their families, *Brady Bunch* style. Susan had two girls from her first marriage and Cyril had two boys. The couple started over in a house near the ocean where the girls shared a room with a bunkbed and so did the boys. Life was as optimistic as the Southern California sitcom.

The couple wanted to have a child together, but a doctor said that it wasn't possible, so they gave up on the idea. Already busy with two jobs and four energetic kids, it was a delightful surprise in 1979 when Susan became pregnant—with a miracle baby.

They were going to need more space, so the couple found a new house in the Brentwood hills of Los Angeles. It had a view of the ocean, seven bedrooms, and a pool in the backyard. The house's price tag kept Cyril up at night, but they scraped together enough to buy it. Liz was born on Yom Kippur, the holiest day of the Jewish year. The parents brought their little angel to a house full of moving boxes where her four older siblings took turns holding the baby.

By the time Lizzie was a year old, they were already calling her precocious. She talked nonstop and showed signs of her father's intellect and her mother's compassion. She was adorable and loved, but times were hard. When both parents were at work, her sister Julie had to hitch rides home from middle school. Her brothers brawled with each other and her parents shouted at each other about what to do. As the only child of the five living with both of her parents, Liz grew up feeling guilty for her relative privilege.

When Liz was still little, her brothers were expelled from the house because of their violence, but also because they had somewhere else to go, their mom's place. Apparently, being there was no sitcom either. As a result, Liz grew up feeling like she didn't *deserve* anything. She had survivor's guilt before she was even old enough to make decisions.

Liz's journey to Asia was a long walk away from her past. Her diminishing bank account and half-empty backpack were signs of a purge. She and Fran were like wandering ascetics, experiencing enough suffering to bring them closer to their families' pain, closer to the poor young Indian mothers they worked with in Tamil Nadu, closer to God.

I think Liz's background was at least part of the reason why she found it hard to give herself things like nice lodgings, new clothes, or a two-dollar tofu lunch at a fancy restaurant in a bright hotel lobby as we traveled from Laos back to Bangkok: She couldn't bear to dine in luxury in a country with so much poverty. Even though vegetarian dishes were hard to find in meat-hungry Laos and we needed protein to get our strength back, Liz took one look at the crystal chandelier in the lobby and turned around. I tried to persuade her, but she fled the sparkling hotel, refusing to even let me buy her lunch. Instead, she bought another baguette. As we ate the bread on a curb across the road from the fancy hotel, I told Liz that I accepted her, I was happy to be with her, and I loved her.

Liz didn't feel that she deserved my love any more than she deserved that two-dollar tofu. For her, love stories were safer on paper—she could experience desire through poetry without dealing with any real heartbreak. She had love poems memorized or written down, and began transcribing them onto handmade Thai paper with leaves woven into it. They would be a wedding gift for her sister. She planned to put one on each table at the reception.

> "The minute I heard my first love story,
> I started looking for you, not knowing
> How blind that was.
> Lovers don't finally meet somewhere.
> They're in each other all along."
> – Rumi

We had four more days together—just enough time to visit Angkor Wat in Cambodia. We spent two days among the ruins of the Khmer empire, which reigned in present-day Cambodia for around six hundred years until the fifteenth century. The Khmers built their capital at Angkor, a lush jungle region with fertile land for farming. At its peak, the city had hundreds of thousands of residents and they built temples for their kings. When the empire fell, the temples were overtaken by the jungle and abandoned until they were rediscovered in the early 1900s. Liz and I explored by bicycle and marveled at the architecture. Though many areas had been restored, some were left as they had been found a hundred years earlier, with trees growing on top of temples and roots changing direction around reliefs of Buddha and other deities.

After Cambodia, we returned to Thailand and an island called Koh Chang. Raindrops dove into the ocean as we sat in a thatched hut on a wooden pier. While working on the gift for her sister, Liz said to me, "There's lots of paper. You should make some for *your* sister." I didn't have a gift planned for her wedding and felt that she would appreciate something creative, so I started transcribing. The immersion in love poetry kept us warm on the cold, rainy, island days. At one point, Liz sat back from writing and asked me how many women I'd been with. "Enough," I said. When she complained that that answer was a dodge, I said, "It's true, though. Now that I've found you, I don't need to be with anyone else."

"What if it doesn't work out for us?"

"I'll be sad...and then I'll have to move on." To break the tension, I grabbed Liz by the shoulders and added, "But that's never gonna happen!"

She smiled and asked, "Do you want to come to my sister's wedding with me?"

I already had a ticket home in time for *my* sister's wedding a month later. "Wow, I appreciate the invitation. It would be cool to meet your whole family, but when I come to California, it's going to be a little later and on a one-way ticket."

Liz was impressed with my confidence, which I think helped her to believe that her love story wasn't ending on that Thai island in the rain.

I held her hand a bit tighter on the mainland bus through rice-paddy countryside toward Bangkok, knowing she was leaving the next day. Writing about love, falling in love, and being in love, I felt like I was soaring. Those final days together felt like a celebration.

Liz said to me, "It's like, *swoosh*."

"*Swoosh*?"

"You know, in basketball. When you get a basket, and it goes *swoosh* through the net?" She explained that in Kochin, we kept missing each other and it felt like the shots were falling short. Then, on our Himalayan honeymoon, the shots were going over the backboard. Lizzie was a character in a snowbound love story and expected the credits to roll after a magical kiss. "But now it's *swoosh*," she said. "I feel connected with you and grounded. It feels right."

We returned to the Shanti Lodge in Bangkok, where we had stored our extra things. It was raining, so we lit a candle by the bedside and stayed up late in the green-walled guesthouse room and talked. When we tried to sleep, I laid in bed wondering, "Where will we lay side by side again?"

Liz couldn't sleep either. I asked her, "Any advice for my last three weeks?"

"Find that balance that you had before you met me."

In the early-morning darkness, I wondered if I had surrendered a part of myself to be with Liz. I didn't think so. The parts of me that were changing were the ones that I wanted to change. I couldn't think of anything more beneficial than to be able to grow along with someone who understood and supported me.

I must have slept at some point because I awoke to Liz packing up her bag. Rain pounded the street as I walked her to the guesthouse door, where an awning shielded me from the deluge. Liz told me, "Don't get wet. Go back to bed." I squeezed her tight and we kissed.

Then I looked her in the eye and said, "I'll see you soon."

Back in bed a moment later, the room suddenly felt huge, empty, and quiet. The candle had burned to the bottom. I wondered what I could hold onto and then noticed an earring that Liz had left behind. It had blue beads dangling between a crescent moon and a star. I clutched it and closed my eyes. I recalled the sight of her on the street, flashing a smile in the transitional rain before getting into the taxi. This time, she truly was a memory. I cradled the earring in my palm and cried. I didn't know when I would see her again, but she was still with me. In a way, we were already a part of each other. It didn't feel like surrender *or* attachment. It was a gift: I gave you me and you gave me you.

CHAPTER 47

Chiang Mai: Solo

Three weeks in Thailand sounds like a luxury vacation, but when Liz left, I realized that I hadn't devoted any thought to the rest of my trip. That day, I ventured through the rain for one of Thailand's famous massages. Unlike in Kerala, where I laid naked under a towel before getting oiled up, Thai massage was a fully clothed acrobatic adventure. I rested on a raised mattress surrounded by curtains and a small Thai woman introduced herself by walking on my back in her bare feet. It felt amazing. She pressed her full weight into the strained backpack-carrying muscles of my shoulders and then swung my arms back as she pulled me into a deep backbend. Then she had me arching in the air with her knees while balancing me by my bottom. She was doing the yoga for me.

The experience oscillated between relaxing and terrifying. Still, I came out of it feeling more limber, and that feeling made me curious about the technique. I recalled seeing Thai massage schools in Chiang Mai and thought that classes might be good for my time alone. It was raining everywhere in the country, so a beach trip didn't make much sense. I pulled my tabla out of storage and bought a bus ticket back north to Chiang Mai.

I checked into the same motel where Liz and I had shared the transitive nightfall of diamonds, but this time, the most special thing about the room was the toilet paper folded into a triangle. During a break from the rain, I went out to get a Thai iced tea. The vendor asked me where the "no straw" girl was. I tried to imagine Liz at home, getting all dressed up for a wedding.

Walking through town afterward, I discovered a Thai massage school with a tidy lobby and promotional materials in English. The young man at the counter suggested that I have a massage before deciding if I wanted to sign up for their four-day course. I thought that was a great idea. The small, muscular Thai masseur had short hair, wore a snug white shirt and loose cotton pants, and smelled like fresh herbal tea. He rested a strong but soft hand on my back as he led me to a mattress on the floor.

It was less stressful than my last massage, because his manipulations felt more deliberate. He kneaded my muscles like dough and twisted my legs and arms in every direction, plucking the nerves as he traveled through each area. It was painful at first, but I could feel the nerves relaxing after the shock subsided. He concluded the session with heated herbal packs that filled the room with a delicious aroma.

When we were done, I asked about plucking the nerves. He explained that our nerves carry even more tension than our muscles, but that most massage styles avoid the nerves because stretching them is uncomfortable. At their school, called Nerve Touch, they worked both the nerves and the muscles in order to allow energy to flow freely through the body.

"Like yoga," I said.

He nodded and pointed to a portrait atop an altar on the wall. The man in the print was a thin swami with a trimmed beard wearing a light robe and a necklace of prayer beads. The swami sat board straight with his legs crossed.

His name was Chivaka Komarpaj and he lived near Varanasi around 450 BCE. Komarpaj was a medical doctor, yogi, and an expert on herbal remedies, diet, and mysticism. He is also known as the father of Thai massage. Komarpaj was a renaissance man before the Renaissance. Legend has it that he was born as the illegitimate son of a courtesan and abandoned in a pile of trash before being adopted by a prince. When Komarpaj was old enough, his adopted father told him of his origins. The story moved him to devote his life to nurturing and healing others. He became a prodigy in the medical sciences and served kings and princes, but his most famous patient was Siddhartha Gautama, the Buddha. Komarpaj became Buddha's friend and disciple. When Buddha needed a bandage or a remedy, he turned to Komarpaj. When Buddha became ill before passing away, Komarpaj attended to him.

After Buddha's death, Komarpaj left India to share his knowledge. He traveled to what is now Thailand and influenced the country enormously with two gifts: Buddhism and massage. The style of massage that Komarpaj taught was an active mind-body exercise that became a meditation for the giver and the receiver. He and his traveling group of Buddhist monks would massage each other and attain spiritual benefit in the process. The practice caught on, merged with traditional Chinese medicine, and Thai massage was born.

This history explained why Thai massages felt like a guided yoga class. Once I was able to trust the masseur, it could be a meditative experience. With training, I could use it to benefit others. I signed up for the course that was beginning the next day. The class was a small group, and after a couple of days, I started to feel comfortable with the technique. The students practiced on each other, so I was getting massaged all day.

Another benefit of the course was that it allowed me to fill every hour with activities and not notice the emptiness of my motel room. I started my days with yoga, went to massage class until the early afternoon, studied my massage textbook, practiced tabla, and wrote.

I wondered if my regimen was bringing balance or simply distracting me from my lack of it. I wanted to believe that, since I wasn't seeking a partner, I could be happy alone. I wasn't convinced, though, because I thought about Liz all of the time. Our relationship had deepened in our time together and I missed her more than I had before—it felt like a part of me was missing. The rain made it harder because I was stuck indoors most of the time. It was not transitional rain, it was *same* rain. The same rain every day, draining the sunshine away.

Thankfully, I made a friend, a Chinese Canadian fellow around my age named Bryan. He hung around the motel when it rained and rode a motorbike in the hills around Chiang Mai when it was dry. One day, he asked, "Want to see the new *Star Wars* movie tonight?" I'm a big fan of *Star Wars*, so I was surprised that I didn't know that *Episode II* was out in theatres. *Star Wars* films were the first movies that I saw in a theatre. When I was five, my dad took me to see a double feature of *Star Wars* and *The Empire Strikes Back*. Those were pivotal hours in my young life. From then on, all I wanted for my birthday were *Star Wars* ships and action figures. I played with them in my basement, content in a universe where magic existed and the struggle between good and evil was clear.

By the time I was an adult, I had seen the original trilogy enough times to have every line memorized. When the movies were rereleased in the 1990s, I saw each one on opening night. I also waited in line to see a midnight showing of *Episode I* when it came out. I was excited to see the next episode, but this wasn't *my* Star Wars anymore. Young Obi-Wan Kenobi and his doomed-to-darkness prodigy, Anakin Skywalker, were just characters in a movie, not the role models that Luke Skywalker, Princess Leia, and Han Solo had been in my childhood.

I didn't identify as much with Luke, the hero whose very name—Skywalker—implies ascension. I related more to the character with the name that suggested that being alone was his natural state. Han Solo was worldly and cynical. He believed in what he could see, calling the force a "hokey religion" that was no match for a blaster at your side.

Solo kept busy and pretended not to care about anyone but himself. At first, Princess Leia took Han at his word, but over time she saw that he actually did care, a lot. He wouldn't reveal it, though. The last thing Solo wanted was to be vulnerable, which may be why I relate the most to his character. As I grew up, my parents always gave me space and told me to ask for help if I needed it. I usually didn't.

Han Solo acted fearless when he was frightened, and aloof when he became involved. He pretended to not need other people, but he was also the one character who always had a loyal friend, Chewbacca, by his side. The others could call Han a "scruffy nerf-herder" or General Solo, but he didn't care. What mattered to Solo were his relationships. He didn't fight for the Rebel Alliance as much as for his friends and the woman he loved.

Like Han Solo, I was learning that my destiny wasn't in a life of solitude. It took me a while to trust people, but that's because I *really* wanted to trust them. I wanted to be surrounded by a circle of support, and I worried that I might not have that support if I moved to another country. I only hoped that if I was with Liz, I would start with a strong foundation.

The day after seeing the movie, I heard from Liz. She had made it home after a week in Japan, but things were tough. As soon as she put her bag down, her mom had loaded her back into the car with the family's geriatric dog. He was hardly moving anymore, but unbeknownst to Liz, her parents had kept him alive all year so that Liz could say goodbye to her childhood pup. They drove to a veterinarian's office that afternoon to put the dog to sleep. Before shaking off jet lag or even sleeping, Liz found herself sitting on a curb outside the vet's office crying into her hands. She wrote to me, "Savor your trip, because it really ends."

It sounded like a miserable way to return home. She was also having a hard time with her family. In her time away, they had become even more entrenched in their positions. Her parents and brothers still weren't talking to each other, and she felt stuck between immovable objects. The next family gathering at her sister's wedding weighed on her mind.

While I considered how to savor my time in Thailand, Liz was facing the reality of her troubled family. The princess didn't need saving, but she did need support. I wrote this poem and sent it to Liz:

> *Liz hurt hits Mark heart.*
> *In an instant, I feel,*
> *not what you feel, but for it.*
> *I don't know how to help,*
> *But you, already wise,*
> *are growing every day.*
>
> *Still, it's harder,*
> *more real,*
> *more now.*
> *I know.*
> *You knew,*
> *it wouldn't be easy.*

CHAPTER 48

Koh Phangan and Koh Tao: Enjoy Being

Endless travel sounds romantic, but it wasn't for me. It was hard to find purpose while on the move. As the rain subsided along with my massage course, the motel courtyard filled with loud travelers. Overhearing them discuss the best bars and largest golden Buddhas in Thailand, I wasn't in any mood to introduce myself. Only half-jokingly, I muttered, "White people…"

Bryan had left to attend a famous Full Moon island party and he invited me to join him. Every lunar month, revelers gather on Koh Phangan and dance to electronic music on the beach. As I boarded the ferry, I wondered if I was making my best choice or only doing what travelers are *supposed* to do. Those doubts were magnified when I signed in on a clipboard: Mark Halpert, Canada, 27. The list was filled with the ages 21, 22, 19, and 20. As sunscreen smells and bikini-clad bodies filled the boat, I wondered if I was getting too old for an all-night dance party. I had danced at a hundred and twenty beats per minute plenty of times, but it was always with chemical assistance. Lacking that kind of fuel, could I still enjoy being there?

The question reminded me of the bumper stickers that say "Enjoy Being." I liked the message, but I had an ethical issue with it—yes, an ethical issue with a bumper sticker. Observing the privileged few who filled the ferry, I thought that "Enjoy Being" wasn't the best mantra for young people. But what would be a better message for "light workers" to spread? I recalled my Tibetan monk friend, Kunchok, saying, "It doesn't matter if you are a monk, nun, married, or single, just as long as you are helping."

"Helping what?" I had asked. His response might have made a better bumper sticker.

"Helping all sentient beings to be happy."

As backpackers cracked open breakfast beers on the boat, I recalled the phrase "third-world wonderland" that Liz had heard in Hampi. I think it bothered her at the time because it made her question her own intentions. The same thing was happening to me. I looked at the plastic water bottles strewn across the ferry floor and wondered if our group would create more garbage than happiness. Our trash would add to Thailand's gross domestic product, but that seemed like a poor way to measure success. Was our indulgence helping all sentient beings to be happy?

When Bryan and I went to see *Star Wars, Episode II: Attack of the Clones*, I'd noticed spiritual teachings hidden in the movie. It wasn't just that Yoda's name sounded like yoga and the character Padme was named for the lotus flower, a Buddhist symbol of creation. Philosophy appeared throughout the dialogue, and the Jedis, the warrior monks of the series, sounded particularly familiar.

In the film, Padme says to Anakin, a young Jedi, "I thought Jedis weren't allowed to love."

He replies, "Attachment is forbidden. Possession is forbidden. Compassion, which I would define as universal love, is essential to a Jedi's life. So, in fact, you could say that we're encouraged to love."

The young monk wanted the girl more than he wanted a spiritual life, but more significantly, George Lucas was using his billion-dollar franchise to secretly teach Buddhism.

When George Lucas was twenty-seven years old and writing his "space opera," he discovered a book called The Hero with a Thousand Faces *by the mythologist Joseph Campbell. Campbell's book analyzes the commonalities among myths around the world. He describes the Hero's Journey as a tale that can be told and retold in different forms and still remain relevant.*

Star Wars *is popular for the characters, special effects, and music, but one reason that it resonates with so many people is the universality of its messages. Though the story occurs "a long time ago in a galaxy far, far away," the myth is timeless. When Campbell watched the films, he said that Lucas had "put the newest and most powerful spin" upon the classic story of the hero.*

We all want to ascend. Figuring out how is often the hardest part.

When Bryan and I arrived at the Full Moon party, the sun was setting while the moon rose. Four large stages faced the open ocean and bodies boogied to a buffet of beats. The music mingled with rolling waves, fresh air, and cool sand to form a blissful sensory blast. Being sober and not knowing anyone other than Bryan, I didn't dance much and felt more like an observer, watching a timeless ritual. Barefoot in the sand under the full moon, devotees shared a peak experience. It would end for some with their arms around a stranger or a toilet bowl, but it still held greater spiritual potential than the religious traditions that our generation had rejected.

Joseph Campbell also observed, "People say that what we're all seeking is a meaning for life. I don't think that's what we're really seeking. I think that what we're seeking is an experience of being alive, so that our life experiences on the purely physical plane will have resonances within our innermost being and reality, so that we actually feel the rapture of being alive."

When asked how to achieve the "rapture of being alive," Campbell distilled his advice to "Follow Your Bliss," which is pretty close to "Enjoy Being," and just as easy to misconstrue as frivolous. Both aphorisms remind us to find what we love and spend time doing that. By doing what we enjoy the most, we discover who we are and that's what makes being yourself okay. I'd wondered if I could love myself as much as I was loving Liz. Alone again without her, I wanted to know the answer before my trip ended.

After the party, I said goodbye to Bryan and went to an island called Koh Tao to reflect on my journey before going home. With the tabla back in storage, I carried a traditional Thai long drum over my shoulder as I walked off the ferry. I tapped the drum in beat with my footsteps and some locals smiled as I bobbed past them. Like Hampi, Koh Tao had boulders seemingly sprinkled by giant-handed gods, though on this island they were sand-colored.

Rounding the top of a hill, I saw a head bouncing to the patterns that I was playing on the drum. As I approached, I saw that it was a Thai man with dreadlocks sitting in front of an outdoor shop made of bamboo. The shop sold jewelry, drums, and tapestries mostly in the red, yellow, and green of Jamaican Rastafarians.

The Thai Rasta called to me, "Marching to the beat of your own drum!"

"You, too, it seems…" His style was familiar to me but rare in Thailand.

"You want a drum?"

I stopped walking to have a look at his djembes. When I told him that I already had one at home and that I'd be going back soon, he said, "You are a musician."

"No. I just like to drum."

"You're a musician, man. You've got the rhythm."

Despite all of my hours of tabla practice, I hadn't thought of myself as a musician until he said it. We jammed together for a while and I asked if he knew of a good place to stay. He directed me to a lodge overlooking the ocean. I wound my way around rocks and up a hill to a hut among trees and boulders. On the way up, I noticed a flyer stapled to a palm tree advertising yoga classes. After checking into the lodge, I followed the yoga signs downhill to a beachfront bar. The bartender introduced me to the yoga teacher, a tall, brown-haired Irishman named Chris. He taught ashtanga yoga every morning and asked how long I'd been practicing. I counted on my fingers. "About five months."

It had become hard to imagine not doing at least a little bit of yoga every day. Then Chris told me, "We're going snorkeling tomorrow if you want to come. Oh, and check out the yoga platform." He pointed in the direction of my cliffside hut. I climbed up the hill and found a concrete floor surrounded by palm trees and almost as big as a tennis court. It had a half-wall with a handpainted, multicolor mural. As I approached the floor, I saw the familiar image of Shiva, with his bare chest and dreadlocks, sitting cross-legged and gazing at me. I paused for a moment. I'd been on Koh Tao less than an hour and I'd already played music and found a yoga class. I was thrilled to be there, but Shiva reminded me that I had only three days left in Thailand before everything would change again. I walked away thinking, "Okay, okay, I won't get too comfortable."

When I checked email, I was excited to see my first message from Liz in a while. Her sister's wedding was a lovely experience and her family had been civil with each other. She'd enrolled in summer school at her alma mater in Berkeley. The classes were prerequisites for medical school. Once those were done, she would study for the Medical School Admissions Test. I laughed to myself, remembering her denials of an interest in medicine. Being home had focused Liz's mind on her future. She asked if I'd be coming to the San Francisco Bay area to look for a job before the end of the summer. She wanted to concentrate on her studies until August, but was encouraging me to come after that. She concluded with, "You should enjoy your time in Thailand. Don't feel rushed to make any decisions."

I wrote back and told Liz that I *did* want to look for a job in San Francisco—something that would help "all sentient beings to be happy"—but I wasn't sure when I could get to California. I would need to make some money at home first, in case my search took a while.

My mom had emailed, too. In response to quotes I'd been sharing in group messages, she'd asked, "Are you a Buddhist now?" I didn't answer right away, but back at my cliffside hut, I thought about how to respond. I had left home an atheist and become a believer. A believer in *what*, though? The yogis taught me about Atman and Brahman. I'd always found nature's beauty to be divine. If Brahman resided in nature, I could accept it as holy. I wasn't a Hindu, but each time I saw Shiva, it reminded me of how I'd felt in Varanasi: of being stripped to my emotional core, alone in the world and desperate for something to hold onto. Something about Shiva's calm gaze while a snake slithered around his neck brought me to the realization that the "I" behind all of this isn't a person at all, it's a spirit that is a part of everything: Atman is Brahman and Brahman is Atman. The realization made me feel that I would never be alone. It wasn't something I could prove, but somehow, in India, I had *experienced* it. George Harrison wrote about this feeling in one of his songs:

> "When you've seen beyond yourself
> Then you may find peace of mind is waiting there
> And the time will come when you see we're all one
> And life flows on within you and without you"
> – *Within You Without You*, The Beatles

I gazed out at the ocean with my journal on my lap. The wind chimes were still and so was I. I hadn't figured out how to tell my mom if I was a Buddhist or not, but I decided that I'd start with no and try to explain myself later.

Chris's ashtanga yoga class was a different style than I was used to, but I enjoyed the combination of movement and stillness. I felt great as I walked back to my hut. When I got there, a Canadian woman visited from next door. She asked a question—"Sorry, but do you have any weed?"—that prompted another, deeper question.

My answer was no, but behind it was, "Did I *want to* have any weed?" The combined yes and no responses were new to me. I hadn't smoked since arriving in Thailand and a puff would surely complement the island sunsets, but part of me knew better. If I had a puff, I'd focus more on the next one than on what I was trying to figure out, and I was running out of time.

That afternoon, I boarded a wooden boat with Chris, his girlfriend, and some other travelers to go snorkeling. It was a pleasant and relaxing time. Two pretty Frenchwomen on board asked me to put sunscreen on their backs, and I complied. It wasn't until after they said goodbye with kisses on both of my cheeks that I realized that they could have asked each other.

I smelled of salt water as I followed a dirt path to the top of a hill, where I sat on a rounded rock to write. I considered the deeper question hidden in the soft skin of the Frenchwomen: Did I *want to* pursue their beauty, or simply appreciate it? They were attractive and friendly, but my connection with Liz was far too special to mess up. If one of the women *was* interested in me, I would sublimate my desire—for my own good.

As I finished writing that entry, a voice said, "Allo?" I looked down from the rock to see the two Frenchwomen, still radiant in their bikinis. One of them said to me, "Do you 'ave your camera? Dis would be a *great* picture." I *did* have my camera and I had just taken a photo of the view, but she was talking about *me*. She wanted me to remember *that* spot in *that* moment.

When I look at the photo now, of course I look younger and thinner, but there's something else as well: I look like I'm glowing. My shirt billows like a sail in the wind and my crossed legs form as stable a foundation as the ancient stone I'm sitting on. Smiling out at the view, I seem as light as the clouds. It *was* a moment worth capturing. I was comfortable on my own and didn't feel compelled to *be* anywhere else or *doing* anything else. In that moment, I *was* loving myself. I loved who I was becoming and I was able to *enjoy being*.

CHAPTER 49

Canada: Man of Honor

"Friends and relatives welcome with joy a loved one,
Returning from abroad after a long absence.
In exactly the same way will the fruits of right action
Welcome the doer as he travels from one life to the next."

– *The Dhamappada*

I had never heard of a "Man of Honor" until my sister Kara emailed me while I was in India and asked me to take on that role at her wedding. She had many close friends, but chose me. Instead of a Maid of Honor, she wanted her brother by her side at the ceremony. I was touched. I wanted to do all that I could to support her, even as I was getting reoriented to being back.

When I arrived in Edmonton, my hometown felt quiet and spacious. After all that I'd seen and done, it was so *normal* that it seemed strange. Our two-story house felt huge, and bunnies ran across the front lawn. My old bedroom had a single bed and the few posters that I didn't take with me to college a decade earlier. Out of habit, I continued to live out of my backpack.

My parents were relieved to have me home. Giving their daughter away in marriage had become real, and their reaction was to try to control the wedding itself. Problem was, their little girl wasn't so little anymore.

She was thirty years old and she and her fiancé knew what kind of an event they wanted to have. Coming from different religious backgrounds that neither felt connected to, Kara and Paul decided to eschew priests and rabbis and have a civil ceremony. My parents had expected something traditional and voiced their objections at a high volume.

As my mom and I drove to Vancouver in advance of the wedding, she lamented Kara not using a rabbi and my "becoming Buddhist" as two sides of the same betrayal.

Driving through the Rocky Mountains, I said, "Just because Kara doesn't want to have a Jewish wedding doesn't mean that she's rejecting our family. She and Paul are starting their own family, the way they want it to be."

My mom remained unconvinced and also wasn't keen on my going to California. When she asked, "Can't you just be *here* for a while?" I told her that it was important for me to follow my heart. In Vancouver, my sister and I stayed up late talking about wedding preparations and my year away. During the day, I returned to my yoga and tabla routines. Paul and his best friends were preparing songs to perform at the wedding, and he invited me to join them on tabla. The guys were hilarious. Paul was focused on everyone getting their parts just right and they teased him relentlessly.

Kara had numerous bachelorette parties and I jokingly complained that as the *Man* of Honor, I wasn't invited to any of them. The truth was that I was much happier at the groom's jam sessions. The final one was before the wedding rehearsal. Friends and extended family were rolling into town and excitement was in the air. The ceremony would be held on the lawn of a mansion facing the coastal mountains and the ocean. The forecast indicated perfect weather.

It was fun to see so many familiar faces after my time away. I left the rehearsal dinner happy that the pre-wedding debates were over and everyone was celebrating, but that happiness was dashed as soon as we arrived at the car. The trunk was wide open and empty. While we were at dinner, someone had broken in and stolen my tabla as well as Paul's friend Kevin's guitar. Also gone was my journal, which contained the speech I planned to give the next day.

I was angry. After being robbed multiple times in India, it was somehow more insulting for it to happen back home; I had to face my newest test with *everyone* around. I'd played that tabla on so many rooftops, porches, and beaches. I'd carried it through Indian snow, rain, and traffic. I *was* attached to it. Imagining a Canadian thief trying to garner a few dollars for it made me mad. Kevin spent some time in the following days scouring pawn shops for his guitar and with an eye out for my tabla, but to no avail.

That night, I stayed up in Kara and Paul's guest room, rewriting my speech from memory. I wanted to give my best to my sister on her big day and not let it be about me. To do that, I needed to process my feelings privately and quickly. I told myself that no thief could take away the music that I'd learned from Keshav in Varanasi—it was already a part of me. I could find another tabla, but by tomorrow's sunrise I needed to move on from the loss of my biggest material attachment to India. As Man of Honor, I needed to be supportive, not sulking.

> "Whoever controls his anger
> Is like a true charioteer,
> In command of the rolling chariot
> And not just holding on the reins."
> – *The Dhammapada*

As usual, I had more than one drum with me. I'd brought along my djembe, which could easily reach a hundred sets of ears. I told Paul that I still wanted to play and that I was confident I could keep the beat on the djembe even though I'd practiced on the tabla.

The wedding was wonderful. My sister sparkled under blue sky framed by the mountains and the sea. I placed the passages of love poetry on the tables and delivered a speech befitting a little brother: loving and mischievous. By the time the groom's party belted out *When I'm Sixty-Four*, my parents were too charmed by the whole experience to care that the wedding was officiated by a justice of the peace. While they had argued with Kara about ancestral traditions, they hadn't realized that she and Paul were planning something meaningful *and* spiritual. They were happy for

their daughter, enchanted by the gorgeous natural setting, and uplifted by music that everyone could relate to:

> "Will you still need me, will you still feed me, when I'm sixty-four?"
> – *When I'm Sixty-Four,* The Beatles

When it was all over and the newlyweds had left for their honeymoon, my dad had a proposition for me: A client of his back in Edmonton needed help. "Their controller left abruptly. They need someone right away while they look for a replacement." I was intrigued. "It'll be easy for you and good practice for your next job. It pays two hundred dollars a day." I was sold. Now I would have the cash I needed for California.

It was surprisingly easy to get back into the work groove. I biked to work with a jacket and tie in my backpack. The client appreciated every day that I was at the company, and the temporary nature of the position made everything feel light. One weekend, I visited my friend Matt in Calgary. He asked me, "Is this a homecoming or a farewell tour?"

"I think it's both."

"So, the goddess search is over?"

It was. I wanted to be with Liz and I was working to make it happen. Matt had found his goddess, too, and would marry her a few years later. When I said, "You only need one, right? As long as she's the right one," he nodded in agreement.

While I was at my parents' house, Liz was staying with her sister Julie and Julie's partner, Marni. One Saturday morning in early August, Liz called to tell me that she had been offered a research job starting in September and her team was heading to Nepal on a forty-day blindness prevention mission. She still really wanted me to come in August and added that I was welcome to stay with her at Julie and Marni's house.

I thought it over while biking across town to a yoga class. During the class, the teacher guided us through a challenging sequence of postures. I felt strong and able, but I was definitely pushing myself. When we rested on our backs in savasana at the end, fatigue set in from working and biking all week. My body sunk completely into the floor. I fell into a daze and then to sleep.

When the teacher tapped a singing bowl to bring us out of the meditation, my eyes snapped open and, for a moment, I didn't know what city I was in. My first thought was that I didn't want to stay in Edmonton. I needed to continue my journey.

On the ride home, I recalled that feeling of reconstruction. What *did* I want my life to include? My hometown had a foundation of support from friends and family, but down in Berkeley, Liz was a cornerstone that I wanted to build my future around. She understood me and I wanted to continue our growth together. She was about to begin a career that would involve a decade of training. If I wanted to be with her, I had to go to California.

I considered waiting to go until after Liz returned in late October, but realized that by then, it would be almost half a year since we'd parted in Thailand. I trusted that our connection was strong, but worried that *something* might get in our way. I also didn't want to stay in my childhood bedroom for much longer. I had to make the move as soon as possible. I felt like an athlete with a big game coming up and I was ready for it to start.

All these thoughts were rolling through my head when I entered the house after my long bike ride back from yoga. My mom and her friend Darlene were sitting on the couch in the living room, and Darlene wanted to hear about my plans. I told her that I was planning to look for a job in San Francisco. As I spoke, Darlene took aim and shot down each point one by one.

"You won't find a company to sponsor your visa. San Francisco is *very* expensive."

"Thanks. I'm going to go anyway."

"Good luck. You won't last six months."

Not believing that she had said that, I bit my tongue, went upstairs, and waited for her to leave. Once I heard the front door close, I came down, shook my head at my mom, and said, "Well, that was encouraging…"

"Oh, you know Darlene…"

"She says what everyone else is thinking, but won't say?"

"That's not what *I* think."

I was surprised to hear that my mom disagreed with her friend. She explained, "You're going to do what you always have. You'll make a plan and follow through on it. You'll find a job and be with Liz, whom I hope to meet very soon. I'm sad because it's far away, but I'm not going to try to discourage you from what you want. There's no point. You're going to do it anyway."

It meant a lot to have my mom's blessing, but why did Darlene's negativity bother me so much? I think it was out of fear that she was right: I had no idea how hard it would be to get a job and a work permit. I had a free place to stay, but only for a month. Darlene's discouraging words made me angry—but what was I going to do about it? Buddha said that the one who controls his anger commands the chariot. Before saying goodbye on Koh Chang, I told Liz that I would come to California on a one-way ticket. She now had ten more days until her courses ended on August 16th. Before inertia, habit, or pessimism took hold, I wanted to follow through on my promise. I booked a flight to San Francisco for August 16th.

CHAPTER 50

Saturn Return

On August 9th, a week before my flight to San Francisco, I went to a bar where my friends' band was playing. The singer noted the musical significance of the date from the stage, but I was already well aware of it.

In May 1995, I attended five Grateful Dead shows in Washington state and Oregon. I was twenty years old and had one year left of college. After the Dead shows, I spent the summer working in my first accounting job as an intern at a big firm. At the bottom of the corporate totem pole, I wore a jacket and tie and I hated it. The interns competed with each other, the managers picked favorites, and the partners—the kindest of the bunch—were mostly off golfing. I counted the days to our local folk music festival in August.

On the first day of the festival, we learned that Jerry Garcia of the Grateful Dead had died at the age of 53 while in a treatment facility for his heroin addiction. There were a few tributes from the stage, but the most poignant one came when the headliner, Elvis Costello, sang the Grateful Dead's song Ship of Fools. *My friends and I mourned together in the beer garden and shed tears in the warm summer night. Not only was Garcia gone, but so was our favorite escape from the mundane. Those shows had been our sanctuary. Combined with the grind of my new job, Garcia's death represented a transition from youthful exploration to adult responsibility.*

Seven years later, in that noisy bar on the anniversary of Jerry's death, I prepared for my next transition. Friends wished me luck in Garcia's old hometown and I had at least one reason to be optimistic: Liz was there.

When I arrived at the San Francisco airport a week later, I looked around but couldn't see her. I picked up my green backpack off of the luggage carousel and walked in circles, looking for Liz as the carousel cleared and families reunited.

Then I saw her, walking slowly, shyly toward me—she'd seen me first. I sensed a combination of joy and nervousness in her smile, her beautiful smile. Her eyes sparkled as I gave her a gentle hug and a kiss on the forehead. I had been excited to leave for San Francisco, but arriving felt more like relief. I'd left friends and family behind in Canada, but with Liz in my arms, I was home.

After that short but beautiful moment, it was time to face the rest of the world together. I met Liz's sister Debbie on the curb outside the airport. She'd been married that spring and was already pregnant. Life in California was moving fast and now I was on the freeway.

At Julie and Marni's house, Liz and I shared a room and practiced yoga together in the mornings. I finally told Liz about my being with Robin in Varkala. She wasn't happy to hear it, but she told me that she had kissed a guy while in Rajasthan. We were both making sure that what we were feeling for each other was as special as we'd suspected.

Liz's medical research job was across town, so the house emptied during the day. One afternoon when Liz was back from work, Fran came over to welcome me. "I thought I *might* see you here..." she said. Then, "Lizzie, you're really going back to the land of Never Ending Peace And Love?" Nepalis use that acronym to describe their country; Fran and Liz had learned it when they visited Nepal for a week before going to Thailand. Back to me, Fran asked, "Where is the tabla?" She didn't know about the theft. When I told her, she said, "You get robbed a lot."

"I get tested a lot."

"Do you know what the Nepalis' acronym for India is?" She asked.

"I'll Never Do It Again." We all laughed.

"Would you?"

"Definitely." As tumultuous as my time in India had been, the country had given me something that I hadn't found anywhere else: myself. Or rather, the person I wanted to be. It turned out that my mom was right all along about that. Somehow, that distant and dirty place brought on more clarity than I'd ever had before. I'd been so glad to leave, but I missed it a lot.

Each of those first few days in California, I spent time on the computer looking at postings for accounting jobs. One of them stood out: a fledgling nonprofit car-sharing organization seeking its first Finance Director. Transportation was a problem in the Bay Area, and City CarShare aimed to make it easy to borrow a car for an hour or two by reserving it online. The cars were parked all around the city and members accessed them with electronic keys. I liked that the venture merged entrepreneurship with community benefit. I wrote a personal but professional letter and sent it in with my resume.

The day that I sent in the application, I sat alone on the couch in the afternoon sun and turned on Julie's CD player. It had a carousel of a hundred CDs set to shuffle. The first song that came on was Elvis Costello singing the Grateful Dead's *Ship of Fools*. I looked through the CD cases and figured out that it was a compilation of performances at a San Francisco radio station. An audience member must have requested *Ship of Fools* knowing that Costello had played it before. I replayed the track and heard him say, "What do you say? You want me to sing that, yeah?... I haven't sung this song since... a night last year, I was up in Edmonton... on that particular day... I hope I remember it all." Costello did remember all of the words. As he sang, the lyrics warned:

> "Though I could not caution all, I still might warn a few:
> Don't lend your hand to raise no flag atop no ship of fools."
> – *Ship of Fools*, Grateful Dead

The music built a bridge from San Francisco to Edmonton and back again, and tears ran down my cheeks. I wasn't crying for Jerry, but for the end of innocence. For 1995, when the music stopped and I began working for a living, and also for 2002. I was back from the road again, looking for another job in an office—hopefully a better one. I wasn't going to raise the wrong flag, not this time. I was ready to serve a cause greater than myself. I'd laid my proposition down and all I could do was wait for the call.

Two days later, the car-sharing organization sent me an email. They wanted me to come in for an interview and was I available tomorrow? I put on my accountant's uniform of dress pants, tie, and sports jacket, and got on the subway. Less than an hour later, I was at the Powell Street station in downtown San Francisco. Before the escalator even reached the street, I was impressed by the architecture of the city. The grey office towers made it feel like I was going somewhere important. People on the sidewalk carried shopping bags, briefcases, or the day packs of travelers.

My tie immediately looked out of place in the nonprofit's small live/work space. Young people hustled between desks lined with colorful iMac computers. They smiled at me and a couple of them introduced themselves. The Executive Director seemed to be the only one older than I was, and probably not by much. Her name was Elizabeth and she had long, wavy red hair and a bright smile, and she was pregnant. "My second baby," she said from a mouthful of almond butter-covered rice cake, indicating that the organization had been her first.

In their small conference room, Elizabeth and her colleagues asked about my work experience and recent year off, but they did most of the talking. I took copious notes. They probably could have used me a year earlier, but time flies when you're in startup mode. Now they were desperate to have an in-house accountant. I left feeling confident. On the train ride back to the East Bay, I organized my notes and began planning for my next interview.

The company emailed again the following week saying they wanted me to meet more members of their team. With a couple of days to prepare, I wrote up a document with my objectives for the job listed in three main bullet points. Each of those points had three subpoints. Each item was drawn directly from the problems that the staff had told me about during my first interview. I had plans to resolve all of the issues in three months. For the second interview, I ditched the jacket and tie. I noticed impressed reactions as I passed out my white paper, and I began using "we" as the interview wore on. As things wrapped up, they asked what type of work visa I would need. Turned out, all I needed from them was a signature. It was a non-issue.

For over a week, I waited to hear back and I started to wonder if I'd only imagined rocking the interview. Then, the following Friday afternoon, I got a call from Elizabeth.

"Mark, I'm so sorry."

My heart sunk.

"I meant to call you earlier. We've been so busy… We want to offer you the position!"

"Oh, you scared me there… I mean, great! I'm so glad."

After I hung up the phone, I found Julie, Marni, and Liz huddled outside the door. I exhaled with relief and said, "Well, that's a good way to end the week."

They all hugged me in celebration. I couldn't believe that things were working out already. I had prepared myself for many rejections, but this was the role that I wanted and my only interview. I had a job in San Francisco!

I'd been in the Bay Area for almost a month and had been noticing the concert listings. I was impressed by how many acts visited every week. Not wanting to drain my cash flow, I held off on attending anything. But now that I was employed, I invited Liz to see Robert Plant, the lead singer from Led Zeppelin, at the Berkeley Community Theatre. It was three days after my job offer and three days before Liz would leave for Nepal.

Just as we were about to leave the house, Julie surprised me in the kitchen with a bag of pot and a tiny bong. "Marky, you like to smoke, right?" The contents of the green baggie looked fresh and enticing. "It was a gift, but Marni won't smoke it with me…"

I was in the mood to celebrate, so it took me a moment to decide what to do. I wanted the night to be a celebration for both Liz and me, but if I went to the show high, I wouldn't be on Liz's wavelength. I told Julie, "Thanks for the offer, but I'll pass."

"Aren't you supposed to get high for Led Zeppelin?"

I looked at Liz and smiled back at Julie. "I don't believe in suppositions."

At the show, Robert Plant sang what he called "an old song for the Californians." I wrapped my arms over Liz's shoulders as music poured through beams of green light. I knew the song, but it felt like I was hearing the words for the first time.

> "Spent my days with a woman unkind
> Smoked my stuff and drank all my wine
> Made up my mind make a new start
> Goin' to California with an aching in my heart
> Someone told me there's a girl out there
> With love in her eyes and flowers in her hair
>
> Took my chances on a big jet plane
> Never let 'em tell you that they're all the same"
> – *Going to California*, Led Zeppelin

Our dream was a story that had already been told, but for us it was *real*. I had a job that I felt good about *and* permission to stay in the country. Most importantly, Liz and I had each other.

The day before Liz departed for Nepal, we visited her friends Janet and Leon in San Francisco. Leon had long blond hair and wore baggy earth-toned clothes. They lived in an apartment full of tapestries and crystals.

When Janet asked how Liz and I met, Liz told her India story and then I told mine. Leon, intrigued by my journey, asked, "How old were you?"

"I turned twenty-seven in Nepal."

"I thought so. It was your Saturn Return."

"My what?"

"Saturn takes twenty-seven years to revolve around the sun. In your twenty-seventh year, Saturn is back where it was when you were born. It's a pivotal time in a person's life." Feeling stunned by the accuracy of his description, I indicated for Leon to continue. "People change their way of living. They face challenges and make big decisions. The transformation defines their life until the next return. Is that what happened?"

I nodded, not knowing what to say. I felt so different than I had a year earlier. I couldn't say if a planet was involved, but I knew that things could have gone another way if not for my instincts, good fortune, and effort.

When Liz left for Nepal, I was offered a housesitting gig for my sister's friend Sue, who lived in San Francisco. Sue's place was close enough for me to bike to my new job. Before Sue and her husband left on their trip, my fellow Edmontonian had words of wisdom for me: "Be careful. People run red lights here."

The next day, I headed out on my bike to sign my employment contract. Just after a light changed, a car flew up a San Francisco hill and through the intersection. I silently thanked Sue for saving my life. I'd come too far to get quashed now.

When I arrived at the office this time, all of the staff came over to welcome me to the team. Once the fifth and sixth person came by, I felt humbled. I'd achieved my goal of getting a job in San Francisco, but in my moment of triumph, I remembered the real reason that I was there: they needed help. The organization's finances kept these people up at night and I was there to put an end to that anxiety. My hiring wasn't a seduction—they just wanted to get some sleep.

I mounted my bike for the ride back to Sue's place. The ride down had been a breeze, but the ride back up to Pacific Heights was a grind. I pumped my legs as streetcars and taxis passed me. At one point, I dismounted to give my knees a break and pace myself for the climb.

I was climbing physically and personally. Less than a month after arriving in San Francisco, I was alone in the city and I had *responsibilities*. My nine-point plan had looked great in the interview, but now I was going to be evaluated on it. As I pushed my bike uphill by the handlebars, the scent of sandalwood wafted onto the street from an Indian restaurant's open door. Curry aromas blended with the incense and piqued my memory. The smells brought India back, warming my being.

I paused outside the restaurant's door and noticed a colorful image on a poster in the window. It was Shiva. He'd also traveled from the Ganga to San Francisco. As the destroyer looked upon the street with his customary calm, I looked back, smiled, and remembered: Everything changes and life happens now.

EPILOGUE

Eighteen Years Later

> "If life were easy, and not so fast,
> I wouldn't think about the past."
> – *Roggae*, Phish

Three years after I arrived in San Francisco, my friend Matt asked me to be a groomsman at his wedding. He surprised me there with a gift—a leather-bound book of the emails I had sent in the year that I was traveling. The book was titled *A Long Strange Trip* (from the Grateful Dead's *Truckin'*) and included a card that read:

> *I had the chance to look into the soul of a close friend and gain inspiration from him on his travels… I hope you enjoy this gift for years to come… It was a treat to put together. You are an amazing guy.* – Matt

I was appreciative and humbled, but my next thought was, "that's not even half of the story." Matt's gift planted the seed to revisit my time in Asia. I began compiling emails and journal entries into a draft and I've been working on it since then.

By 2005, Liz was in medical school and we were living in a small house together. I'd been at my job in San Francisco for three years and was about to start my own nonprofit-focused accounting firm. I was playing tabla with other musicians in Berkeley and traveling whenever possible with Liz. We enjoyed our nieces and nephews, and continued to study yoga.

Around that time, Liz came to understand that it wasn't only her family conflicts that made her hesitant toward relationships and intimacy. She came to accept that she had a history of sexual trauma. We processed it together, and that experience guided Liz in her choice to become a pediatrician and advocate for vulnerable children.

Liz and I were married in 2010 on a beach at a nature center on the Northern California coast. Matt was the Master of Ceremonies and Fran described how Liz and I had met in India. We wrote our wedding vows based on the yamas and niyamas of yoga:

I will selflessly serve our household and wholeheartedly support you
    in your service to our community.
I will honor you and offer my humble devotion.
I will self-reflect and bear responsibility for my actions.
I will approach you with non-violence in thought, word, and deed.
I will be truthful with you.
I will hold your touch as sacred.
I will appreciate the abundance in our lives
    and I will be generous with you.
I will cultivate a healthy and harmonious home.
I will live simply and joyfully by your side.
I will nurture your learning and spiritual growth.
I will walk with you in beautiful places, and when it grows dark,
    I will be a light for you.
I will surrender my ego and value your feelings as my own.

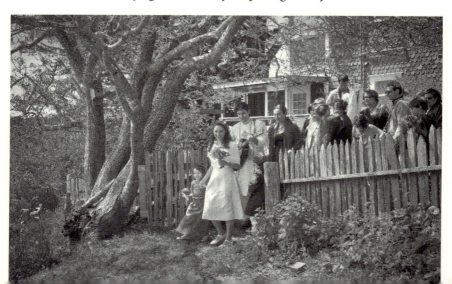

In 1965, George Harrison was on Paradise Island in the Bahamas filming the movie Help! *with his bandmates. It's a goofy chase movie with the Beatles constantly on the run from evil characters. The bumbling antagonists are a human-sacrificing religious cult from the "Far East" led by a potbellied swami. In the film, an Indian character is doing a headstand before going to lie down on a bed of nails. Those were common racial jokes of the time, but it was while filming the final scenes that Harrison met a real swami. Swami Vishnu Devananda was establishing an ashram on a donated plot of land right there on Paradise Island.*

Swami Vishnu Devananda had been sent to the west by his guru, Swami Sivananda, to spread the practice of yoga. In support of that mission, he gave signed copies of his book, The Complete Illustrated Book of Yoga, *to each of the Beatles. Harrison read the book and it sparked his interest in yoga, which led to meditation and, of course, Indian music. He stopped mocking Indian culture and started studying it.*

That chance encounter changed the course of George Harrison's life, and it wouldn't be a stretch to say that it altered mine as well. I arrived in India curious about the classical music that the Beatle had exposed me to. Days after Harrison's passing, I met a Keralan yogi on a beach in Palolem—Krishna had studied yoga at Swami Vishnu Devananda's ashram.

Around the time of our wedding, Liz and I went to Paradise Island to study to become yoga instructors. We trained at the Sivananda ashram where the swami had met the Beatles. At the end of our course, we were to be given "spiritual" names. Seven years after my trip to India, I still didn't buy into the idea of calling yourself one of God's names. It went against my Jewish tradition and also felt pretentious. The teachers assured me that it was quite the opposite—spiritual names are meant to sublimate the ego and to equalize everyone. I decided it would be okay, and the swami named me Maha Dev, which means "great god" in Sanskrit and is one of the titles of—you guessed it—Shiva.

Was any of this fate? I believe that if we know what we're looking for, we end up finding it eventually. It's the knowing that can be difficult. In India, I found my personal trinity of teachers because of my intention. I wasn't looking for a tabla guru, a yogi, or a young woman from California, but I *was* following my love of music and a desire to reopen my heart.

Keshav was the destroyer, dispelling my preconceptions and guiding me toward the blissful quiet that comes from performing music. It was in that space that I found the clarity to move forward with my life.

Once I realized how stuck I had been, I followed a sign that said "Yoga Class" because I was open to trying something new. Krishna, like his namesake, was the preserver. He helped me to find the goodness in myself by guiding me beyond the chatter.

And Liz. Sweet Lizzie… I wasn't looking for a girlfriend when I found her, but when I saw her, I couldn't look away. She was the creator, a goddess. When I was with her, I could more clearly see who I wanted to be. Meeting someone special helps you learn about yourself. In our case, that process has never ended.

Perfect endings are possible in love stories and ragas, but not in the quest for spiritual growth or in real relationships. No guru will slip you the answer, and relationships take work. Still, I feel *so* lucky to be with Liz. She's a beautiful and wonderful woman.

It's now 2020 and eighteen years since I met Liz in Hampi. I run an accounting firm that focuses on supporting nonprofits. Liz is a pediatrician and researcher. I'm proud of the work she does in support of children's health. I've continued to study yoga through the Sivananda organization and with other teachers. We practice yoga as often as we can, and these days I'm more likely to strum a ukulele in a park than tap on my tabla.

We've been in Los Angeles for eight years. It feels great to put down roots in one spot after moving frequently while Liz completed her medical training. I've come to know myself even better by committing—there's that word!—to being with Liz for the rest of our lives. The bond of marriage has forced me to look at how I behave every day. It's important that I bring forward the best of myself and observe the impulses that get in the way of that intention.

While Liz and I make sure to have fun alone together, most of our time is focused on our two young children. Our six-year-old son, Jonah, is a delightful bundle of energy. He looks like me but reminds me more of Liz. Our eight-year-old daughter, Zoe, is brilliant and beautiful, with a zest for life.

The kids are the gurus now. Nothing in my life has been as humbling or challenging as having two small, vulnerable people depend on me. I try to approach parenting the same way that I approach other passions: to be the best at it that I can. I know that I'm not perfect (just ask my family!), but I'm there, available for them and always striving to improve. Sometimes it's hard, but no one said that parenting was going to be easy.

I am constantly aware of how temporary this all is. The kids have gone from being tiny and delicate to smart and strong in such a short time. I know that before long they'll be off on their own adventures. I want to savor the time that the four of us have together.

I still go to see live music with my old friends, including Matt and Josh. It's always fun to be with friends and the bands keep our middle-aged legs moving. Though I kept my vow to not hold my own stash after India, I smoked pot occasionally over the years. It was while revisiting my year in Asia that I created a new rule for myself: Before arriving at a show, I'd plan to abstain because smoking even just a little bit makes me think about when the next puff will be. This rule has made it easier for me to ignore the craving and to focus on the music. My family has a long history of addiction and I want to break the cycle.

Liz wasn't allowed to read the book until it was done, but the other day she took a look. She enjoyed what she read and joked, "I'm a pain in the ass." That response was cute, but what pleased me more was that, when we left on a trip a couple days later, she had packed the *Bhagavad Gita* in her bag. Wisdom speaks to us all the time and it's our job to attune ourselves to it. Sometimes, a book or a song can point us inward on just the right trajectory to reach the pure goodness inside us.

Writing this book has reminded me of what nourishes and diminishes me. If reading it has helped you to do the same, then I'll feel that it has been successful. Thank you for journeying with me to the end and remember: Don't get too comfortable—everything changes.

Postscript

Everything changes, eh? While I complete final edits for this book, our world is embroiled in the COVID-19 pandemic. Eighteen years after I left Canada for California, our family of four has relocated to Victoria, British Columbia, where compliant Canadians create a more stable setting for our children's education. I deeply hope that this swirl of change leads to improvements for our world.

Acknowledgements

"And you may find yourself in a beautiful house
With a beautiful wife
And you may ask yourself, well
How did I get here?"
– *Once in a Lifetime,* Talking Heads

I began documenting this journey in internet cafes and railcars and have finished it at playgrounds and in the quiet of a sleeping house. Thank you for riding along. If it prompted thoughts or memories for you, I'd love to hear about them. You can email me at saturnreturn5762@gmail.com.

I am so grateful to the people who have supported me in sharing this story. Matt Singer has brought inspiration and support all along. Sam Polk guided me to Author Accelerator, where Jennie Nash led me through each stage of the book process. My book coach, Dawn Ius, told me that completing this memoir would be like nothing I've ever experienced. She was right and I will be forever grateful for her teaching and confidence in me.

I want to thank everyone who has taught me about music, yoga, and life, especially Keshava Rao Nayak, Unni Krishna, Swami Sitaramananda, Krishna Darshan, and Alice Hiatt. Thank you to all of the memoir writers who gave me the confidence to share my story and to the musicians who color our lives, especially The Beatles, Grateful Dead, and Phish.

Thank you to my supportive friends in Los Angeles and around the world, particularly Jamie Phillips and Amanda Rosen-Prinz for valuable guidance with the manuscript. Josh Cohen provided direction *and* focus and I'm so thankful for all of the friends who I've met on the road.

I appreciate Jill Angel for editing, Donna Jean Bishop for artistry, and Carla Green for book design and guiding me to the finish line. Now in 2020's pandemic, I especially want to acknowledge everyone who contributed to this book's publication, including programmers, publishing staff, and delivery people.

Mom and Dad, you've always loved me with all of your heart, even when you weren't sure what I was up to. Susan and Cyril, thank you for your kindness and support. Kara, you're the greatest sister I could have. Thank you to my sisters-in-law, brothers-in-law, aunts, uncles, nieces, nephews, and cousins. You bring light to my life and I love you all so much.

Lizzie, you're an incredible partner for this journey called life, and definitely the right goddess for me. I love you. Zoe and Jonah, I expect that you're much older as you read this and I hope I didn't embarrass you too much. I love you. Now hit the road and get your shoes dirty!

Om Namah Sivaya

Manufactured by Amazon.ca
Bolton, ON